The Backcountry
Horseman's Guide
to WASHINGTON

by
John and Roberta Wolcott

D0048278

FALCON®
HELENA, MONTANA

A FALCON GUIDE®

Falcon® is continually expanding its list of recreational guidebooks. All books include detailed descriptions, accurate maps, and all the information necessary for enjoyable trips. You can order extra copies of this book and get information and prices for other Falcon® guidebooks by writing Falcon, P.O. Box 1718, Helena, MT 59624 or calling toll free 1-800-582-2665. Also, please ask for a free copy of our current catalog. To contact us via e-mail, visit our website at www.falconguide.com.

©1995 by Falcon® Publishing, Inc.
Helena, Montana.

Printed in the United States of America.

All black-and-white photos by John and Roberta Wolcott unless credited otherwise.
Cover photo by Features Northwest, John and Roberta Wolcott.

Library of Congress Cataloging-in-Publication Data

Wolcott, John, 1940-
    The backcountry horseman's guide to Washington / by John and
Roberta Wolcott.
      p. cm.
   ISBN 1-56044-338-3
   1. Trail riding—Washington (State)—Guidebooks. 2. Trails—
Washington (State)—Guidebooks. 3. Packhorse camping—Washington
(State)—Guidebooks. 4. Campsites, facilities, etc.—Washington(State)—
Guidebooks. I. Wolcott, Roberta, 1942- . II. Title.
   SF309.256.W2W64 1995
   798.2'3—dc20   95-17176
                                              CIP

 Text pages printed on recycled paper.

CAUTION

    Outdoor recreational activities are by their very nature potentially hazardous. All participants in such activities must assume the responsibility for their own actions and safety. The information contained in this guidebook cannot replace sound judgment and good decision-making skills, which help reduce the risk exposure, nor does the scope of this book allow for disclosure of all the potential hazards and risks involved in such activities.

    Learn as much as possible about the outdoor recreational activities in which you participate, prepare for the unexpected, and be cautious. The reward will be a safer and more enjoyable experience.

CONTENTS

ACKNOWLEDGMENTS

No one writes a book alone. Even two writers can't do it alone. We relied on the expertise, support, and cooperation of so many helpful people to make this book as complete and detailed as possible.

Forest Service and National Park Service rangers and volunteers were valuable resources for us, offering their personal insights as well as the official pack-and-saddle trail guides, wilderness regulations, and horse camp information that riders need to know.

Throughout the researching and writing of this book, we were encouraged by the enthusiasm of forest rangers, tack shop managers, horse owners, and groups such as the Back Country Horsemen of Washington and the Washington Trail Riders Association. They all agreed this first Washington State trail riders' guide is long overdue.

Without the encouragement and patience we received—from each other as well as from others—this guidebook might have remained only a fine idea in the minds of the editors at Falcon Press. We thank guidebook editor Randall Green for his understanding and great patience and our copy editor, Will Harmon, for his fine touch in shaping the contents of each chapter and trail.

Our thanks also go to our families and to our son, Jim, and daughter, Teresa, who have shown such genuine interest and support in this verbal adventure, and to good friends and fellow writers who offered their own encouragement and enthusiasm—Debby and Swede Miller, Patrick Kearney, Phil Noble, Debbie Hoyt, Steve Giordano, and Lynn Rosen. No doubt they are nearly as relieved as we are to see this book in print rather than in process.

Protecting mountain and meadow beauty like this is part of every rider's responsibility. Caring for the environment is as important as caring for yourself or your horse when you ride Washington's multitude of scenic trails. Photo by Robin Barker/Courtesy of High Country Outfitters.

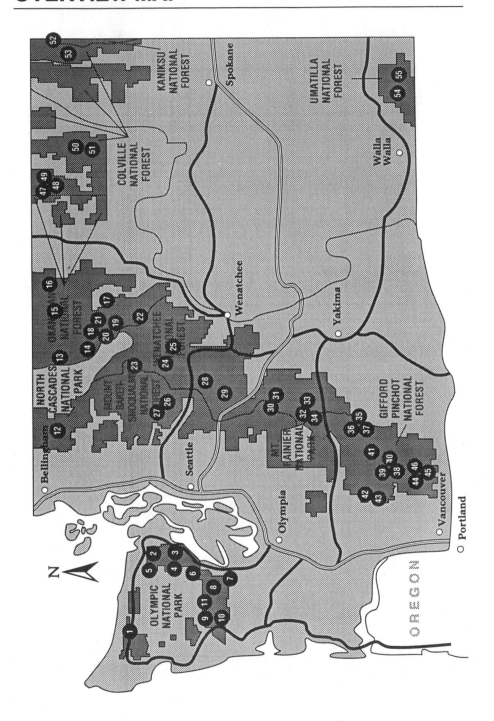

MAP LEGEND

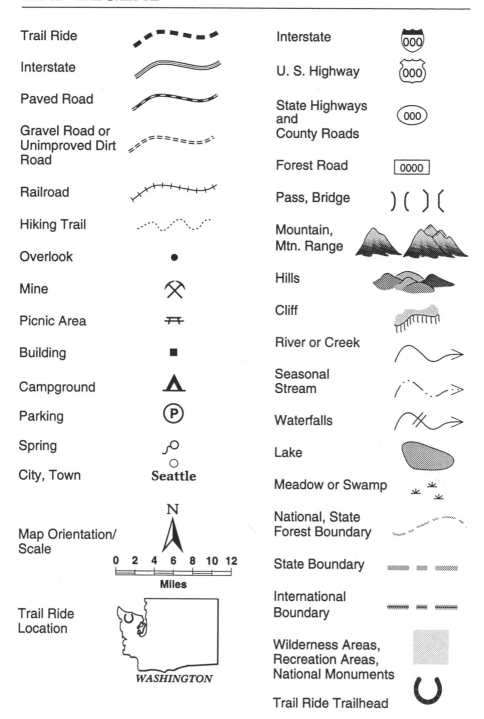

Trail Ride		Interstate	
Interstate		U. S. Highway	
Paved Road		State Highways and County Roads	
Gravel Road or Unimproved Dirt Road		Forest Road	
Railroad		Pass, Bridge	
Hiking Trail		Mountain, Mtn. Range	
Overlook		Hills	
Mine		Cliff	
Picnic Area		River or Creek	
Building		Seasonal Stream	
Campground		Waterfalls	
Parking		Lake	
Spring		Meadow or Swamp	
City, Town		National, State Forest Boundary	
Map Orientation/ Scale		State Boundary	
Trail Ride Location		International Boundary	
		Wilderness Areas, Recreation Areas, National Monuments	
		Trail Ride Trailhead	

Esmeralda Peak in the Teanaway Valley looms over trail riders.

INTRODUCTION

The back country is one of the few remaining sanctuaries for modern man. Away from everyday tensions a person can make an objective evaluation of oneself or a situation and gain a firmer sense of true values.

Perhaps we need an occasional reminder of what insignificant creatures we really are when viewed in comparison with the magnitude of nature. Today's young generation will be the guardians of the resources of tomorrow. We could offer them no finer course than a lesson from nature's classroom on a backcountry trip.

—*Back Country Horsemen Guidebook*

Skylines without skyscrapers, a canopy of stars undimmed by street lights, the warmth of a campfire, craggy mountain peaks, and flowered valleys are luring people into some of Washington State's most scenic mountain wilderness—on horseback. Trail rides and horsepacking trips offer a great time for togetherness and opportunities to experience scenery few people are ever able to see. Considering Washington's geographic profile, the lure of sightseeing on horseback is an irresistible enticement.

This great state's diversity is worth riding out to see, particularly since one-third of Washington is public land, including more than four million acres protected wilderness. Half the state is mountainous, and many rugged and scenic areas are close to metropolitan cities and suburban communities. Some of the most spectacular mountain and valley scenery in America is here.

It's no surprise, then, that trail riding is rapidly gaining popularity in Washington State. Membership in the Back Country Horsemen of Washington has grown from two hundred some fifteen years ago to nearly three thousand today in more than thirty chapters throughout the state.

Trail riding is a great way to relax—saddling up for rides into the North Cascades' Pasayten Wilderness near the Canadian border or seeing where forests once stood tall at Mount St. Helens, riding the rain forest trails along the Humptulips River or basking in sunshine on Diamond Peak in southeastern Washington's slice of the Umatilla National Forest. Wherever you ride and explore in Washington state, you'll be enjoying the varied scenery of one of America's most abundantly blessed outdoor environments.

For the first time, *The Backcountry Horseman's Guide To Washington* presents the information you need to take advantage of these opportunities with your horse. Knowing some of the best trails open to horses, where they go, what you'll see, which maps to bring, where to graze your horse, and where to park your horse trailer will make your trips easier, safer, and more rewarding.

Camping as well as riding will be a great part of your trip memories. With tips from USDA Forest Service and National Park Service rangers and leading horse groups such as the Back Country Horsemen of Washington, you'll be better prepared to Leave No Trace—to protect the environment you came to enjoy—while camping and traveling.

The fifty-five trails profiled here were selected from all over the state. They offer a wide variety of scenery, terrain, and trail difficulty, rated by the Forest Service

A lone rider enjoys the view of the Mount Stuart range near Cle Elum. Photo by Robin Barker/Courtesy of High Country Outfitters.

as "easy" to "more difficult" and "most difficult" treads. Those who love valleys, streams, forests, and mountains should have their fill. Most of the trails are in non-wilderness areas, where scenery is often as superb as in wilderness regions but easier to reach. Some are remote, but many of these trails are close to highly populated metropolitan areas.

There are hundreds more trails open to stock than the ones mentioned here. But we specifically selected scenic areas with developed horse camps or horse facilities at the trailheads. We wanted this first Washington guidebook on horse trails to have an exciting array of trail rides that would provide trail riders with years of recreation and exploring.

Few of the trails are in national parks, for a reason. Except for North Cascades National Park, where there are numerous horse camps and stock trails, the national parks seem to be more oriented toward hikers than horse riders.

In fact, Mount Rainier National Park discourages horse use, noting that most of its stock trails are in forested areas without scenic mountain vistas. Due to snow conditions on the mountain, stock use is only practical from mid-July through late-September. Also, glacial rivers must be forded but rarely can be during the summer months when flows are high and forceful. The National Park Service provides information on trail ride opportunities but warns that there is "extremely little demand for, or actual use of stock" within the park.

Olympic National Park has 300 miles of horse trails, but there are many restrictions on where people can ride, making it difficult to plan trips inside the park compared to the ease of planning national forest trail rides outside the park. There are

Trail riding offers a relaxing way of seeing some of Washington's most scenic mountain realms.

horse camps in the park at several locations, but in many other areas trails are closed to stock. Also, most park roads are closed to stock use, whereas in national forests most roads are open to stock use.

In North Cascades National Park, there is frequent use of the trails by horse riders and horse camps have been developed in several areas. This is a much less congested realm than either Mount Rainier or Olympic National Parks.

Along with describing some of the best scenic trail rides in Washington, this book features information on how to Leave No Trace in the wilderness—and everywhere else you go; surprises your horses may discover on the trail, from mountain bikers to llamas; where to experience your first trail ride or overnight campout with professional outfitters; and a chapter about horse camps being built in Washington. There's information about trail riding horse groups, such as the Back Country Horsemen of Washington, and we've even included recipes and tips for Dutch oven cooking, the kind of hearty camp cuisine that cowboys devoured on cattle drives and settlers depended on during long overland wagon train journeys.

Whether you're riding, camping, or cooking a backcountry meal, you'll find plenty of uses for this practical, saddlebag-sized guidebook to Washington horse trails and horse camps. And the trails it takes you on will be memorable reminders that the outdoors, the backcountry, the wilderness, the valleys, and the mountains of this state are indeed sanctuaries for modern people—a place to ease tensions, enhance friendships, and rekindle a love for our natural world.

HOW TO USE THIS GUIDE

The Backcountry Horseman's Guide to Washington is the first book of its kind for horse riders who love to take to the Evergreen State's trails. In the past, trail information, trailhead locations, and tips for traveling and camping were not easily found. More often than not, trail guides and maps are geared toward hikers, neglecting information important to trail riders. This book weaves together such information from Forest Service maps, ranger interviews, horse groups, professional pack-and-saddle outfitters, and the authors' trail-riding experiences to provide everything you need to know in a single source. The heart of the book is the section with trail ride descriptions. Here's how each one is organized and how to interpret the information.

Trail Ride number and name: We've given each ride a number for easier cross-referencing throughout the book; the name usually is borrowed from the main trail or destination for the trip. Rides are loosely grouped by region, beginning on the Olympic Peninsula, moving through the Cascades from north to south, and then heading east to rides in the northeast and southeast corners of the state.

Location: A nearby town, highway, or landmark is referenced so you can find the general trail area on a state highway map. See page 170 for a list of addresses for specific ranger districts or park offices to contact for more information about each ride.

General description: This is a brief summary of the ride's length, where it goes, type of terrain, and whether it's a day trip, overnighter, or loop ride. Scenic highlights are mentioned here.

Trailhead horse facilities: A wide variety of horse facilities are found at trailheads throughout the state. Which facilities are available will influence your decisions about what to pack for the trip and which trails to ride. Some trailheads are nothing more than wide pulloffs on remote forest roads, others are comfortable camping areas with hitch rails and firepits. Some qualify as luxury horse camps, with amenities to please both horses and riders.

Trailhead elevation: It's always important to know your beginning altitude.

High point: Subtracting the trailhead elevation from the high point of the trail offers some notion about the scenery you might see and how much climbing your horse will have to do. Be mindful that on mountainous trail rides the altitude alone is not a precise indication of how strenuous or difficult the trip might be. Difficulty—or lack of it—depends on the tread. It may be rocky and full of shale, or filled with pine needles and sand. The trail grade may be a slight but steady incline or it may switchback up a 1,500-foot-high ridge and drop down the other side 1,000 feet before you arrive at a destination only a few hundred feet higher than the trailhead.

Wrangler Rob Wottlin of Tacoma is one of High Country Outfitters' top hands. He takes care of horses, saddles, and gear for guests who explore Washington's mountain trails on horseback with professional outfitters Swede and Debby-Gallie Miller.

Maps: The maps in this book are meant to show the general route of each trail, some of the landmarks in the area, neighboring trails, and the route to the trailhead. The maps have been simplified as much as possible, while still including salient points you'll need to understand about where you'll be driving and riding. For the actual trip, you may want to carry more detailed USGS, Green Trails, Custom Correct, or other topographic maps to guide you.

Forest Service offices will sell you national forest maps, but these only give an overview of an area. They can be very helpful in finding trailheads.

U.S. Geologic Survey (USGS) topographic maps show elevations, trails, terrain, and other features that are essential information for most trail trips, particularly in wilderness backcountry. Ranger districts and park offices often have special local maps too, such as the Salmo–Priest Wilderness map issued by the Forest Service for the Colville National Forest.

Finally, most good outdoor recreation retail stores also have an array of commercial maps for hikers, and these work just as well for guiding horse riders, of course. Highly detailed and easy to use Green Trails topographic maps, for instance, are very popular and cover much of the state. For the Olympic Peninsula, a Port Angeles company publishes a special line of Custom Correct maps for Olympic National Park and Olympic National Forest.

Season: Weather is an important consideration when riding in high mountain country, where many of these trails go. Seasonal temperatures and precipitation amounts vary greatly depending on elevation and whether you're west or east of the Cascade Range. Some high trails bear snow into June and July, even into August. They will be snowed in again, or at least very wet, by late October or early November. When you plan your trips, be aware of these shorter "good-weather" seasons at higher altitudes. Also realize that sudden snowstorms can occur at high elevation any day of the year, even in August.

Water availability: This heading refers to stock water. Water for human consumption can be found in many places that horses can't get to, or personal supplies can be carried in canteens. Water from outdoor sources, even in the high country where streams run crystal clear, should be boiled or purified with an approved filter for human consumption.

Horses don't seem to be bothered by the same parasites in streams and lakes that trouble their riders. Check out creeks, stream crossings, campground watering troughs, and other sources of water when you're planning trail rides, to be sure your horse has an ample supply during the trip.

Feed availability: Some grazing areas are found in many of the camps, along valley lowlands, or in high-elevation meadows. We've noted these, but we urge you to pack processed feed or some form of pelletized feed for your stock, whether you are in wilderness or non-wilderness country.

Busy trails mean that even ample grazing areas can be easily depleted. If you count on native forage you might be surprised when you arrive. Another reason to resist using meadows for grazing is to protect them from pawing and excess hoof traffic.

When you do carry stock feed always make sure that it's certified weed-free, processed feed to avoid introducing noxious weeds or non-native plant species into the backcountry.

Permits/restrictions: This section is primarily to tell riders about restrictions or permits required in wilderness areas. Most other trail areas have no strict regulations. The most common items listed here are permits needed for backcountry camping, trail closures, and limits on group size.

Finding the trailhead: Some of the most frustrating memories of many trail trips aren't about wrecks on the trail. They're about unexpected "adventures" finding the trailhead. That can take the fun out of the start of any trail ride.

We have been careful to describe in this section, and on the accompanying maps, the exact location of the trailhead. Be aware that over a period of years, trailheads may be relocated by the land managers. Where this has recently occurred, we note it in the trail description. Trail coordinators, wilderness rangers, and trail crews keep close watch on trail conditions and changes. Check with ranger districts for the latest information.

The ride: The ride descriptions are meant to give riders an understanding of where the trail goes, what the terrain is like, and what scenery they might see. There are also notes about camping sites and special historical or natural landmarks in the area.

Signs at the start of most trails indicate the difficulty of the route. "Easiest" trails, marked by a circle bisected by a gentle "wave" line, require limited skill and offer little physical challenge. These trails often run along river valleys or through low foothills. The tread is smooth, level, and wide, with generous clearing of trees, limbs, and other vegetation above and to each side of the trail to permit easy passage. Elevation gain or loss is minimal. Streams are most often crossed by bridges.

"More difficult" trails, signed by a square with a more exaggerated wave, require a moderate skill level and provide a moderate physical challenge. Tread surface may contain roots and embedded rocks. Clearances of trees, limbs, and other vegetation above and to each side of the trail result in occasional contact by users. Elevation gain or loss is moderate. Streams are most often crossed by fording. River crossings are usually easiest at the wider parts of the river, which are usually the most shallow.

"Most difficult" trails, shown by a diamond-shaped sign bisected by a vertically jagged line, require a high degree of skill and provide a great deal of physical challenge. The slope is often steep. Minimal clearing of trees, limbs, and other vegetation often hampers the progress of the trail user. Elevation gain or loss is usually severe. Streams are crossed by fording and are sometimes difficult.

The level of trail use in national forests is generally rated as light, from 0 to 5 encounters per day on the trail in non-wilderness areas and 0 to 3 in wilderness areas. Medium use is 6 to 15 encounters per day outside the wilderness and 4 to 9 in wilderness. Heavy use on a trail is rated at 16 to 50 encounters per day, or 10 to 18 in wilderness. Extra-heavy use is rated at more than 50 encounters on a non-wilderness trail and more than 18 on a wilderness trail. Remember that trail use may be heavier than normal on weekends, holidays, and during warmer seasons.

Even though all of these trails are rated as accessible for horses, there is as much difference in horses as in trails. Try to find the right match for yours. A tough trail, of course, will demand a well-conditioned horse. A lowland, river valley trail is a good one to start on after a wintering season when the horse has been inactive.

Always check with local ranger districts before a trip—outdoor conditions can change rapidly. Early in the year, winter storms may have blown trees across a trail and crews may not have cleared the route yet by late spring or early summer. Wet trail conditions will also be noted by backcountry rangers and trail crews. Forest Service and Park Service rangers can be immensely helpful for planning your trail ride.

Horse Camp Descriptions

Because this book is devoted to useful information for trail riders, special emphasis has been placed on featuring good horse camps. We've found a dozen of the state's best horse camping locations and focused on nearby trails. Fortunately, there has been increased attention given to horse camps in recent years. Increased cooperation between government agencies, horse groups, and individual riders in siting and building these camps has resulted in some fine horse camps, such as the Kalama, Lewis River and Chiwawa horse camps.

Many more horse camps are being developed in Washington State. Some of them will be opening during 1995. Check with local ranger districts in the area where you want to ride.

The horse camp descriptions are organized much like the trail ride descriptions.

Name of the Horse Camp: based on area or surrounding trails.

Location: A brief description locates the horse camp site to help you plan your trip.

Horse camp facilities: Facilities will vary widely. Look for such amenities as stock ramps, hitch rails, water troughs, and corrals, all important factors in planning your trail rides and camps.

Finding the horse camp: A detailed description of the route to the horse camp is provided. Most horse camps are well marked. Many were developed by horse groups and government agencies; others are only trailheads with horse facilities and some camping space.

Horse camp elevation: Camp elevation is usually of interest to riders, even if it plays no significant role in your camping or trail ride. It's always helpful, of course, to know if the elevations are high enough to be concerned about snowfall in the early summer and late fall months.

Trails: Each horse camp description includes a list of trail rides that meet at that camp.

The growing number of horse camps built in the state in recent years, plus new ones planned for construction, reflect a strong trend. Washington now has more than

Riders enjoy the Esmeralda Basin Trail.

170,000 horses, one of the largest equine populations of any state. And their owners are increasingly interested in trail riding.

Membership in horse groups, for example, is growing. Back Country Horsemen of Washington, part of the Montana-based Back Country Horsemen of America, was founded in 1977. Fifteen years ago the group had two hundred members. Today the group has close to three thousand people who are trail riding, horse camping, and practicing leave-no-trace ethics. And the national organization has nine thousand members in ten western states.

Another trend is the increasing involvement of these groups as they actively work with government agencies to design, finance, and build new horse camps. With tightened budgets and pared staffs, the federal overseers and protectors of our public forests are teaming up more and more with horse groups to clear and build trails, design and construct horse camps, and promote environmentally sound leave-no-trace information.

One of the places this concept has worked best so far is in the Gifford Pinchot National Forest, in areas administered by the staff of the Mount St. Helens National Volcanic Monument. Two well-planned, well-equipped horse camps in that area have proven how well this teamwork has paid off, aided by the financial support of the Washington State Interagency Committee for Outdoor Recreation (IAC).

Kalama Horse Camp, near the town of Cougar in the southwest sector of the Mount St. Helens National Volcanic Monument, offers a prime site for horse riding into scenic mountain realms, all in non-wilderness areas. Facilities include large parking spaces with pull-throughs for trucks and horse trailers, a stock ramp, water

9

trough, hitch rails, a high hitchline, multiple corrals, and a mounting assist area. The camp also has ten campsites, a double-tank composting toilet, a staging area with manure bins, and a picnic area with a horseshoe pit. There's even a "horse lounging area" where stock can roll or relax before or after trail trips.

This "donation" campground uses contributions to maintain and improve the large facility, which was built as a cooperative effort of the Washington Trail Riders Association, Mount St. Helens National Volcanic Monument, Gifford Pinchot National Forest, and the Washington State Interagency Committee for Outdoor Recreation (IAC).

A few miles east of Kalama Horse Camp is Lewis River Horse Camp, another well-appointed site developed through a joint effort of the Mount St. Helens and Thunder Mountain chapters of Back Country Horsemen of Washington, Mount St. Helens National Volcanic Monument, Gifford Pinchot National Forest, and the IAC.

North of Leavenworth and Lake Wenatchee, in the Mount Baker–Snoqualmie National Forest, is Chiwawa Horse Camp, with twenty-one campsites. This is one of the newer horse camps in Washington, completed through a cooperative effort between the Lake Wenatchee Ranger District of the Forest Service and the Cascade Horse Club of Lake Stevens, affiliated with Back Country Horsemen of Washington. Together, the ranger district and the horse club applied to the IAC for a grant to help develop the camp, under the Nonhighway and Off-Road Vehicles Activities (NOVA) program.

Already club members have built trails to connect with Finner Creek Campground and helped to reconstruct other trails in the area. Work remains to be done, and both the Cascade Horse Club and Lake Wenatchee Ranger District welcome other individuals or groups who want to volunteer to complete the area riding trails. Contact Paul Sandford at the Lake Wenatchee Ranger District, (509) 763-3103.

Horse Camp Etiquette

To ensure an enjoyable stay at these large horse camps, the Washington Trail Riders Association, Back Country Horsemen, and the rangers of the Mount St. Helens National Volcanic Monument and the Gifford Pinchot National Forest urge campers to observe a few rules of conduct that can be applied to any campground where horse enthusiasts use public facilities.

In camp:

- Keep riding and pack stock at a walk through the campground.
- Keep dogs under control at all times.
- Use caution when walking or riding near stock since some animals are skittish and unpredictable.
- Obey posted speed limits.
- Park only in designated areas, with camp site registration cards on your vehicle dashboard.
- Use provided facilities to contain or tie stock. Use a high picket line and tree savers for extra stock.

Before leaving:

- Clean corrals and picket lines of all manure and excess feed. Place in manure bins.
- Clean camp areas of all garbage, leftover feed, twine, etc., to leave the facility as clean as you would like to find it.

The appendices located in the back of the book provide additional information. Appendix A, The Trail Rider's Checklist, is a reminder of all the items you might want to carry with you on your next trail ride; Appendix B, Agency Addresses, lists the statewide land managers for each ride; Appendix C, For More Information, offers further references and sources of leave-no-trace information, trail information and maps, horse groups and publications, and the U.S. Geological Survey address for topographic maps; Appendix D, Riding With the Pros, includes information on the Back Country Horsemen of America and its Washington chapter, Washington Outfitters and Guides Association, and outfitters in the state, the Washington Trail Riders Association, and therapeutic riding programs; Appendix E, Packstock Regulations on Washington Public Lands, highlights the most important regulations; and Appendix F, Camp Cooking With Dutch Ovens, offers special tips and recipes for camp culinary delights.

LEAVE NO TRACE

Many exciting opportunities for horseback riding await in the national forests, national parks, and wilderness areas of Washington State. But some people oppose the use of horses in any of these areas because of the damage these 1,500-pound, four-footed animals do to trails and campsites.

According to dictionaries, some synonyms for "treading" are squashing, crushing, tromping, and trampling. That's the image that many people have of horses on public trails and in public campsites. That's why Back Country Horsemen of Washington and other riding groups promote "Tread Lightly" or "Leave No Trace" concepts and practices to protect the environment.

Most riders use good horse sense about their traveling and camping. Unfortunately, though many riders pride themselves in being stewards of the land, even cleaning up hiker camps and packing out others' trash along with their own, a few riders are part of the problem rather than part of the solution. Careless treatment of the outdoors creates problems—eroded trails, polluted creeks, manure piles, exposed and damaged tree roots, overgrazed meadows, and worn-out campsites.

Just as overuse of the popular Alpine Lakes Wilderness Area east of Seattle has led to new restrictions on hiking and camping in that area, the overuse and misuse of trails, campsites, and wilderness by horse riders will lead to increased restrictions on trail use by stock in national forests and wilderness areas. One of the best ways to protect the environment and in turn protect all riders' access to this land is to practice the philosophies and techniques of leaving no trace. The following guidelines were developed by experienced horsemen and women; they are surprisingly effective yet painless adjustments to most riders' backcountry routines.

Trail riders return to the trailhead of the Wolf Creek trail after a trek to Gardner Meadows near Winthrop. Single-file riding reduces trail wear, one of the goals of "Tread Lightly" trail ethics.

Plan Ahead to Prevent Problems Before They Occur

Know your animals. Ideally, all pack and saddle animals should be healthy, reliable, calm, and well trained. High-strung, mean-spirited, or sick animals are more likely to cause trouble in the backcountry.

Take the time at home to familiarize your animals with the packs, restraints, foods, and other equipment they will encounter in the backcountry. A storm on a remote, rocky ridge is no place for your horse's first skirmish with a wildly flapping rain poncho.

Consider using the flat plate style of horseshoe. Heel and toe caulks give the horse better traction on rocky, icy, or steep trails, but they also cause more trail damage than flat plates. Flat plates work well in most conditions and also cause less damage to the home pasture if horses remain shod between outings.

Pack lightly and keep the number of packstock to a minimum. Horses are big, heavy animals. Their weight and power can cause serious harm to plants and soils. To reduce trampling, limit the number of animals. Generally, one average-sized mule or horse can carry 150 to 200 pounds of gear, regardless of terrain. One pack animal for every two to three people is more than adequate on trips of a week or less. Longer trips may require additional packstock. Lightweight gear—such as nylon backpacking tents and one-burner stoves—saves wear and tear on the animals and, consequently, on the trails. Fewer animals also means fewer mouths to feed and less manure.

"Stay on the trail. Shortcutting switchbacks causes erosion and could lead to injury to you and your stock." Courtesy of USDA Forest Service, Pacific Northwest Region.

"Use a nosebag to feed supplemental grain to stock. This enables a full ration to be eaten without waste." Courtesy of USDA Forest Service, Pacific Northwest Region.

Carrying your own feed is particularly important in areas where forage is scarce or packstock use is heavy. An overgrazed meadow is a sign to others of careless packstock use (and not much of a welcome to the next pack train that pulls in). The meadow also will be more vulnerable to erosion and provide less forage, at least for a while, for resident wildlife. Using certified processed feed also ensures that no undesirable plants (such as spotted knapweed or leafy spurge) will be introduced to the backcountry. Remember to feed your stock on it for several days before the trip so their manure will be weed free. Also, a radical change of diet in the backcountry could leave you walking.

Ask beforehand about local regulations or restrictions concerning horses and packstock. Some trails and sometimes entire zones of a park or forest are closed to packstock use seasonally or year-round. More common are restrictions on the number of packstock and type of feed, and regulations on the use of fire. Know the rules and please obey them—to ensure that you and other riders will be welcomed back to the same area in the future.

Designated wilderness areas and national park lands tend to place greater restrictions on all types of visitors, trail riders included. For this reason, and to help protect these pristine lands from being loved to death, *The Backcountry Horseman's Guide to Washington* describes primarily non-wilderness trails where horse use is well established. Make no mistake—these trails sample the whole spectrum of spectacular scenery and pleasing destinations that Washington has to offer. And we couldn't resist including some of our favorite wilderness routes as well.

Just remember: rules and regulations are not meant to punish but rather to help preserve opportunities for everyone to enjoy our wild lands. See page 179 for a list of regulations specific to public lands in Washington State.

On the Trail

Ride only in areas and on trails open to horse use.

Always stay on the trail. Cutting across switchbacks or taking shortcuts off the trail tramples plants, loosens soil, and creates unnecessary paths. Subsequent erosion damages the trail, scars the land, and muddies nearby streams and lakes.

Trail rider Don Craddock of Friday Harbor prepares to cinch up a prized saddle during a ride into Gardner Meadows on the Wolf Creek trail. If you tie your horse, make sure the tree is sturdy enough and look for hard ground that won't be disturbed by the horse's hooves.

Try to keep your stock from skirting shallow puddles, small rocks, and bushes so you don't widen the tread or create secondary trails. Keep packstrings short to reduce this tendency. A short string also travels faster with fewer problems.

Trail riders should carry an axe or small bow saw to clear downfall when traveling forested trails. Clear downfall only if it blocks the trail itself; this will prevent a detour path from forming around the obstacle. If the downed tree is too big to cut, keep your detour as short as possible. On steep slopes and fragile ground, dismount and walk each animal around the obstacle. Resist the temptation to use the axe or saw for other chores (such as gathering firewood or crafting camp furniture).

Yield the right-of-way whenever it's safe and sensible to do so. The rule-of-thumb is that strings going uphill have the right-of-way in the morning; strings going downhill have it in the afternoon. Longer strings generally have right-of-way over shorter strings, and riders without packstock should yield to packstrings. When in doubt, yield to the other party and enjoy a break from the trail.

When overtaking hikers, call out a friendly "howdy" so you don't sneak up on them. Realize that not all hikers know how to react when meeting packstock on the trail. Be helpful, and remind them that you're concerned as much for their safety as for your own. Hikers should all stand on the same side of the trail, and downhill from it. Horses and their kin have a long history of being prey animals; they're wary of predators attacking from above. Standing on the downhill side is perceived as less of a threat.

If you stop to visit with hikers or other trail users, give them the courtesy of talking face to face: take the opportunity to get out of the saddle and stretch your legs.

"Stock that tends to wander while grazing can be restrained by using a hobble on the front legs." Courtesy of USDA Forest Service, Pacific Northwest Region.

During rest stops—even short ones—lead your stock off the trail as a courtesy to other trail users and to help reduce wear and tear on the trail. Look for trample-resistant ground (sand, gravel, or dry meadows are best) for rest stops. As much as possible, avoid tying stock to trees. Rope can girdle a tree's bark, and the animal's hooves will quickly trample and pack the soil around the tree's base. If you do tie up, choose a sturdy tree at least 8 inches in diameter (about as big around as your thigh). And don't leave the animal tied up for long in one spot. Never tie horses to anything they can drag around or break off. They will. Before you move on, scatter any manure to help it decompose.

Watering and Feeding Stock

Except when stock are being watered, they should be kept at least 200 feet from streams, rivers, and lakeshores. Some areas require only a 100-foot buffer zone. Remember that these are *minimum* distances; the greater the distance, the better. When leading stock to water, look for an established ford or low, gentle banks with firm footing. Steep banks are more difficult for stock to negotiate and are easily eroded by heavy hoof traffic. Avoid wet ground and lush vegetation.

When stock are grazing, rotate animals throughout the area to reduce trampling and prevent overgrazing. A few trails listed in this book have ample grazing resources for stock. But even those areas will benefit from horse riders using processed feed instead of depending on grazing. If you do let animals graze, make sure enough natural forage is available to leave plenty for elk, deer, and other wildlife. If possible, graze stock on north-facing slopes, where, come winter, forage will be buried beneath snow. Leave plenty of forage on south-facing slopes, where snowcover is typically thin and wildlife can feed throughout the winter.

Riders carrying processed feed won't be disappointed if the anticipated grazing area is too dry or has been overgrazed by others. As a rule-of-thumb, plan on two to three quarts of oats morning and night and 10 pounds of hay pellets daily for each animal.

Nosebags are great for reducing waste when you feed your stock pellets or grain. They also help to minimize pawing and chewing of the ground cover. If you want to feed stock from the ground, conserve your feed and protect the ground by pouring the pellets or grain on a mantie, a canvas packing tarp.

Choosing and Setting Up Stock Campsite

When choosing a campsite, remember that foot traffic—both human and horse—will be heavy around camp, with a high risk of damage to plants and soil. If a well-worn backcountry campsite exists, use it. The idea here is to concentrate use in places already damaged by previous use. Such sites can usually tolerate continued use and suffer little or no additional damage. But stay away from sites that are lightly worn or just beginning to show signs of use. If left alone, these sites will return to their natural condition. Where no well-worn campsites exist, try to find a patch of durable, trample-resistant ground such as sand, gravel, or bedrock for the main camp area. Dry meadows also work well for short stays. Look for pasture that will hold your stock without damaging the country. Dry grass meadows are best, preferably in sight of camp so you can keep an eye on your animals and put a quick stop to any damaging or dangerous behavior. Also try to camp at lower elevations, never above timberline. Plants and soils at high elevations tend to be more fragile and slow to recover from trampling.

Keep packstock out of established campsites. This reduces campsite damage, keeps manure from underfoot, and curtails the number of flies and other pests in camp.

Don't construct rock walls, log benches, wood shelters, or other "improvements." They detract from the natural landscape. In a designated wilderness area, permanent structures are prohibited.

When you're breaking camp, scout around for stray trash, including unburned waste in the ashes if a fire was built. Animals will dig up any buried trash, so please pack everything out. Make sure all fires are out cold and scatter any ash or charcoal. Also break up and scatter horse manure. Scout the area to make sure nothing will be left behind. Fill in any pawed holes. Return the site to its natural state as much as possible.

Corralling Your Stock in the Backcountry

When horses are confined to one area for more than a few hours, the risk to soils and plants from trampling and grazing is greatly increased. Given careful consideration and planning, however, the method you use to corral your stock can reduce the damage done to backcountry pastures. We've already mentioned that it's best not to tie up to trees because this concentrates the trampling within a small circle around the tree. Using a picket rope and pin often leads to the same problem—a ring of pawed dirt and smashed plants around the pin. So what method works best?

"To form a hitch line, stretch a rope, a horse's head high, between two eight-inch diameter trees." Courtesy of USDA Forest Service, Pacific Northwest Region.

The most convenient yet still effective way to keep stock from wandering off is a high hitchline. And most horses seem more relaxed on a hitchline than with any other restraint. Look for a hard, rocky area or dry grassy clearing and run a line between two trees. Protect the trees with webbing, nylon Tree-Saver straps, burlap bags, or some other cushioning material, then tighten the hitchline about seven feet above the ground, as high as the horses' heads. This allows horses more freedom to move and reduces chances of them getting tangled or hurt. Tie the lead rope to the hitchline, or better yet, tie a loop into the hitchline with a ring or swivel attached. Run the lead rope through the swivel to keep it untangled. Whichever method you use, make sure the lead cannot slide along the hitchline—horses will tangle with each other or end up pawing the ground by one of the trees.

Half-inch hemp or multifilament poly ropes are best for hitchlines; nylon is too stretchy. Many packers use the lash ropes as hitchlines.

If you plan to use hobbles, let your stock become familiar with them before your trip. Besides hampering wandering, hobbles are good for horses who like to paw—hobbling prevents them from tearing up the ground. Hanging a bell on a hobbled horse that likes to stray will help locate the animal in brushy or heavily wooded country. Bells are usually needed only on lead stock. (Don't use them if you are camping close to other parties.) Hobbles work for some animals who like to wander but others have learned how to move fast even while wearing them. If that's the case with your horse, try adding a half-hobble on one rear leg and attaching it to the hobble in front.

If you do use a picket pin to anchor a horse, move the picket frequently to prevent excessive trampling and to reduce overgrazing. Avoid areas with obstacles so the rope doesn't get hung up as the horse moves. When you break camp, be sure to take the picket pin with you and clear manure from the area.

Temporary Fences and Corrals

When you plan to spend several days in one spot, temporary fences and corrals are good ways to keep your stock in camp. Make sure the horses or mules are trained to stay in temporary corrals. It's also best to limit the number of animals enclosed.

There are at least three kinds of temporary fences that can be used to corral horses:

- Plastic snow fences are lightweight and easy to pack and set up. Some people use a strand of electric fence at the top to prevent stock from escaping.
- Portable electric fences also make convenient temporary corrals for stock if the animals are trained to respect the wires. The fences are lightweight and run on D-cell batteries. Some models are available that run on solar power. Wildlife may run into electric fences so place the fence away from likely game trails.
- Rope corrals are relatively easy to rig and move but they do require extra rope. One method uses two parallel ropes tied with loops or bowlines and threaded with cross ropes to make a more secure enclosure.

Regardless of which method you choose, plan ahead and familiarize yourself and your stock with the chosen form of restraint before you leave home.

Disposing of Human Waste

Many people are surprised to learn that human waste, even when properly buried in a "cat hole" under ideal conditions, requires a year or more to decompose naturally. Any fecal bacteria present also will remain viable (that is, ready to infect) for that length of time. And the decomposition process is slowed even more when waste is concentrated (as in a group latrine) or deposited in excessively dry, wet, or cold conditions.

Understanding this, it is easy to see that natural composting can't always keep pace with the amount of human waste unleashed, particularly at heavily used backcountry campsites. The problem is compounded when the site is near a lake or stream (as are most popular campsites) because runoff or groundwater can easily carry fecal material and disease to the surface water. Wildlife—and other campers— then rely on the same source for drinking water. Not a pretty picture.

Increasingly, land managers are asking (and in some places *requiring*) people to pack out human waste. Boaters on many western rivers have been doing this for years, and mountain climbers are now handed plastic bags for this purpose in several national parks (including Mount Rainier). Thanks to the staff at Yosemite National Park, trail riders (and all other types of backcountry visitors) now have a clean, easy, and secure way to join the ranks and pack out waste. It's called the "poop tube."

You can make your own poop tube from a piece of 4-inch diameter PVC plastic pipe, the kind used for plumbing. Cut the pipe to length as needed for the number of days you'll be in the backcountry; a 2-foot section is enough for five to seven days for most folks. Then glue a cap on one end and a threaded adapter for a screw-on plug on the other end. Some people duct tape a piece of nylon webbing onto the side of the tube so it can be strapped onto a pack or pannier.

To use the tube, defecate into a paper lunch bag. Then sprinkle in a handful of kitty litter to absorb moisture and reduce odors. Shake the bag to distribute the kitty litter, then roll it up and slide it into the tube. Used toilet paper can go in the tube too. Screw in the plug and you're done. At the end of the trip, empty the contents into a non-flush vault or "pit" toilet (ask land managers beforehand to recommend a specific outhouse). The paper bag will quickly decay (to ensure that it does, use only unwaxed bags) and won't clog the pump used to periodically clean out the vault. Never put human waste into trash cans or dumpsters—it creates a health hazard and is illegal.

If you decide instead to use the cat hole method and bury your waste in the backcountry, follow a few simple guidelines:

- Look for an out-of-the-way site in stable soil at least 200 feet (about seventy paces) from surface water. Avoid places that show signs of flooding, carrying runoff, or groundwater seepage.
- Make sure the site is at least 200 feet from campsites, trails, and other centers of human activity.
- Look for a site with a healthy layer of topsoil at least 6 inches deep. The ground should be moist (but not saturated) and easy to dig in.
- With a small hand trowel, dig a cat hole 6 to 8 inches deep. Keep the sod lid intact. Set it aside and pile all the dirt next to the hole.
- Squat and aim for the hole. Deposit used toilet paper in the hole (burning it is unnecessary and risky if conditions are dry or windy).
- When covering the waste, use a stick to stir in the first handful or two of soil. This hastens the decomposition process. Add the remaining soil and replace the sod lid. Scrape leaves and duff around to camouflage the site. Remember to clean your hands well before handling food or cooking utensils.
- Unless local regulations state otherwise, it's usually best to dig individual cat holes rather than a group latrine. And always use the outhouse if one is provided.

Washing

The key to cleaning up in the backcountry is to keep soap, oils, and all other pollutants out of the water cycle. Remember that aquatic plants and fish are extremely sensitive to soap, even biodegradable soap, and can die from contact with it.

To wash cooking and eating utensils, carry water in a bowl or tub at least 200 hundred feet from water sources. Use little or no soap—water warmed on the stove will unstick most food and grease. Use a plastic scrubbie and a little muscle for stubborn residues. Scatter wash water over the ground in an out-of-the-way spot at least 200 feet from surface water and 100 yards from any likely campsite. In bear country, pick out food scraps before scattering the water; pack them out with other garbage.

For personal bathing, a good dousing and scrubbing with a soapless washcloth will suffice for all but extended trips. Again, carry the water at least 200 feet from surface water. If you use a shower bag, try to protect the soil from saturation and trampling. Choose a spot where you can stand on a large rock or sandy area, or move the shower bag between uses.

Campfires and Cook Stoves

The advent of lightweight cook stoves for camping has made campfires a luxury, but one many people look forward to at the end of a long day in the saddle. Every luxury, of course, has its price. Campfires are "costly" because they use up wood, sterilize the soil, blacken rocks, and leave long-lasting scars on the land.

Avoid these costs by using a gas or propane stove for cooking, or carry a ventilated metal can-with-a-handle charcoal starter to prepare briquettes to use with a portable grill or Dutch oven. Save the firewood for an evening social session or for unusually wet or cold weather.

Where campfires are allowed, use fire responsibly:

- Do without a fire in windy or dry weather.
- Build a fire only if downed, dead wood is plentiful. Use only sticks that can be broken with your bare hands, no thicker than your wrist. Leave larger branches and trees where they lay; many wildlife species rely on such downfall for food and shelter.
- Gather firewood over a wide area, well away from camp. Pick up only as much as you need. Pack wood with you if possible.
- Keep fires small and brief. Small fires burn more efficiently, with less smoke, and are easier to control.
- If there is an existing fire ring, use it. But do not build a rock fire ring if none is present. Instead use a fire pan—a 3-foot square of flame-retardant canvas or an old steel pan. Cover the fire pan with a mound of sand or dirt (scooped from a stream bank or the hole left by an uprooted tree) and build the fire on top. This insulates the ground and plants from the heat and eliminates the need to dig a hole or build a fire ring.
- Never leave a fire unattended.
- Burn the fire down to a fine white ash. Douse it completely with water and stir to be sure it's out cold. Disperse ashes by sprinkling them over a wide area well away from camp and surface waters. Return any sand or dirt to the hole it came from.
- Leave existing fire rings clean and attractive for the next camper. Pack out any scraps of incompletely burned garbage. Never put aluminum foil in a fire— it won't burn.
- If a campsite has more than one fire ring, dismantle all but one. Scatter the rocks widely, black side down. Also scatter the ashes, and sprinkle leaves, pine needles, and twigs over any remaining scar.

Leaving No Trace Is Everyone's Responsibility

Everyone who enjoys Washington's backcountry has a responsibility to respect the land and to do everything possible to maintain the environment for others to enjoy—or for their own return trip.

Park and forest service rangers can help you with any questions about leave-no-trace techniques or recommendations—just ask at any office or ranger station. Often, the most knowledgeable folks are the rangers you will meet out on the trails; don't hesitate to ask questions or offer feedback about problems or new ways of leaving no trace.

For more detailed advice or to participate further in the effort to protect our lands, contact the National Leave No Trace Skills and Ethics Education Program at (800) 332-4100. Or write to 288 Main St., Lander, WY 82520. You can request free brochures on leave no trace skills and techniques, including specific pamphlets on backcountry travel and camping with horses.

TRAIL RIDING TIPS

Preparing for Trail Rides

Wise preparation will save you from many of the problems, disappointments, or wrecks on the trail that every rider shares in from time to time. This is advice all of us have heard and ignored before. But it's repeated here with the hope that some of these warnings and tips will save you the experience of learning everything the hard way.

What Makes a Good Trail Horse

You may know about horses in general, and about your horse in particular. But unless you've been on trail rides with your horse, and in the company of other horses, consider these helpful tips from the Back Country Horsemen of America.

No doubt the most important item you will take into the backcountry is your horse. Sadly some folks do think of a horse as just another piece of "equipment," but a good trail horse is much more than that. Your horse should also be your friend. And a friendly equine disposition is 75 percent of how well a horse will work for you and with you. An ideal mountain horse should have a quiet, gentle disposition, good stamina, and be reliable under all conditions. Few horses possess all of those qualities without training.

A good trail horse should also have "feet with eyes." It will walk with a natural, balanced gait and seem to know where to place its feet to avoid obstacles. Some horses are born with this and others learn it on the trail. A few may always trip up, slide off trail, or stumble over their own hooves; they make good pasture ponies, but don't bring them into the backcountry.

A horse with trail experience will be much easier to handle in the backcountry than a youngster or an old homebody that's never left the pasture. If you're in the market for a new horse, ask about its trail experience. If you're new to riding, consider taking lessons from a good trainer. Try to find one who ventures beyond the show arena and at least occasionally rides trails.

Several physical characteristics are also the mark of a good trail horse. Withers—the bones at the top of the back just behind the neck—should be large and well-defined (not buried under muscle). This will help to keep your saddle in place. Flat-backed, round-sided horses don't do as well over long distances as longer backed, flat-sided horses. Some folks call them "slab-sided"—a good image to distinguish the leaner body shape from barrel-sided, halter-type horses. It's a shame that over the years the judges in halter classes have favored highly muscled, round-backed, short-legged horses. They tend to tire too quickly and just don't do as well on trails because they carry too much muscle.

Like most domestic animals, horses have a descending order of authority, a "pecking order." A mare will usually lead a herd, unless a stud is present. Also exercise caution when placing horses in a packstring, at a hitch rail, or in a truck to avoid trouble or injury.

Above all, horses are individuals. They usually follow general behavior patterns, but new situations can cause unexpected reactions. When you know the bad habits or attitudes of your horse you are better prepared for anticipating possible problems on the trail.

Even gentle horses can become nervous and unpredictable when they first experience bogs, creeks, deadfalls, trees, and narrow trails, not to mention dropoffs. In addition, mountain trail horses need to become accustomed to sudden movements of birds, wildlife, and dogs; hikers with bright, large packs; fast-moving mountain bikes; and loud motorcycles on the trail.

If you're using an inexperienced horse, there are several things to teach the horse before leaving familiar home territory. A horse must be halter-broken and accustomed to standing tied for extended periods. For practice, tie your horse in the home corral for various periods over several days.

Train your horse to be accustomed to hobbles, pickets, electric fences, or a high hitchline at home. Also, get your horse used to being mounted from both sides. In many steep mountain-trail situations, it's nearly impossible to mount a horse from the downhill side. There may not be a stump or a rock around, or an opportunity to turn the horse around to mount from the uphill side.

Shoes should be checked often. In the spring, they loosen more because the hoof grows faster. Know how to nail a shoe back on and carry extra shoes and nails, a rasp, and a hammer. For emergencies, bring along a slip-on shoe made of urethane. It slips over the hoof like a boot and is held in place by a buckle and cable.

A green horse, like a green dude, will gain confidence by making the first trip with seasoned horses and riders, with either Back Country Horsemen or Washington Trail Riders Association members.

Saddle Up

You and your horse will be happier with a lightweight saddle designed for trail riding and well matched to the contours of your horse. Too many people worry more about how a saddle fits their own backsides, but a saddle that fits your horse poorly will cause a whole litany of problems—cinching difficulties, sores, early tiring, unnatural gaits, and poor behavior.

If possible, buy your horse before you buy a saddle, and then take your horse with you when you go saddle shopping. Saddle makers and shop owners are understandably balky about loaning out new saddles for people to try at home. But they can hardly refuse to let you bring the horse to them for a fitting—after all, it's your money and their livelihood. It also helps them learn what fits and what doesn't. Here are a few tips:

• The leading edge of the bar should fit right behind the horse's shoulders, not on top of them. The shape of the tree should follow the contour of the horse's back. Use a narrow tree for a high-withered, thoroughbred horse, and a wide tree for a mutton-withered, quarter-horse type.

Selecting a good saddle that fits horse and rider is as important as a horse with good trail sense.

• If you use your horse for roping, cutting, bulldogging, or other competitive, short-duration events, then the full, forward-rigged saddle should be your choice. But for a horse that works long hours on the trail, it is better to have the rigging farther away from the elbow so it won't cause galling. A 3/4-rigged saddle works well, but so may a 7/8 or 5/8 saddle, depending on the size of your horse.

• Avoid saddles that are too long; they should not rub either the shoulder or hip.

Too often people try to compensate for a poor match between saddle and horse by adding extra pads. Typically, more pads only make the saddle fit too tightly or raise it so high that it becomes unstable. Then the rider cinches it down tighter, which only annoys the horse.

Polyester pads are the most popular, but tests clearly show that wool is still the coolest material. Foam pads have an unfortunate memory—that is, they want to return to their original shape. You have to cinch them tighter to prevent them from working out from under the saddle.

Of course the saddle also must fit another animal—you! Here's what to look for.

• The length and width of the saddle are important. Average saddle length is 15 inches, measured from inside the pommel (the front, where the horn is) to the center back of the cantle (the rear of the saddle that supports your fanny). Children usually fit in 13- or 14-inch seat sizes and adults in 15- or 16-inch seats. Some custom-made saddles can be fit in half-inch increments.

• When you sit in the saddle there should be a minimum of 1 inch between your thigh and the pommel with your legs hanging down and your feet out of the stirrups.

• When you put your feet in the stirrups and have just a slight bend in the knees, you should be able to freely swing your legs forward and back for climbing and descending steep grades. If you don't have a free-swinging stirrup you will soon be on a first-name basis with aches and pains you never dreamed of after a 15- or 20-mile ride.

• Avoid rough-out seats. Padded seats are okay, but just make sure the seat is covered with a smooth grain leather.

When you find that perfect saddle—the one that fits your horse, you, and your wallet—you're ready to spend many hours and miles breaking it in. First, ask the store where you bought your saddle to turn the stirrups for you. If the store can't, you can do it yourself by soaking the stirrup fenders in water. Water won't harm the leather unless it is left wet for a long time, and then it will rot. So, soak the leather and then put your saddle on a saddle stand (a sawhorse will do). Then turn the stirrups so they face away from the saddle; stick a broom handle between them to hold them until the leather dries, usually in about 24 hours. This will save your knees from twisting in a direction they weren't meant to go.

Protect Your Saddles and Tack

If you haven't camped out before with your horse and tack, you might want to know that saddles, cinches, and other sweaty gear ought to be stored near camp and covered. Small rodents, porcupines, and deer seeking salt will chew on them while you're sleeping. They may destroy expensive equipment or leave it in a weakened condition.

Packstrings and Packing Tips

Know your stock: which animal leads best and which ones follow best. Know their pace. The slowest animal determines the speed of the packstring.

Be sure you understand proper packing techniques—especially the right rope knots and weight balancing—before hitting the trail. A knowledgeable packer could fill a library shelf with books on how to pack, and some of them have. See the sources of more information on page 172 for more on this topic. You can also learn about packing by taking trips with professional outfitters.

There is plenty of lightweight, compact camping equipment on the market, including sleeping bags, tents, cookware and utensils. These make the loads lighter on the pack animals as well as reducing the number of animals needed for carrying camping equipment and supplies.

Transporting Your Horse

You've found the right trail horse and your trailer is hitched and waiting. Now how do you put the two together, preferably without a lot of cussin' and sweat?

Ideally, a horse should be taught how to load and unload from a trailer while still a youngster. If it's already too late for that, at least take the time to practice the maneuver before you actually need to take the horse somewhere.

A horse's reluctance to get into a trailer is nothing less than good horse sense. How many of us would want to be winched into a tight, dark, noisy cell and then swung down the highway, careening around corners and jolting back and forth at every stop and start? It's a lot to ask of an animal accustomed to open spaces.

So take some time with your horse. Leave him with the trailer to get used to its smells, noises, and feel. Keep it clean. Make that first ride in the trailer as pleasant (and short) as possible—do a brief loop on smooth roads close to home. Put good shipping boots on the horse's legs and guide his head when he's backing out of the trailer.

Also make sure that the trailer is safe. Check its lights, brakes, and tire pressure each time you use it. The trailer should be level when rolling with its load, not tilted to the front or rear. A slant-load rig is easier on your horse than a front-load type. Horses can balance from side to side much better than from front to back, so when they face the front in a trailer they tend to scramble up the sides whenever a turn is made at speed.

Before you start down the road, think about how long the drive will be, both in miles and hours. Plan to unload your horse at least once every 4 hours, to give him 30 minutes to walk the kinks out and drink some water.

Finally, although it is rare to be questioned about your stock while traveling, it's worth the peace of mind to always carry proof of ownership when traveling with your horses. A brand inspection certificate issued by a brand inspector is the best form of horse identification. But a temporary certificate, the kind commonly issued at sales, is only valid for a few weeks. In Washington you can obtain a permanent certificate—a card with the horse's photograph on the back—for about $15. Another helpful piece of paper is a health certificate from a veterinarian. These cost between $25 and $30, but you can put several horses on one form. Keep this packet of papers in your saddlebag or other pouch, one that always accompanies you on trips. That way it will be there when you need it. And double-check to make sure you have all the paperwork before crossing state lines or the border into Canada.

Training Rides on Roads Closed to Vehicles

For those who are new to high-country trail riding the trips described in this book should be a wonderful experience. But there is a great difference between valley riding and mountain riding. Most of these trips demand much more preparation than a pasture ride or a day ride close to town. Get your horse and yourself in shape, and do it gradually. Don't try an 18-mile marathon into the Pasayten on your first trip. Start out with valley rides early in the season, when the snow is deep on the higher trails, and you'll be more prepared for the challenge of steeper routes during summer and fall.

An excellent way to familiarize you and your horse with the surprises of the trail is to start out on forest roads gated and closed to vehicular traffic. Many old logging or mining access roads wind through scenic, wildlife-rich forests, providing interesting yet easy rides. They also offer the perfect environs for giving your horse "trail sense." There are bridges to cross, creeks to ford, hills to climb, and steep descents;

grouse to spook, deer to jump, and ravens to grumble at you. Rain and wind will flap at your slickers, your saddlebags or panniers will slip loose, and the cinch will break or lightning will unsettle your steed, or the scent of bear or cougar will tickle his nose. All without the dangers of steep sidehills, tight switchbacks, cliffs, and narrow trails.

Before You Hit the Trail

Check with Forest Service or Park Service offices for maps, trail conditions, fire conditions, snowy or muddy trails, or other situations that could affect your trip.

Set up a checklist for your trip of items you'll need, for both riders and horses, for all kinds of weather conditions. See the checklist on page 168.

Study maps and inspect the condition of camping gear, saddles, and tack. Keep rain gear or a warm jacket or both, depending on the season, tied behind your saddle. Storms move in quickly in the mountain high country where most of these trails lead. Even blue sky and sunshine at the start of a trip is no guarantee against sudden rain or even snow during your trek.

Also, hot sun can be harsher at higher altitudes, and more searing. High winds, likewise, are often more blustery than back at the trailhead several thousand feet below. Prepare accordingly for the unexpected, even if it only means carrying sunscreen and a Windbreaker on a summer ride.

For one reason or another, people end up wearing a wide variety of footwear on horseback. For the most part, that's a matter of comfort. But there are things to consider. Western riding boots, packer boots, field boots, or work boots provide good support and slip fairly easily in and out of stirrups. Avoid shoes or boots with heavy rubber, composition, or lug-type soles that may hang up in the stirrups and cause problems.

Ride with the ball of your foot in the stirrups and keep your feet loose. Pull your feet partway out of the stirrups when you're riding through a dangerous area and just before dismounting. Those are times you could be hurt if the horse stumbles, shies, falls, or bolts.

Wear soft clothing that doesn't rub against your skin. Hours in the saddle can easily lead to chafing. Moleskin is an excellent protective covering for tender areas, particularly if boots are rubbing or the saddle is causing sore areas where you need to sit. Because those areas are difficult to reach with Moleskin once you're on the trail, you might want to apply some before leaving home or the campground, just as a precaution. You know where your bony parts are and what needs to be covered.

Western hats have always been popular with cowboys for many good reasons. The hat protects from wind, rain, sun, snow, and from small tree branches when you don't duck fast enough. Most riders change between straw and felt hats depending on the season, but even on straw hat days, cold nights at high elevations may make an old beater felt hat stuffed in a saddlebag mighty welcome.

Leather riding gloves are indispensable on a trail ride, and a sharp knife—preferably a cased folding knife with a locking blade—is also highly recommended.

Dress in layers—moisture-wicking underwear; an insulating or ventilating second layer, depending on the season; and an outer layer to shed wind and rain or snow. You can add or take off layers as needed to better regulate body temperature and comfort. Trails pass through a variety of altitudes and weather conditions that demand flexibility in the amount of clothing being worn.

For nighttime, take along a sleeping bag, blanket, and small, lightweight tent. High-country sleeping provides marvelous middle-of-the-night opportunities for gazing at crisp, sparkling galaxies across a blackened night sky. But if you're too cold to care, you may go home with the wrong kinds of camping memories. If the weather is frosty or snowy, your horse may appreciate a blanket, too.

On the Trail

For successful trail rides, observe a few basic rules. Let your stock pick their way through boggy places, across slide zones, along slick and steep trails, and through deep water and snow. When necessary, don't hesitate to get off and lead them through treacherous areas.

Few trails are perfect throughout their whole length or in all seasons. Watch for changes in the terrain and trail conditions. On early summer rides it's not uncommon to find patches of snow on the trail at higher elevations. Some horses, of course, shy from the sight or feel of snow. Even small patches are sometimes enough to spook them.

Follow the guidelines for leaving no trace outlined on pages 11 through 22. Do not smoke while traveling on horseback, especially during the fire season.

Sharing the Trail—Hikers, Llamas, and Mountain Bikes

While traveling on trails, observe basic courtesies to make life easier for everyone involved. Downhill travelers usually yield to uphill travelers, especially in steep, rough country. People traveling on foot, with mountain or motor bikes, or with llamas should yield to horses and mules because it is easier for them to move off the trail.

Trail users are getting better at knowing the protocols for when to yield to whom, but not everyone knows how to behave around horses, especially in close proximity on a narrow trail. If you encounter hikers, bikers, or llama packers who are unfamiliar with horses, ask them to hold up until you pass. Riding in small groups will enhance your own trail-riding experience as well as reduce problem encounters with other trail users. Talk to people when you meet them, take the opportunity for a friendly visit, and reassure them that you're as concerned for their safety as for your own packstring.

If horses have never seen a llama before, they are often spooked by the sight and smell of these strange-looking creatures. Mountain bikes also pose a scare for many stock, particularly if they come up fast and with little warning. Motorbikes seem to be less of a problem because you can always hear them coming.

Ask a ranger beforehand what types of travelers are allowed on the trails you plan to use so you'll know what to expect. If you know of llamas in your area, it may help to arrange a visit to let your horse get close to a llama in a non-trail situation. The llamas will just be curious and most horses soon adjust. If you meet bikers on the trail, take the time to thank them for yielding the right-of-way. Remind them that the horses will be less spooky if the bikers stand quietly on the downhill side. Removing their helmets helps make them more recognizable for the horses. And if someone exhibits truly discourteous or dangerous behavior toward you or your horses, let the local ranger know. More trail users are getting the message, but it's a slow process.

Snake Sense

There are no poisonous snakes west of the Cascade Mountains in Washington. The weather doesn't suit them. On the east side, however, poisonous rattlesnakes are plentiful, though rarely seen or heard.

The Northern Pacific rattler is native to the Pacific Northwest and is a common resident of such places as the Umatilla National Forest, among other eastern Washington regions. Forest Service rangers at the Umatilla National Forest Supervisor's Office offer some "snake sense" advice and information.

Snakes tend to hole up in very hot weather. Although they are cold blooded and need to be warmed by the sun, they cannot take extreme heat so they find shelter under rocks.

Rattlers are most apt to be moving around early in the morning and late in the evening. They like water sources, so the closer you are to a river, lake, or stream, the more likely you are to see them. Elsewhere, they are found in a variety of terrains from grasslands to coniferous forests. Generally, they prefer stony canyons and rocky outcrops near water sources.

Although most Northern Pacific rattlers are 30 to 40 inches long, they can be as long as 5 feet. They have white bellies and large black or brown blotches down the midline of the body. A rattlesnake sheds its skin whenever it becomes too tight, usually a couple of times a year. At each shedding the snake grows a new rattle.

Like most wild animals, rattlesnakes are wary of humans and will usually slither away and hide. Don't panic if you encounter a rattler. Step back slowly and leave it alone. If you enter an area with several rattlers, calling for help won't bother the snakes—they can't hear above-ground sounds—but it could bring help that would scare the snakes off by the vibrations of their approach.

Traveling on horseback in snake country, riders are usually wearing boots, which offer protection if riders dismount and walk off trail. Use a long stick to strike rocks to scare snakes out before you rest on them. Never put your foot or hand under rocks or in areas you can't see.

If you are bitten by a rattler, stay calm and move as slowly as possible to minimize blood circulation. Make sure everyone moves well away from the snake (don't bother trying to kill or capture it—it's not worth the risk of another bite). Remove any constricting clothing, jewelry, or watches from the affected limb. DO NOT apply a tourniquet, cold water, or ice—these increase the risk of gangrene. Splint the injured area to prevent muscle movement, which speeds the venom's absorption. Check the splint frequently to make sure swelling is not cutting off circulation. If possible, ride (don't run) to the nearest trailhead and drive to the nearest medical center. Give fluids and anticipate possible shock.

Camping in Bear Habitat

When camping in areas that are part of bear habitat, check with rangers on bear sightings before you start up the trail. Check your campsite for bear droppings and other sign, and consider moving on if you find some.

Rangers say bears are not attracted by horse flesh. In fact, horseback riders tend to have fewer bear problems than hikers do. A surprise encounter is less likely because of the noise made by a horse or packstring. Horses also may smell a bear before you're right on top of it, giving both you and the bruin an opportunity to back away from an encounter. Finally, a rider on horseback may appear more intimidating to bears than a person on foot. Bear troubles on the trail are uncommon for horsepackers.

In camp it may be a different story, particularly if people are careless in their food handling habits. The best way to keep bears out of camp is to keep your camp clean. Don't rely on panniers to protect food from an inquisitive bear. Hang food from a tree branch at least 15 feet above the ground and 5 feet away from the trunk. In some areas the experts recommend hanging all stock feed as well—ask beforehand. Cook well away from the tents—100 yards or more. Don't sleep in clothes filled with cooking aromas. Be alert and make plenty of noise while picking berries (a favorite bear food) or while hiking in dense cover or along streams.

Safe Drinking Water

Backcountry streams in the wilds of Washington are inviting, appearing crystal clear and pure as they flow over rock outcroppings and through meadows. But it's impossible to see the giardia parasite (*Giardia lamblia*), a microscopic organism in animal and human feces that can reside in seemingly fresh water.

Symptoms of illness in humans, which may take a week or more to appear, include nausea, diarrhea, cramps, and loss of appetite. With proper medical treatment, symptoms will pass quickly. Without treatment, they can continue sometimes for years because it can be difficult to diagnose.

Boiling water for at least five minutes is the best way to kill giardia and other organisms. If you're camping above 5,000 feet, where water boils at a lower temperature, boil your water for 10 minutes to be sure of killing the parasite. There are also effective filters designed to screen out giardia and other impurities. Most sporting goods stores sell several different models. Read the packaging before purchasing a filter to make sure it will screen out giardia and bacteria.

EQUINE FIRST AID

"First" aid means just that—what you do first to alleviate pain, stop blood flow, and cope with any other life-threatening conditions after an accident either to humans or animals. This section deals with first aid for horses, at least for the most common types of backcountry injuries. Bear in mind that no book can teach you how to properly diagnose and treat every emergency that may arise while trail riding. You can gain confidence with experience, but you may also want to enroll in some formal first-aid training to better care for your stock. Horse clubs, community colleges, and some veterinarians offer classes on the subject. Even a first-aid class for treating people will teach you some good bandaging techniques that will work on horses just as well.

The most common equine injuries in the backcountry are cuts and abrasions. Colic and heatstroke come in second, followed by saddle sores, rope burns, and minor accidents.

The first-aid kit that you carry for yourselves and your family has lots of things in it that you can use on your horse. But you should carry a separate kit for your horses packed right with their feed, brushes, and equipment. It doesn't need to be elaborate but should contain bandage materials such as Vetrap, Elastikon, and gauze pads. Some folks use feminine sanitary pads for bandaging wounds on a horse's legs. They provide padding and protection and at the same time are highly absorbent. Disposable baby diapers also work well.

You need some blood stop powder such as Farnam's Quick Stop. It is caustic so be careful not to use it around the horse's eyes. And use it only when there is a copious amount of blood flow. This occurs most often on the legs. After applying the blood stop powder you should have wound ointment such as Furacin or calendula (marigold) ointment. Slather the wound completely and wrap it snugly, not tight, just enough to support the leg until you can get the horse out and to a veterinarian. Remember this is "first" aid; not a cure.

Heat Stroke and Colic

Heat stroke and colic are sometimes confused. The symptoms are similar: the horse wants to lie down and sweats profusely. But the treatment is much different. With heat stroke the horse is just plain overheated. This happens with horses who are out of condition or have been carrying too heavy a load for too long on very hot days. The best thing to do is recognize the problem before the horse collapses. Stop right where you are, unload the animal, get him in the shade, let him rest, and do not walk him! Take a cloth or towel soaked in water and wipe him down from head to toe, especially over the head and neck area and down the insides of the legs where large blood vessels are close to the skin. Don't offer him cold water to drink until his body has cooled. You may dribble water from your towel or scarf into his mouth.

This takes time; you may have to camp on the spot. Heat stroke usually occurs well into the trip, late in the afternoon on hot summer days. Other symptoms of heat stroke include a dazed look to the horse's eye, stumbling, and weaving down the trail. Some horses will not sweat, so another way to tell if a horse is dehydrated is to pinch the skin on the neck. If it does not pop back into place within a few seconds, your horse needs water. Again—be careful about offering cold water, and limit intake to small amounts of water at first. Perhaps it's best to bring him a bucket full rather than allow him to drink his fill from the lake or stream. Some young or green horses will not drink from streams as you cross, and those are the ones you need to watch on hot days.

Always encourage your horses to drink at creek and river crossings as you ride. This is the only way they have to cool off, and they need lots of water to keep fluid levels up. A horse drinks 10 to 15 gallons of water on an average day. When working hard a horse will drink up to 25 gallons a day and perhaps more on hot days. So be aware of how much your individual animals drink and plan accordingly when you ride.

Colic is another crisis that can hit in the backcountry. Some horses are more susceptible than others. Colic usually occurs when there is a change of feed. Perhaps the horse was on pasture at home and then on the trip he switched to a pelletized ration or grain. Be sure your horses are accustomed to this feed at home first.

Symptoms of colic include pawing, rolling, sweating, head tossing, restlessness, and glazed eyes if the horse is in pain. Treatment is to try to keep him walking so that he doesn't roll and twist the intestine. Yet sometimes when a horse rolls the motion releases a gas bubble and relieves the pain. You really have to know your horse and have a good idea what is causing the distress. Walking the horse will aid the circulation in his intestinal tract. You can offer water, but usually a horse in pain will not drink. Try putting your fist up under his belly in different places and lift or put pressure on the stomach area. Move your fist around all under his tummy and see if that won't relieve the gas that usually causes the blockage.

Saddle Sores and Rope Burns

In an emergency, rangers recommend using bacon grease to soothe sores and chafes and using flour to stop minor bleeding.

An Equine First-Aid Kit

Your equine first-aid kit should include:

Vetrap
Elastikon tape
Scissors
Duct tape (for keeping hooves wrapped)
Easyboot to fit each horse
Gauze padding (sanitary napkins work well)
Furacin or Calendula wound ointment
Blood stop powder
*Phenylbutazone Paste
*Banamine

* Must be obtained from your veterinarian for pain and colic.

Euthanasia

As sad as it is, there are times when it may be necessary to end an animal's suffering in the backcountry. There are several factors that must be considered before doing this, and there is a right way to do it.

Euthanasia means humanely killing an animal to end its suffering when it is apparent that it cannot be saved or will not be able to function after recovering from the injury. This is never an easy decision to make, but it is far more fair to put the animal out of its misery than to torture it by keeping it alive. If Forest Service or park rangers are nearby, call them in for help. They can offer options that would not be available otherwise.

When a horse is seriously injured, the first problem is to determine whether the extent of the injury warrants euthanasia. Assuming you are far into the backcountry and the difficulty of getting the horse out to civilization and a veterinarian is going to do more damage than good, then the choice must be made. Also, the value of the horse becomes an important consideration. A broken leg, even if repairable, can be expensive. The healing process can take many months, and there is never any guarantee your horse will be sound and useable again.

Putting down an injured horse is a nasty business under any circumstances. Those horsemen and women who have had to do it often agonize over it long afterward. However, any rider who is more than 10 miles from the nearest veterinarian should know how to humanely kill a severely injured horse.

When the decision has been made to euthanize a horse and you must use a gun, a primary consideration is the selection of the weapon. A handgun is best, but a rifle can be used if you don't have a sidearm. Use the largest caliber available: .38, .44, .45, or a .357 magnum. A .22 caliber will work, but the placement of the bullet must be exact to insure a clean, humane death with one shot.

To locate the correct spot, draw imaginary lines from the base of each ear to the eye on the opposite side of the face. Where the lines intersect in the middle of the forehead is the place to hold the muzzle of the weapon. Hold the muzzle of the gun 0.25 to 0.5 inch from the horse's skull. Carefully squeeze the trigger and immediately step back. While some horses drop instantly, some will flip over backwards or lunge forward.

It may not be necessary on a day ride, but someone in a group of riders should carry a firearm. Be sure to check local regulations before packing a gun on the trail. They are not allowed in national parks and some other areas. If a horse is injured in the backcountry and you don't have a firearm, contact a ranger as quickly as possible. Even in national parks, rangers can carry a gun and are authorized to humanely dispatch injured livestock, after consultation with the animal's owner.

After putting the animal down (or if a horse has died outright) you must report the incident to the nearest ranger station so that they are made aware of a carcass— an unnatural food source—that may attract bears or other wildlife. Horses do not usually die "natural" deaths in the backcountry. They are plains animals and would not venture into the mountains unless taken there by humans. It's wise to carry with you the phone number of the nearest ranger station or park office so a call can be made from the trailhead or nearest town.

(Based on advice from Ruth James, D.V.M., who wrote *How to be your own Veterinarian—Sometimes*.)

1 MOUNT MULLER–LITTLETON LOOP

Location: 31 miles west of Port Angeles near Lake Crescent.
General description: A strenuous 13-mile loop ride along Snider Ridge and east of Mount Muller with spectacular views of Mount Olympus and the Strait of Juan de Fuca. An easier 9-mile ride is also possible.
Trailhead horse facilities: None. Water, restrooms, large parking lot, and trail information.
Trailhead elevation: 1,000 feet.
High point: 3,748 feet at the summit of Mount Muller.
Maps: Ask at the Sol Duc District office for a guide map. Use the Olympic National Forest map to reach the general area.
Season: Early summer to late fall.
Water availability: Ample at the trailhead and at Milepost 10, near Hutch Creek, on the 13-mile trip. Water is scarce or nonexistent at the higher elevations of the loop ride.
Feed availability: Carry processed feed for a horse treat on this short ride.
Permits/restrictions: No permits are required. Camping with horses is prohibited in meadows along this trail; camp only in timbered areas.
Finding the trailhead: From Port Angeles, drive 31 miles west on U.S. Highway 101 (4 miles west of Lake Crescent). At Milepost 216, turn right (north) on graveled Forest Road 3071. Drive 0.5 mile to the trailhead.

The ride: The Mount Muller–Littleton Loop Trail 882 is so new that it isn't on any current Forest Service maps. Parts of the loop date back to the early 1900s, and in the 1930s the Civilian Conservation Corps (CCC) added an extensive network of trails in the area, including an upgrading of the old Mount Muller trail. When the loop was reconstructed in 1994 some of the original trail was rebuilt, but most of this 13-mile loop is new. Our hats are off to the Peninsula Chapter of the Back Country Horsemen of Washington and individual volunteers who worked with the Forest Service rangers of the Sol Duc District, the InterAgency Committee for Outdoor Recreation, and the Washington Department of Natural Resources to put this trail on the ground.

The trail begins in the temperate, forested valley along US 101. Littleton Creek provides stock water at the trailhead. Don't be fooled by the lowland surroundings: horses need to be in good condition for this trail, which has steep slopes and multiple switchbacks.

From here the trail climbs hard 0.5 mile to Miner's Crossing, where traces of old miners' roads are still visible (but not passable) through the forest. From here the grade grows even steeper, switchbacking to Snider Ridge. About 1 mile from the trailhead the switchbacks give way to 1 mile of straight tread, only to revert to more switchbacks climbing to 3,200 feet at Jim's Junction on Snider Ridge. The average grade for these first 3 miles is about 15 percent.

Spring through summer, wildflowers provide weeks of seasonally changing blooms and colors along much of this route. A recent survey by the Forest Service found more

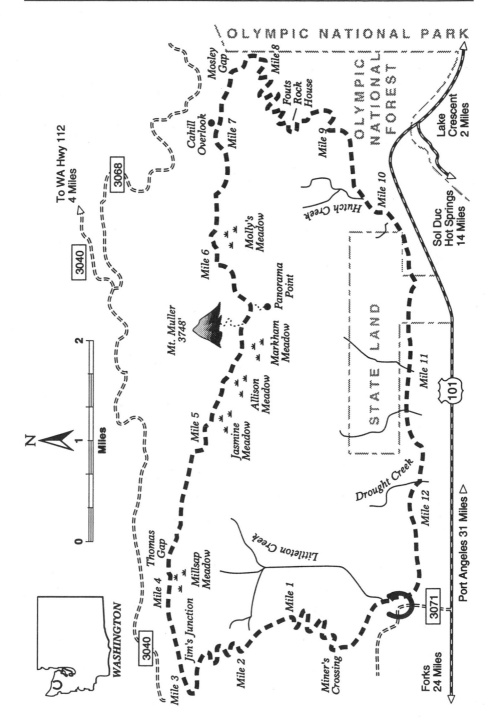

OLYMPIC NATIONAL PARK

OLYMPIC NATIONAL FOREST

STATE LAND

WASHINGTON

To WA Hwy 112
4 Miles

3068

3040

Mosley
Gap

Mile 8

Fouts
Rock
House

Cahill
Overlook

Mile 7

Mile 9

Lake
Crescent
2 Miles

Mile 10

Hutch Creek

Molly's
Meadow

Mile 6

Sol Duc
Hot Springs
14 Miles

Mt. Muller
3748'

Panorama
Point

Markham
Meadow

Allison
Meadow

Mile 11

101

N
Miles
0   1   2

Jasmine
Meadow

Mile 5

Drought Creek

Mile 12

Thomas
Gap

Mile 4

Millsap
Meadow

Littleton Creek

Jim's Junction

3040

Mile 3

Mile 1

Mile 2

Miner's
Crossing

3071

Forks
24 Miles

Port Angeles 31 Miles

than 140 species of wildflowers in just a 1.5-mile section of trail.

Some maps show a short, steep route to Jim's Junction from Milepost 9.7 on FR 3040, but there is no parking space at the trailhead, making the route unsuitable for horses.

From Jim's Junction the trail winds for 4 miles between timbered shelter on the north and meadows and craggy lookouts on the south. Heading east the trail contours along both north and south flanks of Snider Ridge, with spectacular views of Mount Olympus and Lake Crescent. Occasional views north reveal the Strait of Juan de Fuca, Vancouver Island, and, in the distance, Mount Baker.

This trail can be hot on a sunny summer day, so take advantage of the forested sections to rest in the shade and cool off. About 1 mile from Jim's Junction the trail skirts Millsap Meadow and Thomas Gap, named for one of the engineers who worked on the original trail. In another mile the trail arrives at Jasmine Meadow, also on the south side of the trail.

After passing Allison and Markham meadows in the next 0.5 mile, the trail comes within a few hundred feet of 3,748-foot Mount Muller. A fire lookout was established here for horse patrols in 1917, but it often took crews several days to reach the fires once they were spotted because so few trails or roads existed then.

A short path to the north leads to the summit of Mount Muller. A little farther down the main trail, a short spur leads to Panorama Point, which offers outstanding views south. Walk to the point, or take only two horses at a time: the point is too small for a crowd.

About 0.5 mile from Mount Muller (and 6 miles from the trailhead) is Molly's Meadow. One mile farther brings you to Cahill Overlook. Another 0.5 mile, at Mosley Gap (also named for an early trail engineer), the trail begins its descent from the ridge. The route switchbacks over the next 1.5 miles, past Fouts Rock House, a cave-like space about 20 feet deep in a rockfall of giant boulders. This is one of the most unusual boulder gardens in the region. A short spur trail leads to the rock house, but leave your horses by the main trail.

From the boulder garden the trail smooths out and descends over another 1.5 miles to cross Hutch Creek. From here it is 3 miles back to the trailhead, crossing three small creeks, including Drought Creek a little more than 1 mile from the trailhead. Those looking for a shorter, easier ride would enjoy the 4.5-mile one-way trip east from the trailhead to the boulder garden, retracing their hoofprints to avoid the steep ridge portion of the loop.

Also, this is cougar country. Two cougar sightings have been reported in the last two years along older sections of the trail. These big cats are usually wary of humans, but they can be dangerous. If you do see a cougar it will likely run away. If not, stand your ground. Do not turn your back on the cat, and do not run. Pick up small children immediately. If the cougar approaches, throw rocks, wave sticks, and try to make yourself look bigger (spreading a coat or poncho above your head).

2 TUBAL CAIN TRAIL 840 TO BUCKHORN LAKE

Location: West of Quilcene in the Buckhorn Wilderness.

General description: A 12-mile round-trip into a scenic glacial valley on the east side of the Olympic Mountains.

Trailhead horse facilities: None. There is little parking space for trucks and trailers and little turning room. Parking is usually found on the main road turnouts above and below the trailhead.

Trailhead elevation: 3,300 feet.

High point: 5,300 feet at the Buckhorn Lake Cutoff.

Maps: Custom Correct Buckhorn Wilderness; Green Trails Tyler Peak 136; USGS Tyler Peak quad; Olympic National Forest.

Season: Late spring to mid-fall; July through mid-October are best.

Water availability: May be scarce at higher elevations but is abundant at Copper Creek (3.25 miles in) and at Buckhorn Lake.

Feed availability: Carry processed feed.

Permits/restrictions: No permits are required. Fires are prohibited above 3,500 feet. Groups of more than twelve people and eight livestock are prohibited within the wilderness area. For horse riders, that basically means the largest group of riders would be eight people, with no pack stock. Mountain bikes and motorized vehicles are prohibited on this trail.

Finding the trailhead: From the entrance to Sequim Bay State Park, drive south on U.S. Highway 101 for 0.1 mile and turn west onto Louella Road. Travel 0.9 mile and turn left on Palo Alto Road at the T-intersection. 5.6 miles from US 101 this paved county road becomes graveled Forest Road 28. At 7.4 miles, bear right on Forest Road 2860 and follow it into the Olympic forest. At intersections and junctions, there will be signs for the Tubal Cain and Dungeness trails.

After passing the East Crossing Campground the road descends to the Dungeness River, crosses it, and begins climbing to a switchback at 12.3 miles. There is an intersection at that point with Forest Road 2870 but stay left on FR 2860. At 17.2 miles the road descends toward the Dungeness River, crossing it again at 18.8 miles. About 4 miles from the river crossing (or 22.7 miles from US 101) look for the trailhead on the south side of the road.

The ride: From the trailhead it's only a 0.25-mile ride to the Silver Creek Shelter and the boundary of the Buckhorn Wilderness. This is a scenic trail that is particularly enjoyed by photographers and mountain lovers.

The 44,258-acre Buckhorn Wilderness, largest of five wilderness areas adjacent to Olympic National Park, is in the northeast portion of Olympic National Forest. A patented mining claim—Tubal Cain—includes 216 acres of private land within the wilderness, which was established by the Washington Wilderness Act of 1984.

Within the Quilcene Ranger District there are 93.2 miles of trails, with 84.4 miles open to pack and saddle stock. Most of those miles are in the Buckhorn Wilderness and are subject to special restrictions. Wilderness visitors should always carry rain

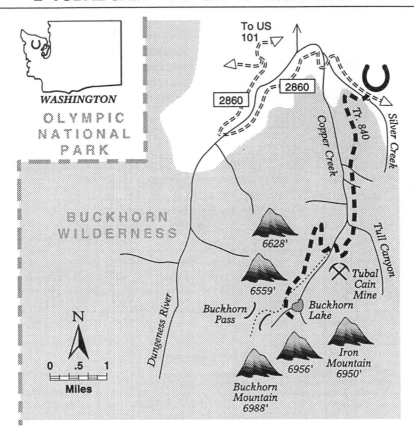

gear plus adequate clothing, food, and water.

There is very steep terrain in many parts of the wilderness. Peaks in the wilderness include Mount Fricaba, 7,134 feet; Buckhorn Mountain, 6,988 feet; Iron Mountain, 6,950 feet; and Tyler Peak, 6,370 feet. Barren ridges and steep, rocky cliffs and peaks are common in higher elevations. Lower slopes support stands of old-growth Douglas-fir, western hemlock, and western red cedar. Higher elevations are marked by subalpine fir and western white pines, with alpine flowers above timberline.

Be aware that nearby Olympic National Park is home to cougars, potentially dangerous animals. Attacks on humans are rare and none have ever been reported in the park. Encountering cougars in the surrounding national forest is even less likely than in the park. Groups traveling together should make enough noise to avoid surprising a cougar. Further information is available from rangers.

Major streams flowing through the wilderness include the Gray Wolf, Dungeness, and Big Quilcene rivers.

There are no officially designated horse camps in the Quilcene District. Among the most popular trails commonly used by horse riders are the Upper Big Quilcene to Marmot Pass Trail (see Trail Ride 4) and the Dungeness Trail (see Trail Ride 5).

Buckhorn Peak (Tubal Cain). Photo by Erik Molvar.

After crossing Silver Creek the trail leads west across slopes filled with Douglas-fir and western hemlock, salal, Oregon grape, bracken fern, thimbleberry, and Washington's state flower, the rhododendron. After 0.5 mile the trail moves south above the Copper Creek drainage.

The trail crosses three small creeks in the first 2.75 miles so ample water is available. At that point a 1.5-mile branch of the main trail angles to the left, reaching to an old mineshaft at the opening of Tull Canyon. Riding another 0.5 mile on the main trail through forest shade brings travelers to the Copper Creek crossing and several riverside campsites. If you stop to camp, remember that stock have to be kept more than 100 feet from the stream except for watering.

From the campsites, at 3.5 miles, the Tubal Cain Mine site, also known as Tull City or Copper City, is found up a short trail on the eastern slope. In the 1890s strings of horses and pack mules brought people and tons of machinery, iron pipes, stoves, and mining equipment here.

From Copper Creek the main trail heads steeply upward 0.5 mile, switchbacking across the western side of Copper Creek Canyon. The hillside is decorated with subalpine firs, Alaska yellow-cedars, white pines, some lodgepole pines, and grassy areas with weathered, bleached snags. Colorful wildflowers cover the hillside in mid-summer.

On the last part of the switchback riders should be able to see the San Juan Islands and the Strait of Juan de Fuca to the north. Along the southbound trail the accompanying scenery includes a variety of Olympic mountain peaks, many nearly 7,000 feet high. Along the way in late July and August, watch for small plants with a five-petaled, bell-shaped blue flower—the Piper bellflower—which grows only in the Olympic mountains.

At 5.6 miles from the trailhead and 5,300 feet elevation, Buckhorn Lake is downhill at the end of a 0.5-mile spur trail to the left. The steep, abandoned trail leads to a bench with scattered creeks. Shaded by subalpine fir, streamside campsites above the lake are popular. The lake, filled with tasty trout, is downhill from the campsites at the end of the trail.

3   LOWER BIG QUILCENE

Location: West of Quilcene in the Buckhorn Wilderness.
General description: An easy 6-mile ride along the Big Quilcene River.
Trailhead horse facilities: Big Quilcene Campground, with picnic tables, a toilet, and firepits, but no horse facilities. The parking area is small.
Trailhead elevation: 1,200 feet.
High point: 2,500 feet.
Maps: Olympic National Forest; Custom Correct Buckhorn Wilderness; Green Trails Tyler Peak 136.
Season: Spring to fall.
Water availability: In 2 miles the trail crosses the Big Quilcene River; the trail meets the river at several points over the next 4 miles.
Feed availability: Forage may not be available; carry processed feed.
Permits/restrictions: No permits are required. Fires are prohibited above 3,500 feet elevation. Groups of more than twelve people and eight livestock are prohibited within the wilderness area. For horse riders, that basically means the largest group of riders would be eight people, with no pack stock. Use existing campsites when possible. Do not camp within 100 feet of water.

Motorized vehicles and mountain bikes have access to the Lower Big Quilcene Trail but are prohibited on the Upper Big Quilcene, past Ten Mile Shelter. (See Trail Ride 4.)
Finding the trailhead: From Quilcene, drive 2 miles southwest on U.S. Highway 101. Turn west on Penny Creek Road and go for 1 mile, then go south on Big Quilcene River Road (Forest Road 27) for 3.5 miles to Forest Road 080, a spur to the left that dead-ends at the trailhead.

The ride: From the trailhead the path follows the Big Quilcene River through heavy forest. The grade on this trip is only 10 to 15 percent, making it an increasingly popular trail for mountain bikes.

Most of the scenery is of the river and forests, including a good variety of old-growth and second-growth trees. It's an excellent ride in spring and early summer. Check with the ranger district about trail conditions.

Just before Bark Shanty Camp, at 2.4 miles along the trail and 1,700-feet elevation, the route crosses the Big Quilcene River downstream a short distance from where Townsend Creek joins it. A short distance up the trail from that first crossing, you'll ride into the Bark Shanty Camp on the Big Quilcene. This is a small space

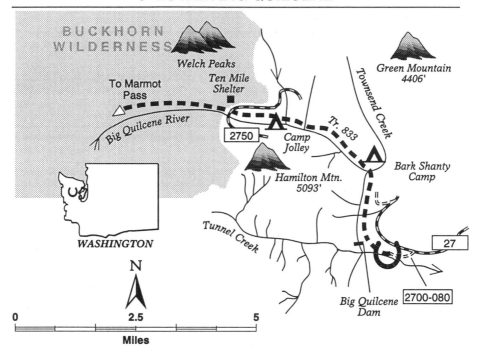

From the map: BUCKHORN WILDERNESS, Welch Peaks, Ten Mile Shelter, To Marmot Pass, Big Quilcene River, 2750, Camp Jolley, Tr. 833, Townsend Creek, Green Mountain 4406', Bark Shanty Camp, Hamilton Mtn. 5093', Tunnel Creek, WASHINGTON, N, 27, Big Quilcene Dam, 2700-080, 0, 2.5, 5, Miles

that could accommodate two horses and riders for camping.

From Bark Shanty it's a 2.1-mile ride along the river, past other inflowing creeks, to reach Camp Jolley at 4.5 miles and 2,000 feet elevation. Jolley Creek flows into the Big Quilcene near the camp. Hamilton Mountain, a 5,000-foot peak, is southwest of the camp. The final 1.5 miles of the route adds only 500 feet elevation, with the arrival at Ten Mile Shelter and Forest Road 2750.

There are campsites at Ten Mile Shelter. Riders may want to ride Upper Big Quilcene Trail 833 to Marmot Pass, a route that begins at Ten Mile Shelter (see Trail Ride 4).

4   UPPER BIG QUILCENE TRAIL TO MARMOT PASS

Location: West of the town of Quilcene in the Buckhorn Wilderness.
General description: A steep, strenuous 10.5-mile round-trip to Marmot Pass with spectacular mountain vistas and wildflowers.
Trailhead horse facilities: None. Parking for trucks and horse trailers on Forest Road 2750.
Trailhead elevation: 2,500 feet.
High point: 6,000 feet.

Maps: Olympic National Forest; Custom Correct Buckhorn Wilderness, Green Trails Tyler Peak 136.
Season: July through mid-November.
Water availability: Plentiful along the river to Shelter Rock Camp, then no water for 2 miles.
Feed availability: Carry processed feed.
Permits/restrictions: No permits are required. Fires are prohibited above 3,500 feet. Groups of more than twelve people and eight livestock are prohibited within the wilderness area. Use existing campsites when possible. Do not camp within 100 feet of water. Motorized vehicles and bicycles are prohibited past Ten Mile Shelter on the Upper Big Quilcene trail.
Finding the trailhead: From Quilcene, drive a mile south of the Quilcene Ranger Station on U.S. Highway 101. Turn west on Penny Creek Road for 1.4 miles to a road signed Big Quilcene River Road on the left. This road becomes Forest Road 27. After traveling about 11 miles to the junction with Forest Road 2750, turn left at the sign for the Big Quilcene Trail. Follow this road 5 miles to the trailhead at Ten Mile Shelter and Wet Weather Creek. This trailhead also serves as the upper end of Lower Big Quilcene Trail 833 (see Trail Ride 3).

The ride: A few paces after mounting up you'll enter the Buckhorn Wilderness, a realm of green trees, moss, and ferns at the start. Late spring and early summer bring blooming rhododendrons at lower elevations of this trail and meadow wildflowers on the higher slopes. There are numerous small creeks crossing the trail's route. Views of the Big Quilcene River are frequent.

Shelter Rock Camp, at 3,600 feet, is 2.5 miles up the trail. This is the last place to get water for the next 2 miles. Beyond Shelter Rock Camp the trail becomes much steeper, trees diminish in size, and sunny weather makes the trail a hot ride. Some grades are as steep as 30 percent. This part of the trail moves through subalpine forests, rocky meadows, and groves of silver fir and western hemlock.

The steep grade tops out at 5,500 feet at Mystery Camp, 2 miles from Shelter Rock Camp (4.5 miles from the trailhead) and only 0.7 mile from Marmot Pass. With no water on the pass, Mystery Camp is a fine place to rest or stay overnight. There are two springs and a grove of alpine trees protecting the campsites.

An evening ride through flowered meadows to the pass may be rewarded with a sunset-lit panorama of peaks, from Warrior Peak and Mount Constance, close by, to the more distant outlines of Mount Mystery, Mount Deception, and The Needles. Below is the wooded valley of the Dungeness River. Another view of Olympic Mountain peaks can be found from the top of the 6,300-foot knoll just south of the pass.

More peaks come into sight riding north of the pass on the Dungeness Trail to Buckhorn Pass, 1.6 miles away, and then up a path to the west summit of 6,950-foot Buckhorn Mountain. Views include 7,300-foot Warrior Peak, 7,743-foot Mount Constance, and views of the Strait of Juan de Fuca and Vancouver Island to the north.

Not surprisingly, Marmot Pass is home to the whistling marmots ("whistlers" and "rock chucks") that gave the area its name. No doubt there will be plenty of the marmots around. Just before the pass is the Buckhorn Botanical Area. At the pass

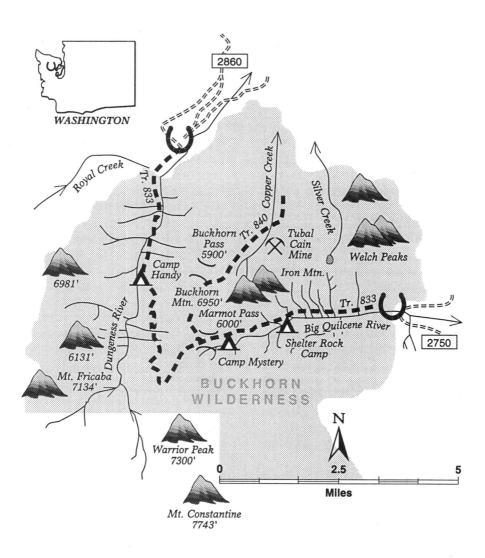

the trail meets with Tubal Cain Trail 840 and the Dungeness Trail, also labeled 833.

If you camp, there are sites at Ten Mile Shelter at the trailhead, at Shelter Rock Camp midway on the trail, and at Camp Mystery near the pass, as well as at several other spots along the trail. Use existing camping areas. Water is scarce at the higher elevations. Boil all water for human consumption.

5 DUNGENESS TRAIL TO MARMOT PASS

Location: South of Sequim in the Buckhorn Wilderness along the northeastern boundary of Olympic National Park.

General description: A popular 8.1-mile ride into the high country around Marmot Pass.

Trailhead horse facilities: None, but there is a vault toilet and room to park trucks and horse trailers.

Trailhead elevation: 2,500 feet.

High point: 6,000 feet at Marmot Pass.

Maps: Custom Correct Buckhorn Wilderness; Green Trails Tyler Peak 136; USGS Tyler Peak quad; Olympic National Forest. See map on p. 43.

Season: Late spring to mid-fall; July through mid-October are best.

Water availability: Generally available over the first 6.4 miles to the Boulder Shelter.

Feed availability: Do not graze in meadows here; carry processed feed.

Permits/restrictions: No permits are required. Fires are prohibited above 3,500 feet. Groups of more than twelve people and eight livestock are prohibited within the wilderness area. No camping within 100 feet of water. Mountain bikes and motorized vehicles are prohibited on this trail.

Finding the trailhead: From Sequim Bay State Park drive north 2 miles on U.S. Highway 101 to Palo Alto Road. Turn left (south) and continue to the pavement's end, where it becomes Forest Road 28. Continue about 1.1 miles to Forest Road 2860. Drive 11 miles on Forest Road 2860 to the upper trailhead of Dungeness Trail 833. At intersections and junctions along the road watch for signs for the Dungeness Trail.

The ride: The Dungeness Trail passes through forest most of the way, until the higher elevations. There are meadows along the river route. As the trail ascends grades are mostly 10 to 15 percent, with some 20 percent inclines. The junction with Royal Creek Trail 832 is reached at the 1-mile point. About 1 mile farther the trail crosses Still Creek, which flows into the Dungeness River.

About 3.4 miles from the trailhead is Camp Handy, a popular camping area at 3,100 feet. Other campsites are located along the trail and should be used whenever possible rather than making a new camp. A three-sided shelter, a popular style in the Olympic National Forest, provides a good place to camp.

From Camp Handy the trail begins moving away from the river and climbing steadily, leaving the forest behind for the scenery of the upper alpine meadows. This part of the trail reveals fascinating views of the mountain peaks in Olympic National Park and adjoining forest.

About 6.4 miles in, the trail arrives at a junction with Home Lake Trail 893, on the 4,950-foot level of the ridge that leads to Marmot Pass. A couple hundred feet south of the junction is Boulder Shelter, another three-sided hut. This shelter is in a smaller area and is not recommended for camping. If you visit the shelter, do not ride through any of the meadows on the way.

From the junction with Home Lake Trail 893 ride on about 1.25 miles to Marmot Pass, 8.1 miles from the trailhead. Here the Dungeness Trail connects with Big Quilcene River Trail 833 to the east. There are marvelous mountain views along this ridge ride, including 6,956-foot Buckhorn Mountain to the north.

6 DUCKABUSH RIVER

Location: Northwest of Hoodsport in The Brothers Wilderness near the eastern boundary of Olympic National Park.

General description: A 12.4-mile round-trip ride along the Duckabush River to the Boundary of Olympic National Park.

Trailhead horse facilities: Stock ramp, restrooms, parking for horse trailers in the lower lot.

Trailhead elevation: 270 feet.

High point: 1,750 feet.

Maps: Olympic National Park; Custom Correct The Brothers–Mount Anderson.

Season: Year-round; best May through November.

Water availability: Plentiful.

Feed availability: Pack processed feed.

Permits/restrictions: Groups of more than twelve people and eight livestock are prohibited within The Brothers Wilderness and the Olympic National Park.

Finding the trailhead: From Hoodsport drive 22 miles north on U.S. Highway 101 to the signed Duckabush Recreation Area. About 0.2 mile north of the Duckabush River bridge, turn west onto Duckabush River Road (Forest Road 2510). Follow this road 3.5 miles to the Interrorem Guard Station, then continue 2.0 miles and turn right onto FR 2510-060, which leads to the trailhead and two parking lots. The trail begins from the upper lot, but park and mount up in the lower lot. Be sure to register at the trailhead.

The ride: The Duckabush Trail is maintained only during the summer months, although it is open all year. The entire trail runs 20 miles to Lake LaCrosse and O'Neill Pass in the heart of the Olympic Mountains. But riders can enjoy a memorable day ride on just the lower end of the trail. It enters The Brothers Wilderness and winds along the Duckabush River in the midst of 200- to 400-year-old trees. At 6.2 miles the trail reaches a sign for the Olympic National Park boundary, a good place to begin the return trip.

The ride begins low in the forest and meets the boundary of The Brothers Wilderness about 1 mile from the trailhead. The route from the trailhead climbs 400 feet in that first mile, to the top of Little Hump. This rise is not a major barrier. After Little Hump the trail descends 200 feet to the river and follows an old logging railroad grade through second-growth trees that date back to the mid-1920s and 1930s. Pieces of steel cable and an occasional old length of rail track can be seen.

At 2.4 miles and 700 feet in elevation the trail reaches the Duckabush River. At 3.5 miles, just before the Big Hump summit, there are cross-valley views of St. Peters Dome and a look downstream on the Duckabush.

Four miles in the trail climbs Big Hump, a 1,000-foot crest. An excellent trail eases the ascent. Elevation at the top is 1,750 feet. This is the highest point of the lower part of the Duckabush River Trail. Past Big Hump the trail arrives at the Duckabush River again at 4.8 miles and 1,100 feet elevation.

Bead lilies and calypso orchids blossom along the trail in the late spring and early

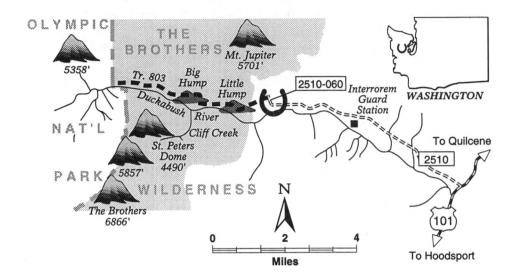

summer months. Beyond Big Hump the trail drops sharply 600 feet to the river and continues on to a fine campsite, Five Mile Camp. There are numerous camps along the trail to stop for lunches or to enjoy the restfulness of the riverside campsites. But the most popular camping and fishing area is at Five Mile Camp, which is open to stock use.

The Olympic National Park boundary is at 6.2 miles and 1,300 feet elevation.

BROWN CREEK HORSE CAMP

Location: West of Hoodsport and south of Lake Cushman on the Olympic National Forest.

Horse camp facilities: Rustic site; no potable water, tables, or individual campsite fire rings. Open area for horses and riders has space for about 10 no-fee campsites with a single campfire ring, vault toilet, hitching rails, and stock ramp. There is room for campers, trucks and horse trailers with a 28-foot maximum length for trucks and trailers. A local chapter of the Back Country Horsemen has developed a trail for taking stock to water, 0.25 mile from camp.

Finding the horse camp: From Shelton drive 6 miles north on U.S. Highway 101. Turn left (west) at signs for the Skokomish River Recreation Area and drive 5 miles on the paved Skokomish Valley Road, past the George Adams State Fish Hatchery, and bear right to follow Forest Road 23.

Drive 9 miles on FR 23 to Forest Road 2353, turn right, and drive 0.75 mile to the South Fork Skokomish River bridge. Cross the bridge, turn sharply right onto FR 2340. Brown Creek Campground is 0.25 mile past this point, on a side road that curves back to Forest Road 2340. Don't go into the Brown Creek Campground. Stay on FR 2340 as you pass the campground. Where the campground road returns to FR 2340, from the right, turn left onto a spur, Forest Road 540. Travel less than 100 yards on the spur road to reach Brown Creek Horse Camp.

Horse camp elevation: 800 feet.

Trails: Two trail rides explore different types of scenery from Brown Creek Horse Camp.

- Lower South Fork Skokomish Trail is located off FR 2353 and leaves from the horse camp (see Trail Ride 7).

- Upper South Fork Skokomish Trail is an extension of the lower river trail. It winds into higher elevations to the boundary of Olympic National Park. Stock are prohibited from entering the park on this trail (see Trail Ride 8).

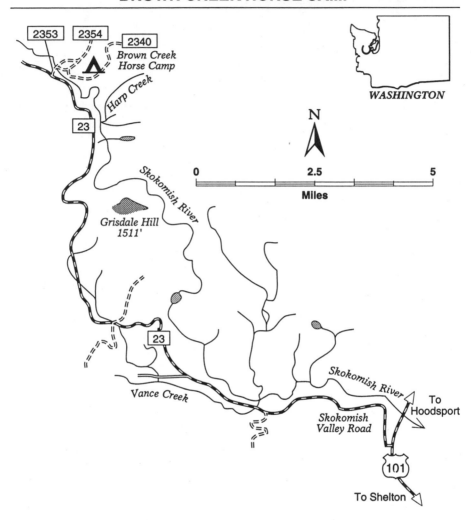

7 LOWER SOUTH FORK SKOKOMISH FROM BROWN CREEK HORSE CAMP

Location: West of Hoodsport on the Olympic National Forest.
General description: An easy ride along a recently improved river valley trail.
Trailhead horse facilities: None. See Brown Creek Horse Camp.
Trailhead elevation: 800 feet.
High point: 1,300 feet.
Maps: Olympic National Forest; Custom Correct Mount Skokomish–Lake Cushman.
Season: Year-round.

Water availability: No water at trailhead but stock can be watered 0.25 mile from the horse camp. On the ride, horses can get to the Skokomish River at some points, and creeks cross the trail.

Feed availability: No grazing. Pack processed or pelletized feed.

Permits/restrictions: There is no fee for use of the horse camp and no permits are required for camping.

Finding the trailhead: See Brown Creek Horse Camp. A trail on the north side of the horse camp, passing the Brown Creek beaver pond, connects with the junction of Forest Road 2340 (paved), Forest Road 2353 (paved), and Forest Road 2354 (gravel). After crossing this intersection, continue on FR 2353, which becomes a gravel road at this point. The trailhead is a short distance up FR 2353, where the road crosses LaBar Creek.

The ride: The Lower South Fork Skokomish Trail 873 stretches 10.9 miles to the start of the Upper South Fork Trail 873.1, about 0.5 mile northwest of the Harps Shelter, at the end of Forest Road 2361. In 1994 the trail was improved in areas that were previously muddy and difficult for horse passage at certain times of the year.

The lower part of the trail wanders along the South Fork of the Skokomish River through forested land, traveling up and down over ridges and along a bluff above the water. The Church Creek and Camp Harps shelters, three-sided huts, are found on the upper end of the trail.

Olympic elk (600-pound Roosevelt elk that are larger than elk found in other parts of Washington) are often seen throughout the river basin. They can be observed if visitors are quiet and don't approach too closely. Wildlife and bird watching are prime attractions on this trip. Also be aware that mountain bikes may be encountered on the trail.

Look for signs marking the Old LaBar Claim at 1.4 miles and 870 feet elevation. Just north of the Church Creek Shelter, at 8.3 miles and 950 feet elevation, is the first "wet" crossing of the river. Cross at this wide and shallow ford. Farther up the trail are logs for hiker crossings. Don't try to cross at the hiker area as the stream is usually too deep to be passable.

Big Bridge is reached at 9.5 miles and 1,070 feet; the Camp Harps Shelter at 9.7 miles (1,200 feet), and the end of FR 2361 at 10.3 miles. The trailhead for the Upper South Fork Skokomish Trail 873.1 is reached at 10.9 miles and 1,300 feet elevation.

8   UPPER SOUTH FORK SKOKOMISH TRAIL FROM BROWN CREEK HORSE CAMP

Location: West of Hoodsport in the Olympic National Forest.

General description: A 4.9-mile ride through old-growth forest and across the South Fork Skokomish River.

Trailhead horse facilities: See Brown Creek Horse Camp if you plan to leave from the bottom of the Lower South Fork Skokomish Trail 873. At the trailhead for Upper South Fork Skokomish Trail 873.1, at the end of Forest Road 2361, there is a large parking area with room for horse trailers and an unloading ramp.

Trailhead elevation: 1,300 feet.

High point: 2,980 feet.

7 LOWER SOUTH FORK SKOKOMISH FROM BROWN CREEK HORSE CAMP
8 UPPER SOUTH FORK SKOKOMISH TRAIL FROM BROWN CREEK HORSE CAMP

Maps: Olympic National Forest; Custom Correct Mount Skokomish–Lake Cushman.
Season: Year-round.
Water availability: Plentiful where the trail crosses several streams.
Feed availability: Pack pelletized or processed feed for horse snacks.
Permits/restrictions: This trail is closed to horses at the Olympic National Park boundary. The trail is in very poor condition as it enters the park.
Finding the trailhead: The start of Upper South Fork Skokomish Trail 873.1 is located at the end of FR 2361. The trailhead can also be reached by Lower South Fork Skokomish Trail 873 from the Brown Creek Horse Camp.

To get to FR 2361, drive 6 miles north of Shelton on U.S. Highway 101. Then turn left on Skokomish River Valley Road and drive to the junction with Forest Road 23. Turn right and drive 15 miles to the junction with FR 2361. Continue 4 miles to the end of FR 2361 and the trailhead.

The ride: This ride is a continuation of the easier Lower South Fork Skokomish Trail 873 from the Brown Creek Horse Camp (see Trail Ride 7). The trail is rated as a "more difficult" trail than average, but it receives annual maintenance and is in good condition up to the Olympic National Park boundary.

Leaving the trailhead, follow the trail for 1.8 miles to an avalanche chute on the mountainside. From there, the trail begins climbing up the canyon above the Skokomish River Valley, but the trail never rises high enough for mountain views.

Scenery changes dramatically on this trail compared to the lower route along the Skokomish River. Whereas the lower trail passes through river bottom forest—where evergreens mix with maples and alders—the upper trail moves through a forest of old-growth timber, including hemlock and Douglas-fir. Near the end of the upper trail the canyon is much narrower than on the lower trail.

There are three wet crossings on the upper trail where horses need to ford, twice over the Skokomish and once over Rule Creek. Signs indicate the Olympic National Park boundary and there is room to turn horses around for the return ride.

9 COLONEL BOB TRAIL

Location: East of Lake Quinault Lake in the Colonel Bob Wilderness.

General description: A scenic 6.5-mile one-way ride through old-growth rain forest to Moonshine Flats, with views of the Olympic Mountains, Cascade Range, and the Pacific Ocean.

Trailhead horse facilities: Parking for horse trailers, stock ramp with wheelchair access, barrier-free restroom, and trail information.

Trailhead elevation: 270 feet.

High point: 3,470 feet at Moonshine Flats.

Maps: Custom Correct/Quinault-Colonel Bob Wilderness (1994 revised); USGS Colonel Bob and Lake Quinault East quads; Olympic National Forest. See p. 54.

Season: July through November. Always bring rain gear.

Water availability: None at trailhead; small stream at 2.4 miles and at Mulkey Shelter, 4 miles in. Water available year-round at Moonshine Flats.

Feed availability: Carry processed or pelletized feed.

Permits/restrictions: No permits are required. Fires are prohibited above 3,500 feet. Groups of more than twelve people and eight livestock are prohibited in the wilderness. No camping within 100 feet of water. Horses are not allowed on the 1.5-mile trail from Moonshine Flats to Colonel Bob Mountain (but it's worth the hike).

Finding the trailhead: From Humptulips, drive 19 miles north on U.S. Highway 101 to the South Shore Road (just south of the bridge over the Quinault River) and turn right. Drive 2.5 miles to the Quinault Ranger Station (ask here about trail conditions if you haven't phoned ahead). Continue 4 miles to a sign for Colonel Bob Trail 851. Turn right onto a narrow road to the large parking lot.

The ride: There are two ways to approach this ride, and which you choose will depend on how much time you have and whether you can arrange a vehicle shuttle. First, as a 13-mile out-and-back ride, the trip to Moonshine Flats makes a full day.

Looking east from Colonel Bob (Colonel Bob Point). Photo by Erik Molvar.

The second option is to camp at Moonshine Flats and then continue south 3.5 miles down Pete's Creek Trail 858 to the trailhead on the West Fork of the Humptulips River and Forest Road 2204 (see Trail Ride 10).

Either way you'll have to negotiate some steep terrain, but the views of Quinault Lake, into the Olympics, and west to the Pacific Ocean are well worth the effort. Plan extra time to enjoy the short hike to the summit of Colonel Bob Mountain from Moonshine Flats.

This wilderness trail receives only low to moderate use. For the first 5.5 miles it climbs in long switchbacks through lush rain forest of giant trees and hanging moss. The trail crosses Ewell's Creek at 3 miles and begins climbing to Quinault Ridge where vistas open up north and south. In about 4 miles the trail arrives at the campsites at Mulkey Shelter at the 2,550-foot contour. There is no grazing available here.

From the shelter the trail climbs hard through a series of switchbacks to a 3,250-foot pass and a junction with Pete's Creek Trail 858 from the south. Both of these trails were reconstructed in 1990, with water bars added to guide runoff, so both are in good condition. Bear left here. One mile from the junction and 6.5 miles from the trailhead is Moonshine Flats at 3,470 feet. About 0.3 mile before the flats, watch for Fletcher Canyon Overlook.

From Moonshine Flats a trail leads 1.5 miles north to the 4,492-foot summit of Colonel Bob Mountain. The summit trail leaves the forest and threads through fields of mountain wildflowers. Horses are not allowed on this trail, but it's worth the walk.

The summit shows little evidence of the old lookout cabin, but views are spectacular. Look west to Mount O'Neil and the ocean, north to the Strait of Juan de Fuca, and southeast to Gibson Peak. Rows of mountains in the Olympics, often partly veiled by banks of mist, are a grand sight. On clear days scan the eastern horizon for the peaks of mounts Rainier, Adams, and St. Helens.

10 PETE'S CREEK TO COLONEL BOB MOUNTAIN

Location: Southeast of Lake Quinault in the Colonel Bob Wilderness.
General description: A "more difficult" 7-mile day ride into old-growth forests and high meadows, with a 1.5-mile hike to the summit of Colonel Bob Mountain.
Trailhead horse facilities: Parking for trailers, stock ramp, and trail information.
Trailhead elevation: 1,000 feet.
High point: 3,470 feet at Moonshine Flats.
Maps: Custom Correct/Quinault-Colonel Bob Wilderness (1994 revised); USGS Colonel Bob and Lake Quinault East quads; Olympic National Forest.
Season: July through mid-October.
Water availability: Ample at trailhead and 2 miles in; also year-round at Moonshine Flats.
Feed availability: Carry processed feed.
Permits/restrictions: No permits are required. Fires are prohibited above 3,500 feet. Groups of more than twelve people and eight livestock are prohibited in the wilderness. No camping within 100 feet of water. Horses are not allowed on the 1.5-mile trail from Moonshine Flats to Colonel Bob Mountain (but it's worth the hike).
Finding the trailhead: From Hoquiam drive north 25.5 miles on U.S. Highway 101 and turn east on an angled road (Forest Road 22) signed Donkey Creek, Humptulips Guard Station. At 8.2 miles the pavement ends. Turn north on Forest Road 2204, signed for Campbell Tree Grove Campground. Drive 10.9 miles to the trailhead.

The ride: The trail begins on the uphill side of FR 2204, almost immediately entering the Colonel Bob Wilderness. Rated as "more difficult," the trail climbs steadily and is rocky in places. One mile in it crosses Pete's Creek, and at 2 miles there is a small scenic viewpoint with a campsite. Soon the trail arrives at Gibson Slide, with 4,309-foot Gibson Peak rising to the east. There are campsites here with a small stream for water, but no grazing is available.

About 2.5 miles in the trail meets Colonel Bob Trail 851 (see Trail Ride 9) at an elevation of 2,900 feet. One mile farther, at 3,470 feet, is Moonshine Flats, a popular high camp on this trail. Just before the flats watch for Fletcher Canyon Overlook, offering more splendid views.

The camping area at Moonshine Flats lies just below the 3,500-foot "no campfire" zone. Water is available here year-round. The flats are forested, but it's a subalpine environment with rolling meadows, scattered trees, and dense woods lining the valley flanks.

From Moonshine Flats a trail leads 1.5 miles north to the 4,492-foot summit of Colonel Bob Mountain. The summit trail leaves the forest and threads through fields of mountain wildflowers. Horses are not allowed on this trail, but it's worth the walk.

The summit shows little evidence of the old lookout cabin, but views are spectacular. Look west to Mount O'Neil and the ocean, north to the Strait of Juan de Fuca, and southeast to Gibson Peak. Rows of mountains in the Olympics, often partly veiled by banks of mist, are a grand sight. On clear days scan the eastern horizon for the peaks of mounts Rainier, Adams, and St. Helens.

9 COLONEL BOB TRAIL
10 PETE'S CREEK TO COLONEL BOB MOUNTAIN
11 WEST FORK HUMPTULIPS AND LOWER PETE'S CREEK LOOP

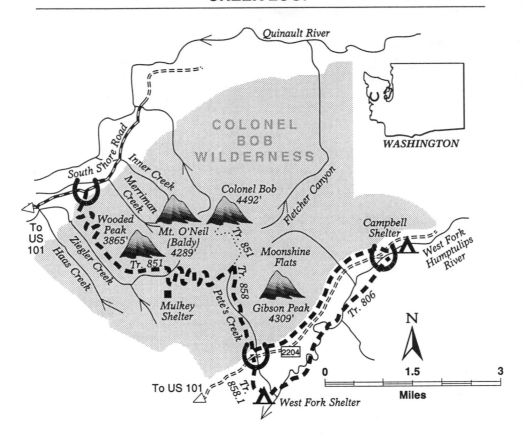

11 WEST FORK HUMPTULIPS AND LOWER PETE'S CREEK LOOP

Location: East of Quinault near the southern boundary of Olympic National Park.

General description: An easy 8.1-mile loop for a day or overnight trip through a scenic, lowland old-growth forest.

Trailhead horse facilities: Park horse trailers at Campbell Shelter on the north side of the Campbell Tree Grove Campground. Trail information is posted here. Also, horse trailers can be parked at the trailhead for Pete's Creek Trail 858, 10.9 miles northeast on Forest Road 2204. Pete's Creek also has trail information, restrooms, and a stock ramp.

Trailhead elevation: 600 feet.

High point: 1,000 feet.

Maps: Custom Correct/Quinault-Colonel Bob Wilderness (1994 Revised); USGS Colonel Bob, Lake Quinault East quads; Olympic National Forest.

Season: June through November.

Water availability: Plentiful at trailhead and at various points along the West Fork of the Humptulips River.

Feed availability: Some grazing in meadows along the river route, but riders are encouraged to pack processed feed.

Permits/restrictions: No permits are required.

Finding the trailhead: From Hoquiam drive north 25.5 miles on U.S. Highway 101 and turn east on an angled road (FR 22) signed Donkey Creek, Humptulips Guard Station. At 8.2 miles the pavement ends. Turn north on Forest Road 2204, signed for Campbell Tree Grove Campground. To reach the West Fork Trail 806 trailhead, drive 14 miles to the Campbell Shelter, on the north edge of the Campbell Tree Grove Campground.

The ride: Although this trail is also open to mountain bikes it receives relatively low use and should afford pleasant riding without interruptions from an overabundance of hikers or bikers. The lush forest here is home to enormous Douglas-fir and spruce, some up to 10 feet in diameter. Alder and maple line the streams, and there are good views of the Moonlight Dome Roadless Area to the southeast and the Colonel Bob Wilderness to the northwest.

This 8.1-mile loop ride begins with a scenic stretch heading southwest along the West Fork of the Humptulips River. This easy, level section crosses the river several times; there are no bridges but fords are well marked.

A more difficult stretch is the uphill ride on Lower Pete's Creek Trail 858.1. Follow this trail northwest to where it crosses FR 2204 at the 5-mile point. (To continue on Trail 858.1 to Moonshine Flats, near Colonel Bob Mountain, see Trail Ride 10.) To return to the Campbell Shelter and the trailhead, ride northeast along FR 2204 for 3.1 miles, shadowing the nearby boundary of the Colonel Bob Wilderness to the northwest. The Pete's Creek Trail 858 trailhead could also be used as a start/end for this loop ride.

12 PARK BUTTE

Location: In Mount Baker National Recreation Area and the Mount Baker Wilderness, east of Bellingham.

General description: A 3.5-mile ride on the southwest flank of Mount Baker, on one of the most scenic and accessible trails in the North Cascades.

Trailhead horse facilities: Stock ramp, toilet, creek water, staging area, hitch rails, and two horse campsites with firepits. Parking for four to five trucks with horse trailers.

Trailhead elevation: 3,200 feet.

High point: 5,400 feet at the summit of Park Butte.

Maps: Mount Baker-Snoqualmie National Forest; USGS Hamilton and Mount Baker; Green Trails, Hamilton 45.

Season: August 1 through November 1.

12 PARK BUTTE

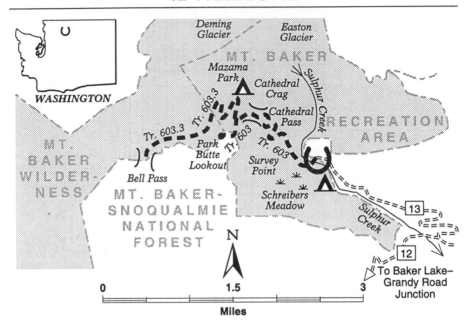

Water availability: Abundant at trailhead campsites and along the route, except on high ridges. There is also water at two horse campsites at Mazama Park.

Feed availability: Pack processed, weed-free feed.

Permits/restrictions: Except for East Bank/Baker Lake Trail 610, all stock trails on the Mount Baker Ranger District are closed to pack and saddle trips from November 1 through August 1 to minimize damage to trails during the worst months of rain, snow, and snowmelt.

On this trail in the NRA and all trails in the Mount Baker Wilderness, pack-and-saddle groups are limited to twelve heartbeats, in any combination of riders and animals. All stock users are required to use processed grain.

Finding the trailhead: From Interstate 5 at Burlington, drive east on Washington Highway 20 to Sedro Woolley and then 14.5 miles to the Baker Lake–Grandy Road junction. Turn left (north) and drive 12.5 miles to a fork in the road just past the signed entrance to the Mount Baker–Snoqualmie National Forest and the Rocky Creek bridge.

Turn left at the fork onto Forest Road 12, the Loomis–Nooksack Road. Drive about 3 miles and turn right onto Forest Road 13, Sulphur Creek Road. Follow FR 13 through switchbacks and a straight northwesterly stretch to the end.

The ride: Park Butte Trail 603 is close to populated areas, yet it offers the kind of remote wilderness trail experience riders seek. Whistling marmots populate the rocks of this mountain-and-meadow trip and there are waterfalls, lakes, and views of Mount Baker and its glaciers to the north.

WARNING: Trail numbers have been changed several times over the past couple years. Check with the ranger district on the current numbering for offshoots of Park Butte Trail 603. Do not take the faint trail through Baker Pass to Mazama Park. Near Cathedral Crag, do not take the old Baker Pass trail to the north; it is too worn to use. A new route from Cathedral Crag, through Cathedral Pass to Mazama Park, is shown on the map. Also, the new Scott Paul Trail 603.1, completed in 1994, leaves the horse camp and parking area at the trailhead, but that route is closed to pack-and-saddle stock.

Park Butte Trail 603 leaves the trailhead horse camps, crosses Sulphur Creek, and almost immediately enters scenic fields of heather and seasonal blueberries in Schreibers Meadow, which is only 5 miles due south of the spectacular 10,778-foot summit of Mount Baker.

Beyond several small frog ponds and an old cabin shelter, the trail enters the forest. One mile from the trailhead, riders will usually find at least three wide streams to ford, the result of melting ice from Easton Glacier to the north. The trail soon begins climbing a switchback trail through a forested slope to lower Morovitz Meadow, where riders get their first close-up view of Mount Baker.

As the trail straightens out, it follows an easier grade into upper Morovitz Meadow, at 4,500 feet elevation. There are scenic campsites in the upper meadow, some of them near groves of alpine trees, others in green open areas beside streams. Campfires are discouraged here, so be sure to carry a propane stove with your gear.

From upper Morovitz Meadow, ride northwest to the southern base of Cathedral Crag on Trail 603, then rein left on Trail 603 for the 1-mile ride to the summit of Park Butte. From the base of the butte, the trail climbs west to the 5,400-foot summit where there is a lookout tower. There are hitch rails at the foot of the lookout to accommodate horse riders who want ascend the tower to see more of the panoramic scenery. The spectacular views include Mount Baker and its glaciers, river valleys, forests, and nearby peaks of the Cascade Range to the south.

After enjoying the views from the summit, ride back to the junction with Mazama Park/Bell Pass Trail 603.3 at Cathedral Pass, then rein right for the return ride to the trailhead horse camps.

For an extended 5-mile round-trip ride to Bell Pass, rein left at the Cathedral Pass junction and follow a new switchback trail down steep terrain for 0.5 mile to Mazama Park. DO NOT follow the old, faint and worn trail through Baker Pass to Mazama Park, which is shown on most maps. The Forest Service has replaced that route with this new switchback route to Mazama Park.

From Cathedral Pass you can see the three-sided log shelter at Mazama Park, where there are also two horse camps. Hitch rails at the site aren't installed yet. Plans call for a 1995 completion of that task, but until then there are trees for setting up high lines for stock.

A couple of small creeks fed by snowfields provide water for the horse camping sites. Normally there is plenty of water, but in the long, hot summer of 1994, the creeks pretty much dried up. If that happens again, riders can carry water from streams a little farther from the campsites. Put a collapsible water bucket in your trail pack.

Near the campsites at Mazama Park is the trailhead for Ridley Creek Trail 696, coming in from the northwest. Don't ride it. Rangers advise the trail is a bad route due for reconstruction and is not suitable for horses. When the improvements are finished, however, the trail is planned to be a new horse route connecting the Mount Baker National Recreation Area with the Nooksack River's Middle Fork and adjacent Lake Forest Road 38.

From Mazama Park, ride southwest on Bell Pass Trail 603.3, passing below Park Butte. You won't be able to see it above the trail because of the forest. The ride provides about a 2-mile tour along the southern boundary of the Mount Baker Wilderness to Bell Pass. Creeks along the trail provide ample watering spots for stock. From Bell Pass, enjoy the scenic views before returning by the same route to the trailhead at FR 13.

13 EAST BANK ROSS LAKE

Location: Ross Lake National Recreation Area, along the east bank of Ross Lake north of Washington Highway 20.

General description: An easy, scenic trail along the shores of mountain-ringed Ross Lake, with six horse camps en route and opportunities for round-trip rides of 8 to 62 miles.

Trailhead horse facilities: Stock ramp and two hitching rails, with ample parking for horse trailers. No camping facilities.

Trailhead elevation: 1,800 feet.

High point: 3,500 feet.

Maps: Mount Baker–Snoqualmie National Forest; North Cascades National Park/Ross Lake and Lake Chelan National Recreation Areas; USGS Ross Dam, Pumpkin Mountain, Skagit Peak, Hozomeen Mountain, and North Cascades National Park Complex; Trails Illustrated Topographic Map.

Season: May through October at the southern end of the trail close to Ross Lake, but June through October in the higher elevations near Hozomeen Campground and the Canadian border.

Water availability: Water stock at creeks along the trail and at horse campsites.

Feed availability: Scant forage, except in the horse pasture south of Hidden Hand Pass.

Permits/restrictions: Stock parties are limited to a total of twelve heartbeats, people and stock combined. To lessen impact on the area, plan trips with as few saddle and pack animals as possible.

Backcountry permits are required for overnight camping. Obtain permits from the National Park Service station at Marblemount, the Park's Newhalem visitor center, or from any Forest Service station in the area, including Twisp, Winthrop, or the Early Winters visitor center (during the summer months). Fires are permitted only in designated fire pits. Use only dead and downed wood, where fires are allowed.

Finding the trailhead: The trailhead and parking area are east of Marblemount near Mile Marker 138 on the north side of Washington Highway 20.

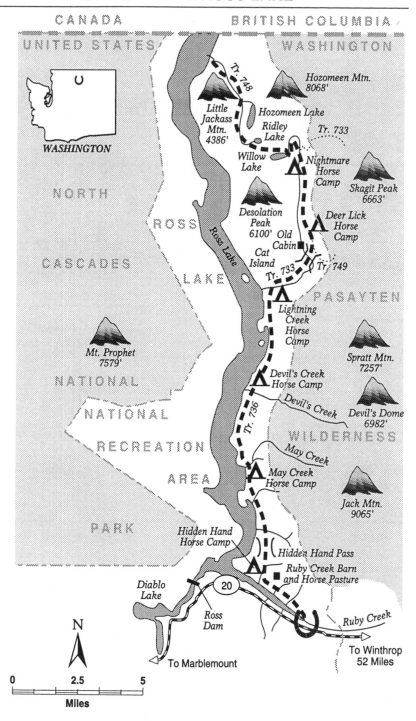

CANADA — BRITISH COLUMBIA
UNITED STATES — WASHINGTON

WASHINGTON

Tr. 748

Hozomeen Mtn.
8068'

Little
Jackass
Mtn.
4386'

Hozomeen Lake
Ridley
Lake

Tr. 733

Willow
Lake

Nightmare
Horse
Camp

Skagit Peak
6663'

NORTH

ROSS

Desolation
Peak
6100'
Old
Cabin

Deer Lick
Horse
Camp

CASCADES

LAKE

Cat
Island

Ross Lake

Tr. 733

Tr. 749

PASAYTEN

Lightning
Creek
Horse
Camp

Mt. Prophet
7579'

Spratt Mtn.
7257'

NATIONAL

Devil's Creek
Horse Camp

Devil's Creek

Devil's Dome
6982'

NATIONAL

Tr. 736

May Creek

WILDERNESS

RECREATION

May Creek
Horse Camp

AREA

Jack Mtn.
9065'

PARK

Hidden Hand
Horse Camp

Hidden Hand Pass

Ruby Creek Barn
and Horse Pasture

Diablo
Lake

20

Ross
Dam

Ruby Creek

N

To Marblemount

To Winthrop
52 Miles

0   2.5   5

Miles

East Bank Trail. Photo courtesy of Features Northwest.

The ride: Hikers and riders come from all over the state to enjoy the awe-inspiring scenery and delightful trails of Ross Lake National Recreation Area. East Bank Trail 736 traverses 31 miles of this remote, beautiful backcountry between WA 20 and the Canadian border. Six horse campsites on this trail allow rides of various lengths. Each campsite has a fire grate, hitching post, and pit toilet.

Ross Lake may not be full during many months, since water is drawn down periodically to produce hydroelectric power at the three dams on the Skagit River below Ross Lake—Ross, Diablo, and Gorge. Shoreline stumps and mid-lake treetops often appear when the water is low.

Washington fishing licenses are required for Ross Lake, which is one of the few lakes in the state that is not artificially stocked. Species include rainbow, cutthroat, bull, and Eastern brook trout. The season is from July 1 to October 31.

Weather around the lake is typically warm during summer, with temperatures reaching into the 90s at times. Even with high temperatures, however, the mountain lake water is very cold. Warm fall days with cool nights are usually very pleasant. Strong winds often whip through this rock-walled natural wind channel, which was cut by the now inundated Skagit River.

Leaving the parking lot, the trail is quickly enveloped in a cool forest as the path zigzags in a gentle downward slope 0.3 mile to the Ruby Creek bridge, about 200 feet below the trailhead. During a gold rush in the 1880s, Ruby Creek was a maze of placer claims for prospectors. Interpretive plaques near the bridge tell the history of the area, although there is now scarcely a sign of that former activity.

Beyond the wood and steel-cable suspension bridge, which offers a fine view of

Ruby Creek during the crossing, the trail meets the Devil's Dome Loop Trail into the Pasayten Wilderness. Turn left (west) as the path becomes the East Bank Trail, following the northern shore of Ruby Arm.

The trail widens as it heads northwest along Ruby Arm. Actually, this grade is the end of a 1930s road-building project that attempted to link the Skagit River with Harts Pass. Riders will pass the Ruby Creek Barn and Ruby Pasture at about 2.8 miles from the trailhead. This is one of the few meadow grazing areas available on the trip. Few horse riders use the campsite since it's so close to the trailhead.

Just beyond the meadow, the route along Ruby Creek swings north along the east shore of Ross Lake. There is a junction here with an 0.8-mile trail to the left to Ross Lake. To the right a trail provides a steep northeastern route to Jack Mountain in the Pasayten Wilderness.

Follow the East Bank Trail as it turns north for a 1.-mile ascent, with a 900-foot elevation gain, to forested Hidden Hand Pass. The Hidden Hand campsite is about 0.3 mile before the pass.

Miners' tales say that prospector Jack Rowley was guided by a pointing hand as he passed through this route in 1879 to find gold on Ruby Creek. Jack Mountain in the Pasayten is named for Rowley. This mountain saddle at Hidden Hand Pass is a fine scenic resting and turnaround point for those who are only out for a short 8.5-mile round-trip day ride.

The trail descends through forests for several miles from the pass, traveling inland from the lake until well past Roland Creek Campground. It then swings close to the lake again at the May Creek horse campsite. From there, the trail remains inland until reaching Rainbow Camp, a hiker's camp on the lakeshore about 8 miles from the trailhead.

For the next 7.5 miles the trail mainly follows the shoreline of Ross Lake to Lightning Creek, passing an easterly spur trail, Devil's Dome Trail 752, at Devil's Creek. A high suspension bridge crosses the mouth of Devil's Creek Canyon, just south of Devil's Creek horse campsite.

Another horse campsite is found where Lightning Creek spills into Ross Lake, and there are spectacular views of the lake and the surrounding mountainous terrain. Another suspension bridge spans Lightning Creek. Both the Devil's Creek Canyon and Lightning Creek bridges are built solidly and do not sway.

The East Bank Trail ends at Lightning Creek, at the junction with Desolation Peak Trail 772 and Lightning Creek Trail 733. Horses are not allowed on the 2.5-mile trail to the top of Desolation Peak, site of a historic fire lookout station where 1950s "beatnik" poet Jack Kerouac spent time as a lookout. He described his experiences in the book *Desolation Angels*.

Riders can follow the other trail east and then north along Lightning Creek, paralleling the boundary of the Pasayten Wilderness, less than 0.5 mile away. This route follows the base of Desolation Mountain, named after a forest fire swept over its slopes in 1926.

From Lightning Creek, the trail to Hozomeen Campground near the Canadian border is 15 miles. First the trail switchbacks up 1,000 feet in 0.5 mile to a ridge with marvelous views of the sparkling waters of Ross Lake. Snowcapped, 9,065-foot Jack Mountain rises to the southeast and Skagit Peak fills the horizon to the northeast, across

Ross Lake. Photo courtesy of Features Northwest.

Lightning Creek Valley. Those who know their mountain peaks in this area can easily spot the 10,775-foot snow cone of Mount Baker, the jagged ridges of Mount Shuksan, the North Cascades' Pickett Range, and other scenic mountains, all to the west.

From here the trail descends into the secluded Lightning Creek Valley. About 4 miles up the trail from the bridge is the Deer Lick horse campsite on Lightning Creek, just north of the junction with Three Fools Trail 749 coming in from the Pasayten Wilderness. The trail was named, supposedly, for three young prospectors who were duped into leaving their claim on Ruby Creek to explore this area.

A trapper's old log cabin near Deer Lick is closed to the public but maintained as a historic structure in this isolated region. Beyond, the trail follows Lightning Creek, crossing a log bridge over the creek to reach Nightmare Camp, situated in a shady cedar grove.

From Nightmare Camp the northbound trail turns west, becoming the trail to Willow Lake, which is set in a long shallow basin 1.0 mile from Ross Lake, at 2,853 feet elevation. Beyond Willow Lake the route becomes Hozomeen Trail 748. About 1.8 miles north of Willow Lake a 0.5-mile spur trail leads to Hozomeen Lake. This deep, clear lake reflects the granite spires of Hozomeen Peaks to the north.

The lake is closed to all visitors early in the summer to protect nesting loons. Gray wolves have been seen in this area, and there is a small grizzly bear population nearby. Black bears also live in the area. Hang your food high and keep a clean camp.

From the junction with the Hozomeen Lake spur trail, the main route continues north 3 miles in a gradual descent, ending at Hozomeen Campground, some 31 miles from the trailhead on WA 20.

14 BRIDGE CREEK TRAIL TO MCALESTER LAKE

Location: South of Rainy Pass on Washington Highway 20 in North Cascades National Park and Lake Chelan National Recreation Area.

General description: A pleasant 14-mile roundtrip into the high country of one of America's most rugged and scenic mountain settings.

Trailhead horse facilities: Paved parking with adequate room for horse trailers; restrooms.

Trailhead elevation: 4,510 feet.

High point: 6,300 feet, Hidden Meadows Horse Camp.

Maps: USGS McAlester Mountain and Washington Pass 7.5-minute quads; USGS North Cascades National Park quad; Okanogan National Forest.

Season: July through September.

Water availability: Abundant.

Feed availability: Grazing is not permitted in North Cascades National Park (first 5 miles of trail). Grazing is allowed in the Lake Chelan NRA (see permits, below), but carry pelletized feed to preserve high-country grasses at McAlester Lake.

Permits/restrictions: Backcountry permits are required for overnight camping. Grazing permits for the Lake Chelan NRA must be obtained at the same time. Coming from the west, obtain permits from the National Park Service station at Marblemount or the Newhalem visitor center. From the east, stop at any Forest Service office in the area, including the Twisp, Winthrop, or the Early Winters visitor centers (during the summer months). Party size is limited to twelve heartbeats in any combination of riders and stock. Fires are permitted only in designated fire pits.

Finding the trailhead: The Bridge Creek trailhead can be found in a clearing on the north side of Washington Highway 20, 1.2 miles east of Rainy Pass or 3.4 miles west of Washington Pass and Milepost 159. Heading east, the trailhead is past the second crossing of Bridge Creek, which is signed. Heading west, the trailhead is just before crossing Bridge Creek for the first time. The trail begins on the south side of the highway, opposite the parking area.

The ride: Since it was completed in 1972 the North Cascades Highway has provided access to views of some of the highest and most majestic peaks in the North Cascades. The beauty of these peaks is the magnet that draws many people to trails, of course, and the McAlester Lake Trail offers some of the best of this high-country scenery.

Bridge Creek Trail starts out on a short stretch of the 2,600-mile Canada-to-Mexico Pacific Crest National Scenic Trail, which crosses the highway here. The trail, easy to follow, parallels the highway for 0.5 mile before descending through a 0.9-mile stretch of subalpine spruce and fir trees. Deer are common here.

Rein left at the trail fork, letting the Pacific Crest Trail go straight ahead. Instead, ride the eastern Bridge Creek Trail, which soon crosses State Creek. This can be difficult to ford in the spring and early summer if flows are high.

14 BRIDGE CREEK TRAIL TO MCALESTER LAKE

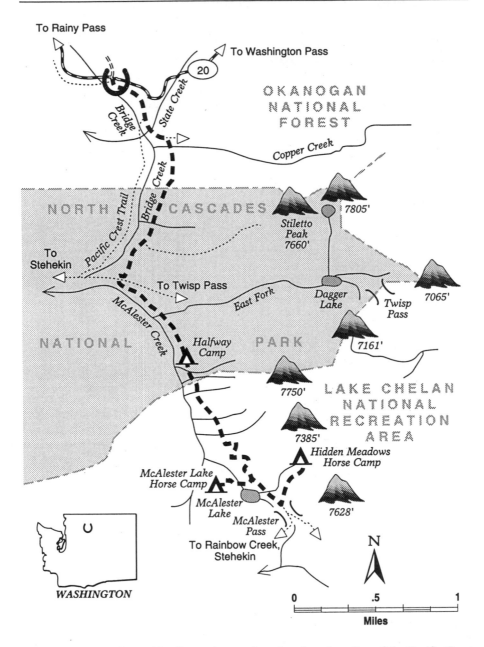

When you reach an old mileage sign, and an abandoned section of the Pacific Crest Trail, bear left. Another trail sign is close by, marking the faint trail eastbound to Copper Pass and the Twisp River. Instead, bear right for 0.25 mile, cross Copper Creek, and ride south. Water is available along much of this route.

At 1.4 miles from the trailhead the trail enters North Cascades National Park, where grazing is prohibited. From that point the trail descends through a dry forest and passes the little-used eastbound trail to Stiletto Peak.

In another 1.7 miles go straight through the junction with the eastbound Twisp Pass Trail. Shortly after that intersection is the junction with McAlester Pass Trail. As it ascends along McAlester Creek the trail crosses McAlester's East Fork. There is no bridge over the creek. This is a potentially hazardous crossing in June and July during peak snowmelt. Be sure to inquire at a ranger station about the current condition of this crossing.

About 1.8 miles from the start of McAlester Pass Trail is the boundary for the Lake Chelan National Recreation Area, where grazing is allowed. Just before the boundary is Halfway Camp, with a picnic table and firepits beside the creek.

Beyond the camp the trail enters a large meadow cleared by avalanches that offers views of timberline mountains at the head of McAlester Creek. A short distance farther the trail enters the spruce and fir forest once again, climbing steep terrain before reaching a series of switchbacks. Just before the switchbacks is a reliable small creek. Through the trees you'll glimpse basins and rocky ridges nearby, lined with rows of stunted timber.

As you approach McAlester Lake, at 5,500-feet in elevation and 6.8 miles from the highway, watch for a spur trail heading west to a hiker's camp at the northwest end of McAlester Lake, where several campsites are set in the woods. Fishing is usually good at the lake; resident 8- to 10-inch cutthroat trout make tasty meals. But please walk to the lake, don't ride. The shoreline is an especially sensitive area.

Follow the trail past the hiker's camp to reach McAlester Lake Horse Camp, newly established in 1994 and early 1995 to replace an earlier horse camp site on the south end of the lake. That area is due for a period of rest and revegetation after years of use. Facilities at the horse camp include a fire grate, hitching post, and pit toilet. East of the lake is Peak 7628, jagged and covered with scrub timber.

To reach the Hidden Meadows Horse Camp, high above the lake to the northeast, continue past McAlester Lake on the main trail. A short distance before McAlester Pass is a signed trail to the northeast. Rein left and follow the narrow trail as it ascends to Hidden Meadows Horse Camp at 6,300 feet. This unofficial path was made by repeated use, but the site has a fire grate, hitching rail, and pit toilet. A small creek usually flows just southeast of the site.

If you continue up the McAlester Lake Trail to McAlester Pass, you'll find a 6,000-foot notch about 1.25 miles northwest of South Pass. There's a junction with two other trails: the South Creek trail to the southeast that connects with the Twisp River Horse Camp (see Trail Ride 19) and the Rainbow Creek Trail that heads southwest to Stehekin.

One mile south of McAlester Pass is 7,928-foot-high McAlester Mountain. From the pass the view encompasses the jagged peaks of the North Cascades, forests, and mountain lakes. Rocky cliffs rise to the west, where ridges are spotted with Lyall larch. Below, McAlester Lake sets in a beautiful subalpine environment that offers scenic views of forests, meadows, and lakes. Western hemlock, subalpine fir, and alpine larch are among the several types of trees in this Cascade crest area.

15 BILLY GOAT LOOP

Location: North of Winthrop in the Pasayten Wilderness and the Okanogan National Forest.

General description: A week-long, 50-mile loop into the rugged Pasayten backcountry.

Trailhead horse facilities: Stock ramp, hitching rails, and parking space for up to eight or ten pickup-and-trailer rigs. Six horse trailers and trucks up to 16 feet long can use the space easily. A watering creek is nearby.

Trailhead elevation: 4,800 feet.

High point: 7,500 feet.

Maps: USGS Billy Goat Mountain, Ashnola Pass, and Ashnola Mountain 7.5-minute quads; Okanogan National Forest.

Season: July through September.

Water availability: Abundant along much of the route.

Feed availability: Forage is scarce. Pack pelletized feed.

Permits/restrictions: No permit is required. Groups larger than twelve persons and eight head of stock are prohibited in the Pasayten Wilderness.

Finding the trailhead: At the west end of Winthrop, turn northwest off Washington Highway 20 onto West Chewuch Road, west of the Chewuch bridge. The latest information about road and trail conditions is available at the Winthrop Ranger Station 0.3 mile from WA 20. The road along the Chewuch River valley is paved for 9.6 miles to the junction with Forest Road 5130. Turn left at the fork, where the sign points to Billy Goat Mountain and Buck Lake. Continue up FR 5130 along Eightmile Creek past several spur roads. The pavement ends after 5.3 miles and the road becomes a smooth, wide dirt road marked on maps as Forest Road 383. It gets rough only in the last mile to the trailhead, about 26 miles from Winthrop and 16.6 miles from the Chewuch River. Park at the equestrian trailhead—switchbacks on the road to the hiker's trailhead 0.75 mile farther are too tight for truck-and-trailer rigs.

The ride: Rolling hills, alpine meadows, lakes, streams, groves of trees, and marked trails characterize the majestic, secluded Pasayten Wilderness. From the ridges, riders are treated to vistas of row upon row of blue-hazed or cloud-wrapped peaks of the North Cascades traversing the border into Canada. Many Pasayten peaks rise to 8,000 feet, yet this land of sculpted valleys and sloping hills provides ample riding opportunities to high elevations without climbing gear, a rare circumstance in most parts of the Cascades.

Although the rides into the Pasayten from various trailheads are often six-hour saddle sessions, the scenery is well worth the journey. It's dry country, receiving one-third less precipitation annually than the western side of the Cascades. But the open meadows, ponderosa pine forests, and scenic ridge views make this prime riding country. The area is laced with trails, covering an area 40 miles wide and 20 miles north to south, from the trailhead to the Canadian border.

While the Pasayten Wilderness is not as accessible as the Alpine Lakes Wilderness near Snoqualmie Pass, where too many admirers have quite literally worn out

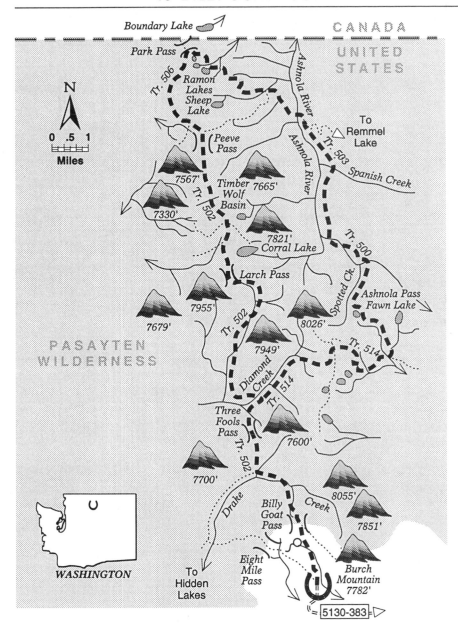

their welcome, fragile Pasayten trails can still easily be damaged by horses. The Billy Goat Trail gets plenty of travel but it's less used than the popular Andrews Creek Trail to the east, a main route into Bald Mountain, Spanish Creek, Cathedral Peak, Amphitheater Mountain, and Remmel Lake. Yet the scenery along Billy Goat is equally majestic.

A Pasayten Wilderness rest break on Amphitheater Mountain.

Temperatures can be hot in this open country despite the high elevation, so keep those wide-brimmed hats on and bring along sunscreen and canteens of water. On my August ride into the Pasayten, the riders basked in 80-degree temperatures. At other times, especially at the beginning and ending of summer, sudden changes from sunshine to rain to snow are not uncommon. Even in clear weather, keep the slickers tied on the saddles. They could come in handy, particularly on a long loop ride such as Billy Goat.

The lakes along the Billy Goat Loop hold pan-sized cutthroat trout. Early summer wildflowers add their color to the scenery, and there are brilliant displays of fall color in the Lyall larch trees at the timberline. This trip includes eight mountain passes, two of them traveled twice during the trip. The region is so distant from civilization that you're more likely to find other riders here than hikers.

Heading up Trail 502 from Billy Goat Corral, continue past the Eightmile Pass Trail that forks to the left. The trail then switchbacks up through an open Douglas-fir and subalpine fir forest. There are good views of Big Craggy Peak, one of the area's most rugged mountains, from the trail across Eightmile creek.

Traveling through another drainage the trail continues to wind upward through subalpine forests and increasingly rocky terrain. There is generally a reliable stream at this part of the trail, worth a stop for the horses to drink briefly before continuing on for 0.5 mile to Billy Goat Pass. On the boundary of the Pasayten Wilderness the 6,600-foot pass is 2.75 miles from the trailhead.

From here, the trail descends past the turnoff for 7,782-foot-high Burch

Mountain, 2 miles to the southeast. As you continue riding down through flowered meadows and open timberline forest, you're likely to encounter a few small creeks, especially in early summer, and occasionally some campsites. To the west is the giant granite shape of Billy Goat Mountain, dotted with larch trees.

Farther along, the downhill trail crosses Drake Creek through an area shaded by lodgepole pine and passes several trailside campsites. It then climbs again, passing Two Bit Creek, usually a reliable source of water.

About 2.25 miles from Billy Goat Pass the trail passes a spur to Drake Creek, a nice opportunity to turn around and for a short ride back to the trailhead if time is limited. Three miles on, the Drake Creek Trail connects with the trail to Eight-Mile Pass, which is 4 miles from the trailhead.

To follow the Billy Goat Loop Trail, stay to the right after the junction with the Drake Creek Trail and continue climbing through a burn area with old snags. The burn is reforesting itself with whitebark and lodgepole pine, Englemann spruce, and subalpine fir.

When the trail crosses Three Fools Pass, you can see Two Point Mountain to the north. Behind you is a view of Billy Goat Pass. Heading down the trail from Three Fools Pass, riders will see the junction of the return leg of the loop, 7.2 miles from the trailhead.

Head left at the junction and cross Diamond Creek. The creek runs full of rushing water in early summer, but it's narrow. From this point the trail leads west across rocky slopes dotted with aspens and Douglas-firs. Then it turns north again, through a forest of lodgepole pines with views of Diamond Creek and Many Trails Peak, to the west.

Pass by the left-forking trail 1.5 miles from the previous junction, the route to Dollar Watch Pass, and continue another mile to the bridge across Larch Creek. The trail follows Larch Creek north through meadows and more stands of lodgepole pine, passing several campsites along the way.

Soon the lodgepole pine forest becomes one of spruce, and the trail crosses to the east bank of Larch Creek, then bridges a westward tributary. After a few switchbacks, the trail jogs northwest to the headwaters of Larch Creek, a scenic area encompassing subalpine meadows set off with wildflowers. The stream usually dries up by late summer in the higher meadows.

There's a scenic campsite at this elevation, near a seeping spring on the way to a long switchback leading to 7,200-foot Larch Pass, marked by a forest of stunted Lyall larch. About 0.25 mile south of the pass another small spring seeps across the trail.

Heading north of Larch Pass, Trail 502 leads to a spectacular view of open alpine grasslands that make the trip worthwhile even to this point. But more amazing scenery is still ahead. Looking south from the pass, views include bald, sloping, alpine mountains, with the broad alpine mesa of Ashnola Mountain to the northwest and the rugged peaks of the distant North Cascades on the western horizon.

Moving along the trail, riders will cross rocky slopes north of Larch Pass and come upon McCall Gulch, a particularly scenic region in the Pasayten Wilderness that is a popular camping area with a small, year-round stream. Scattered stands of timber dot the flowery meadows of the gulch. About 0.75 mile from Larch Pass there's a trail off to the left, destined for Hidden Lakes, but stay on the main route, which climbs 400 feet to a 7,500-foot saddle, the highest elevation on the Billy Goat Trail.

The Corral Lake Trail heads off to the right from McCall Gulch, destined for campsites a mile away near the lake, which is usually only fair for fishing. A faint trail at the pass heads west over Ashnola Mountain for 1.5 miles into Whistler Basin, named for the whistling marmots in the area. This beautiful alpine area offers secluded camping with plentiful water.

At this point, the main trail travels along a spur of Sand Ridge above Crow Lake, a site for good fishing and campsites, then descends steeply into the very scenic Timber Wolf Creek basin. Sheltered campsites in the area are in scattered groves of Lyall larch, Englemann spruce, subalpine fir, and whitebark pine. Nearby streams provide ample water for these sites.

From these campsites the trail rises out of the basin to the northwest, reaching a spur ridge extending from Sand Ridge at a point 2.25 miles from the last pass. Here's an opportune moment to lean on saddle horns and pause to marvel at the beauty of the deep Ashnola River canyon, backdropped by rows of not-so-distant peaks and scenic plateaus.

To the northeast rises the craggy rock of Cathedral Peak, nearly on the U.S.-Canada border, and—much closer and due east —the broad plateau known as Bald Mountain. If the weather is clear, take time to ride 0.25 mile up a faint trail to Sand Ridge for an even better view from the ridge's grassy top.

This is the high-country scenery the Pasayten Wilderness is known for, spectacular sights that have remain unchanged for thousands of years. Being privileged to be among the few people who ever see these scenes is a feeling that stays with you for a lifetime. Prominent among the peaks to the southeast is 8,905-foot Jack Mountain, clad in ice and rising majestically at the westernmost boundary of the Pasayten, not far from Ross Lake National Recreation Area.

After returning to the main trail, head north toward 6,900-foot Peeve Pass, reached by an easy descent past flowing streams and scattered groves of trees. At the pass, which is 18 miles from the trailhead, you'll reach a junction of trails. Ignore the right one, which stretches 4.5 miles to the Ashnola River and passes a spur trail that heads north to Sheep Lake.

Instead, rein left down the trail signed for Hidden Lakes and the Pasayten River, descending 300 feet in 0.4 mile to another junction. A left turn here leads to scenic Quartz Lake, 1.5 miles away, but we want to go right to follow a 2.75-mile up-and-down route across the western slopes of 8,274-foot Sheep Mountain. After leaving a small timbered area, riders will find grassy, open slopes with many flowing springs.

Views from the slopes of Sheep Mountain are wonderfully scenic, particularly to the southwest where Jack Mountain can be seen joined by other peaks of the Cascades. To the northwest is a clear-cut swath marking the international boundary between the United States and Canada, along with a burned area to the north of the border that was logged after the ravages of a forest fire.

The trail descends to 7,000-foot Park Pass, amidst groves of timber and open grassy slopes. The pass is 2.75 miles from the last junction and more than 21 miles from the trailhead. The rounded, grassy mountain north of the pass is just across the Canadian border. Riding farther along, the border clearing is seen again as it stretches east to Cathedral Peak.

For an international side trip from Park Pass, you can ride moderately steep grassy slopes to the northwest to Monument 90, one of the many concrete markers along the U.S.–Canada boundary, located about 0.75 mile from the pass. Lying below to the northeast is Boundary Lake, where cutthroat fishing is good. But don't try it without a British Columbia fishing license.

Returning to Park Pass, the main trail, 503, leads southeast through open grassland and across a low ridge where a faint trail meanders to the lowest and largest of the Ramon Lakes. Pan-sized cutthroat can be found in the lower lake. This scenic basin features grassy slopes, and a thin forest of scattered Lyall larch, Englemann spruce, whitebark pine, and subalpine fir sheltering numerous potential campsites. To the west, Sheep Mountain looms above the basin.

At timberline high above the lake are two smaller lakes on a western bench. While secluded and scenic, these lakes are too shallow to hold fish. By late summer their outlet streams are almost certain to be dry.

Riding on past Ramon Lakes follow the main outlet stream from the lower lake along the southern bank to a point where it crosses a lower basin with well-watered meadows. It traverses another lower ridge into a shallow basin. Eastward, across the Ashnola River, are more scenic vistas, the familiar but never tiresome mountain views on this wilderness trip. Deer are often seen in the meadows and on high ridges near dusk.

Follow the southeastern trail toward the Ashnola River, which flows between Bald Mountain and Fred's Mountain. Over the next ridge, the trail descends to a grove of lodgepole pines, a point where you should rein right and lean back for a steep drop into the Martina Creek drainage. Reaching the bottom of the canyon, you'll be about 23.5 miles from the trailhead on this loop trip. A spur trail from the canyon climbs to Sheep Lake at the head of the drainage, but the path is faint and difficult to find.

Where the faint Sheep Lake Trail meets the main trail, rein left, to the east, to descend through a mile of woods to cross Martina Creek at a junction with the trail from Peeve Pass to the west. Bearing left again, you'll descend a moderately steep trail that loses 800 feet elevation over the next 1.75 miles, arriving at the Ashnola River, a tributary of the Okanogan River.

After fording the Ashnola, look for a log lean-to shelter in the lodgepole forest. Farther on, the trail, now 500, jogs south for 0.2 mile to a meeting with an eastbound trail to Remmel Lake, a marvelous Pasayten Wilderness scenic vista. The large lake spreads out before the 8,590-foot majesty of Remmel Mountain. At this juncture, bear right for 1.5 miles through a wooded area to meet the Spanish Creek Trail running southeastward.

Turning right again, bridge Spanish Creek near a campsite and continue heading south, watching for the deer and moose often seen in this area, particularly early and late in the day. At 2.25 miles beyond Spanish Creek, the trail crosses the boulder-filled bed of the Ashnola River and spruce and fir begin to appear at the edge of the lodgepole forest.

A boggy meadow lies ahead, particularly in the late spring and early summer months. But the trail avoids it and then crosses back to the east bank, passing by several other wet meadows and occasional campsites.

Four miles from the crossing at Spanish Creek, make an easy crossing of the Ashnola, at 29 miles from the trailhead, and start climbing along Spotted Creek as it courses through a narrow meadow edged with lodgepole pines. The route offers pleasant views up the canyon, with the pyramid shape of Diamond Point in the distance. You'll cross the small creek several times on this trail, often through muddy spots, before the route ascends steeply from the creek to the ridge of Ashnola Pass. Beyond is the tree and rock-ringed Fawn Lake at 6,201 feet.

There are numerous campsites beckoning horse and rider to Fawn Lake, and the thought of catching trout up to 12 inches long makes it hard to pass up this mountain lake. Beyond the lake, the trail crosses a rocky rise and then descends along Lake Creek. The 2 miles from Fawn Lake to a log bridge at Newland Creek are rugged, so expect a slower ride on this stretch.

At a junction, rein right and head west toward Diamond Creek along a trail signed for that destination. Crossing Lake Creek, the trail, now 514, begins climbing again but this time to a much smoother path. After the climb, the trail levels off on a bench, crosses several small streams, and skirts a lone campground. There are switchbacks here, but the trail quickly reaches a second bench in subalpine forest and the ride becomes easier. Note that there is no water available in this area.

Some 3.25 miles farther the trail arrives at a 7,100-foot saddle that is 1,800 feet above Lake Creek, with trails leading north to Diamond Point, 1.25 miles away, and south toward Fox Lake and Fool Hen Lake.

Follow the main trail south for about 100 feet along the ridgeline, then turn right and descend to the west toward a giant alpine mountain to the southwest. Pass by a left-branching trail 0.75 mile from the ridge and continue descending through switchbacks into the channel cut by Diamond Creek. The trail levels off near a roofless cabin and passes by several campsites at trailside, near a small creek.

Soon afterward, you'll ride by a scenic meadow and campsite at the base of Peak 7949. Above the creek, travel along a slope that guides the trail to where it crosses a small, reliable stream 2.5 miles from the pass. From there, it's an easy 1-mile ride downhill through woods and past a rocky spring to a junction. Turn left and head south through Three Fools Pass and Billy Goat Pass for the 7.25-mile ride back to the trailhead.

16 CHEWUCH TRAIL TO REMMEL LAKE

Location: North of Winthrop in the Pasayten Wilderness.
General description: An 18-mile scenic valley ride through lodgepole pine and subalpine forests to Remmel Lake.
Trailhead horse facilities: Stock ramp, hitch rails, campsites, toilets.
Trailhead elevation: 3,500 feet.
High point: 6,871 feet.
Maps: Okanogan National Forest; USGS Remmel Mountain, Bauerman Ridge, Coleman Peak quads.
Season: July through September.
Water availability: Along Chewuch River Trail and at Remmel Lake.
Feed availability: Good grazing for much of this trip, but supplement with pelletized feed.
Permits/restrictions: No permit is needed for Pasayten pack trips, but there is a wilderness restriction of twelve persons and eighteen head of stock.

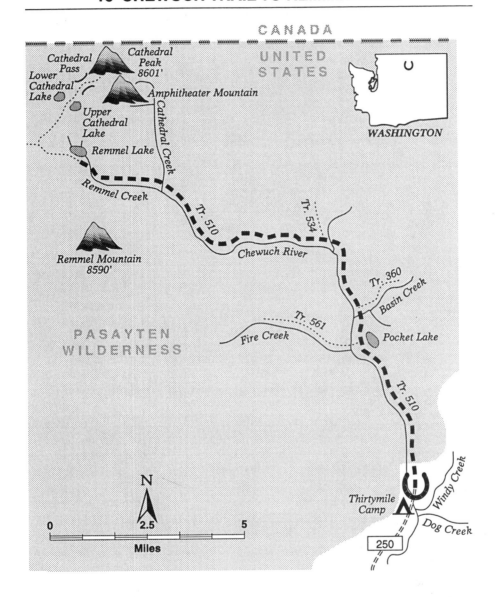

Finding the trailhead: From the west end of Winthrop, turn northwest off Washington Highway 20 onto West Chewuch Road west of the Chewuch bridge. The latest information about road and trail conditions is available at the Winthrop Ranger Station, just 0.3 miles from the highway. Travel 29 miles to the road's end at the trailhead for the Chewuch River Trail 510, by the Thirtymile Camp.

Upper Cathedral Lake.

The ride: Wide and dusty describes the start of the trail, which stays that way for most of the route except when there's mud to contend with after rains or early spring snowmelt. After only a mile the trail reaches the boundary of the Pasayten Wilderness. You're already surrounded by mountains, visible through some of the stands of lodgepole pine.

It's easy going to start with, gaining only 300 feet in the first 3 miles on the way to Chewuch Falls. About 2 miles farther the trail passes Pocket Lake to meet the Fire Creek–Coleman Ridge Trail 561. About 0.5 mile farther is the turn off for the Basin Creek Trail 360. But continue on the main trail for another 2.5 miles to the junction with Tungsten Creek Trail 534, at an elevation of 4,600 feet.

At the Tungsten Creek Trail junction, the Chewuch River Trail turns west through the pass to Remmel Lake. The trail becomes worn and rocky but rises only slightly as the forest fades and open meadows beckon. The rugged north side of Remmel Mountain can be seen from the trail, and the path levels out as the trail leads to the shore of Remmel Lake at 6,871 feet.

There are clumps of trees around the lake, but much of the area is meadow, covered in the spring and early summer with blue lupine and deep red paintbrush and yellow "sunflowers." Deer frequent the area. Mule deer often graze near tethered horses, watching the riders curiously but unafraid.

Temperatures can be hot in this open country despite the high elevation, so keep those wide-brimmed hats on and bring along sunscreen and canteens of water. On my August ride into the Pasayten we enjoyed 80 degree temperatures. At other times, especially at the beginning and ending of summer, sudden changes from sunshine to rain to snow are not uncommon, so keep your rain slickers back of the saddle. Late one August, a snowstorm dumped 6 inches on this area of the Pasayten.

Rolling hills, alpine meadows, lakes, streams, groves of trees, and weathered, wooden-signed trails characterize the majestic, secluded Pasayten Wilderness. Due north of Remmel Lake 3 miles is the Canadian border, with scenic Amphitheater and Cathedral mountains and the two Cathedral lakes only 1 mile from the border.

A loop trail leads to Upper Cathedral Lake, the larger and most scenic of the two. Ride out from the north side of Remmel to the northeast and around the west side of Amphitheater Mountain, a bare rocky crag towering above Upper Cathedral Lake.

For a short side trip, ride to the top of Amphitheater, at about 7,000 feet. Near the top you pass slots in the rock with views Upper Cathedral Lake directly below. Grab your saddle horn—it's a dizzying view. Once on top there is ample flat ground to tether the horses while riders climb the few feet to the top. Large granite boulders here are smooth enough to recline on while enjoying the sun and scenery.

From Amphitheater's summit riders are treated to vistas of row upon row of blue-hazed or cloud-wrapped peaks of the North Cascades that traverse the border into Canada. To the north rises the craggy rock of Cathedral Peak, nearly on the United States-Canadian border, and to the southwest, the broad, meadowed top of Bald Mountain.

On clear days the snowy volcanic cone of Mount Baker rises in the west above neighboring granite sentinels. Many Pasayten peaks rise to 8,000 feet, yet this land of sculpted valleys and sloping hills provides ample riding opportunities to high elevations, a rare circumstance in most parts of the Cascades.

Scenic views greet riders at the top of 7,000-foot-high Amphitheater Mountain in the Pasayten Wilderness.

Returning to the Cathedral Lakes Trail, ride north and continue a short distance to Upper Cathedral Lake. This large, clear lake is lined with boulders on its western shore and the rock walls of Amphitheater Mountain to the south. There are trout in the lake and sunshine often warms the rocks, making them perfect perches for either fishing for cutthroat trout or napping. From here, it's less than 2 miles back to Remmel Lake.

Be particularly aware of environmental considerations in this relatively pristine and scenically rewarding area of the North Cascades wilderness. The Remmel Lake, Cathedral Lakes, and Amphitheater Mountain destination has long been a popular one with horseback travelers. There is ample room to roam, plenty of scenery, good horsefeed, and ample water.

But the popularity and heavy use has been particularly hard on the area, which is also visited by riders on the Billy Goat Loop trails and the even more popular Andrews Creek Trail to Spanish Camp. The same camps are used over and over in this area, resulting in trampled grass and flowers, damaged trees, sanitation problems, and the ongoing enlargement and "improvements" to campsites by users. Lakeside camp areas have especially damaged the environment.

When you arrive at this area try to avoid heavily used sites. Find more secluded, off-trail camps. You'll see plenty of the area on day rides. Avoid camping too close to any of the lakes. When you ride to the Cathedral Lakes, try to tie up before getting there and walk the last 0.25 mile, especially at Upper Cathedral, which has a delicate environment and is already seriously damaged from heavy past use.

Fortunately, requiring six hours in the saddle to get here limits the crowds but it doesn't take much to destroy the beauty in this high country, where everything grows and recovers slowly. When you leave the wilderness leave no trace of your visit. Pack out everything you packed in, plus what less considerate visitors have left behind.

17 WOLF CREEK TRAIL TO GARDNER MEADOWS

Location: West of Winthrop in the Lake Chelan–Sawtooth Wilderness.
General description: A moderately easy 10.3-mile ride along Wolf Creek, with views of Abernathy Ridge, to the meadows beneath Mount Gardner.
Trailhead horse facilities: Stock ramp, hitchrails, toilets.
Trailhead elevation: 3,100 feet.
High point: Gardner Meadows, 5,800 feet.
Maps: USGS Gilbert, Midnight Mountain, Thompson Ridge.
Season: June through September.
Water availability: Good supply of Wolf Creek water along the trail and at the base of Mount Gardner near meadow campsites.
Feed availability: Stock can graze high meadows, which are also grazed by cattle under permit system; bring pelletized feed or grain to supplement horses' meals.

Wolf Creek Trail.

Permits/restrictions: No permit is needed. Groups traveling in the Lake Chelan-Sawtooth Wilderness are limited to twelve persons and eighteen head of stock.
Finding the trailhead: From Winthrop drive south on Washington Highway 20 across the Methow River bridge and turn right on Okanogan County Road 9120. Drive 1.5 miles and stay right on County Road 1131. Drive 4.5 miles, staying right on Forest Road 5505 to the signed trailhead.

The ride: This moderately easy trail follows the banks of Wolf Creek most of the way, offering good access to water and fishing for cutthroat, rainbow and Eastern brook trout. Watch for mule deer near the trailhead—we saw four on the road. They stopped momentarily to watch us saddle our horses, then moved on.

For the first 2.5 miles the trail is nearly level, winding through ponderosa pine forest. Then it climbs steeply for the next 7.5 miles to Gardner Meadows. There will probably be range cattle along the way, especially at the upper ends of the trail during the late summer and early fall.

The Wolf Creek Trail provides an opportunity to see green forests, white foaming rapids, and towering granite peaks in a relatively short ride that takes you from civilization to wilderness beauty in about five hours.

It's easy to spot clearings along the way where there is room for a streamside lunch break, a chance to relax under the tall trees and savor the sound and flow of Wolf Creek. As the trail gains elevation heading west openings allow glimpses of Abernathy Ridge to the south and Wolf Creek below.

Perhaps the strangest section of the ride is the last part, where the trail passes through more than 2 miles of charred, lifeless snags. These eerie sentinels mark the

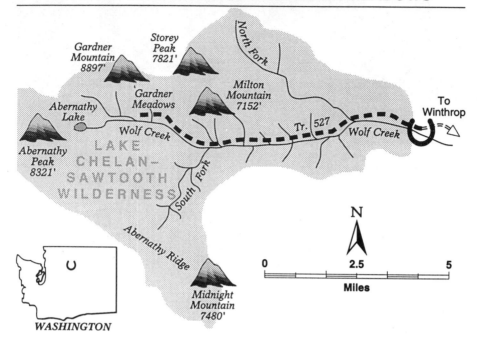

path of a major forest fire that swept through the area nearly twenty years ago. Suddenly the welcoming green forest you've been riding through is transformed into an unsettling world of grey and black, a surrealistic environment that even reaches to some of the forest around the campsite at 6,000 feet.

A thousand feet above the camp is the peak of Gardner Mountain, a familiar sight from the Methow River Valley and the windows of Sun Mountain Lodge above Winthrop. The meadows at the timberline camp area are slightly sloped, but the really steep incline is just above camp. There is no trail toward the peak, but riders can reach the upper meadows, where cattle sometimes graze in the fall, by guiding their horses in a switchback pattern across the meadow. Near the giant rock face of Mount Gardner, at the edge of the meadow, loose shale makes further riding dangerous.

A band of some two dozen mountain goats travels across the summit and adjacent ridges every two to three days. They can easily be sighted from camp, although binoculars are needed to see much detail.

Gardner Meadows.

TWISP RIVER HORSE CAMP

Location: Along the Twisp River, in an area between Lake Chelan National Recreation Area to the west and the northeastern sector of the Lake Chelan–Sawtooth Wilderness on the Okanogan National Forest.

Horse camp facilities: Stock ramp, hitching rails, feeding stations for pack and saddle stock, twelve individual campsites, toilets, picnic tables, and fire pits. The camp has water nearby at the Twisp River.

This is a fine camp for an extended stay. The trail to the Twisp River begins about 150 feet from camp and there is a pool of water by shore for horse watering that is separate from the rushing current of the river.

Remember this is bear country and camp accordingly. Keep spare food hung high. Do not leave cooked food around campsites. Further precautions are noted at ranger district offices and on the Forest Service information kiosk on the Twisp River Road.

Finding the horse camp: The route is clearly signed. From Twisp, the camp is 22 miles up the Twisp River. Drive westward on the Twisp River Road for about 10 miles. At the end of the pavement, by Mystery Camp, turn south at a T-intersection and cross the river to pick up Forest Road 4435 on the south side of the Twisp River. Follow this gravel road about 3 miles to the horse camp. Several turnouts along the road are large enough for trucks and horse trailer rigs.

A sign marks the camp entrance. The gravel road ends abruptly about 50 feet past

Twisp River Horse Camp.

TWISP RIVER HORSE CAMP

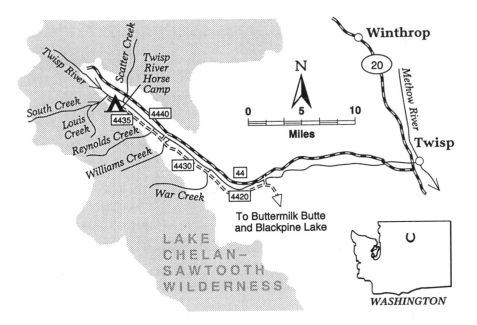

the horse camp entrance, where trails lead to the South Creek and Twisp River trails.
Horse camp elevation: 3,000 feet.
Trails: Several trails suitable for day rides meet at or near the Twisp River Horse Camp, including:

- Twisp Pass Trail 432, Ride 18, which offers spectacular views of Dagger Lake.

- South Creek Trail 401, Ride 19, which enters the Lake Chelan–Sawtooth Wilderness to reach Hidden Meadows Horse Camp in Lake Chelan NRA near Lake McAlester.

- Louis Lake Trail 428, Ride 20, a junction trail that extends off the South Creek Trail through meadows into a deep valley.

- Twisp River Trail 440, Ride 21, an easy journey along the Twisp River that passes by the camp, providing 8 miles of lower valley riding.

Road to Twisp River Horse Camp.

18 TWISP PASS TRAIL FROM TWISP RIVER HORSE CAMP

Location: West of Twisp and along the Twisp River near the eastern boundary of Lake Chelan National Recreation Area.

General description: A 4.5-mile trip to Twisp Pass with spectacular views of Dagger Lake, high-country forests, and jagged mountains, including Stiletto Peak.

Trailhead horse facilities: See Twisp River Horse Camp.

Trailhead elevation: 3,700 feet (horse camp is at 3,000 feet).

High point: 6,064 feet.

Maps: Okanogan National Forest; USGS Gilbert and McAlester Mountain.

Season: Late June through October.

Water availability: Water is available from the North Fork of the Twisp River along the first 2 miles of trail.

Feed availability: Grazing is limited after leaving the North Fork of the Twisp River. Bring pelletized feed.

Permits/restrictions: Twisp Pass is the boundary of Lake Chelan NRA, where permits are required for overnight stays. Also, grazing permits must be obtained from the National Park Service or from Forest Service ranger stations in Twisp or Winthrop. Party size for riders and stock is limited to twelve heartbeats. Dogs and firearms are not permitted in the NRA. Open fires are limited to camps with fire pits.

Finding the trailhead: From the Twisp River Horse Camp, ride the South Creek Trail across the Twisp River to the Twisp River Road. Then head left on the road for about 2.5 miles to the Twisp Pass trailhead.

18 TWISP PASS TRAIL FROM TWISP RIVER HORSE CAMP

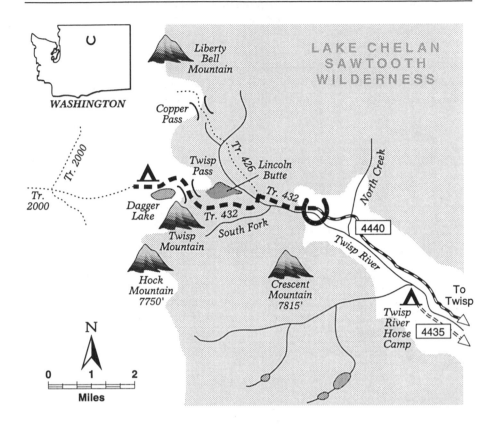

The ride: This trail leads to Twisp Pass, which marks the boundary separating the Lake Chelan-Sawtooth Wilderness in the Lake Chelan National Recreation Area of North Cascades National Park. The first 2 miles of trail are fairly easy. The last 2.8 miles, all in the wilderness area, are very scenic but moderately steep as they climb into the high country. Alpine views from the pass are unsurpassed—riders will want their cameras along for this trip.

The trail ascends through the Okanogan National Forest of central Washington, leaving the Twisp River Valley. Occasional views of Lincoln Butte, a pyramid-shaped mountain on the north side of Twisp Pass, can be seen to the west. The last dependable water is found 2 miles from the trailhead, at the junction with Copper Pass Trail 426.

Rein left, crossing the North Fork of the Twisp River, and head up the increasingly steep trail toward the pass. A mile from the junction is a ridge that offers views of valley forests and the ragged rock of Hock Mountain to the southwest. The mountain rises above the glacier-fed headwaters of the South Fork of the Twisp River. Soon the trail emerges from forest and travels over a rocky side slope where the route had to be blasted from hillsides in some areas.

About 4 miles from the trailhead, and less than 1 mile from the pass, the trail reaches a meadow of heather and flowers. A small stream offers water in about 0.5 mile. Only 0.25 mile more and the pass is reached, the boundary that marks the start of North Cascades National Park and its Lake Chelan National Recreation Area. Below the pass is Dagger Lake, surrounded by trees, with a backdrop of rugged North Cascade mountains.

More expansive views of Dagger Lake and Bridge Creek can be found by riding into the meadows north of the pass. South of the pass about 0.25 mile, at the base of Twisp Mountain, is a smaller lake surrounded by grass, wildflowers, and alpine forest.

Lean back in the saddle for a steep descent if you want to ride on 1 mile to the shore of Dagger Lake. Beyond, another 4 miles from the lake, is Bridge Creek and a junction with Pacific Crest Trail 2000.

19 SOUTH CREEK TRAIL FROM TWISP RIVER HORSE CAMP

Location: Between Lake Chelan National Recreation Area to the west and the north-eastern sector of the Lake Chelan-Sawtooth Wilderness to the east.
General description: A 7.8-mile ride from creek bottom to ridgetop, with opportunities for an extended trip to McAlester Lake in Lake Chelan NRA.
Trailhead horse facilities: See Twisp River Horse Camp.
Trailhead elevation: 3,000 feet.
High point: 5,351 feet at South Pass; 6,300 feet at Hidden Meadows Horse Camp above McAlester Lake.
Maps: Okanogan National Forest; USGS Gilbert and McAlester Mountain.
Season: Mid-July through October.
Water availability: Ample along South Creek but scarce at higher elevations.
Feed availability: Limited forage in Lake Chelan NRA; pack processed or pelletized feed.
Permits/restrictions: Permits for overnight stays and grazing are required for those camping in Lake Chelan NRA. Stop in any office or visitor center of the National Park Service or Forest Service (located in Twisp and Winthrop, Marblemount and Newhalem, Chelan or Stehekin).

Party size for riders and stock is limited to twelve heartbeats. Fires are not permitted except in designated fire pits. Grazing permits may be denied early in the season when grasses are still wet in the highlands.
Finding the trailhead: From the Twisp River Horse Camp, ride a short distance to the end of Forest Road 4435. At the end, follow the trail to the left, to the bridge over South Creek and the junction with South Creek Trail 401. The South Creek Trail actually begins to the right, across the Twisp River in South Creek Campground, but from the horse camp you turn left when you reach the trail junction.

19 SOUTH CREEK TRAIL FROM TWISP RIVER HORSE CAMP

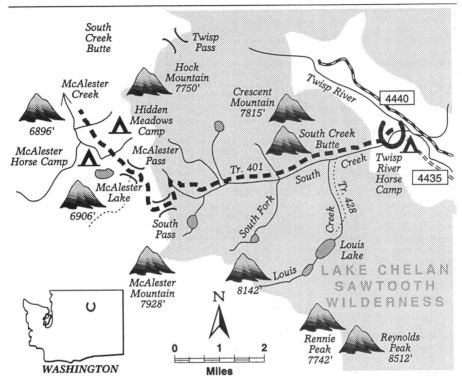

The ride: From the South Creek Trail 401 junction the path climbs gradually westward toward South Pass. Riding along the gentle opening stretch of the trail listen for South Creek rushing down a slot canyon. Within 1 mile the trail enters the Lake Chelan–Sawtooth Wilderness. Two miles up the trail, at 3,800 feet, is a junction with the Louis Lake Trail 428.

Continue up the trail 5.5 miles to South Pass on the ridge that forms the dividing line between the Twisp Ranger District and Lake Chelan NRA. From the pass the view encompasses the jagged peaks of the North Cascades, forests, and mountain lakes. Rocky cliffs rise to the west, where ridges are spotted with Lyall larch. One mile south of South Pass is 7,928-foot McAlester Mountain.

The trail continues beyond the pass about 1.25 miles northwest to 6,000-foot McAlester Pass. Here meet the South Pass, McAlester Lake, and Rainbow Creek trails. Groups larger than twelve heartbeats, people and stock combined, are prohibited on the west side of this ridge. Many people return to the Twisp River Horse Camp from the South Pass vantage point after enjoying a few hours of mountain scenery. But others stay on overnight at one of the two horse camps near McAlester Lake.

To reach McAlester Lake and either Hidden Meadows Horse Camp or McAlester Lake Horse Camp, follow the trail northwest from McAlester Pass through scenic country. The trail negotiates some steep switchbacks on the way down. Those staying overnight in Lake Chelan NRA need a backcountry camping permit and a grazing permit (see "Permits" above). For another approach to this high country see Trail Ride 14, Bridge Creek to McAlester Lake.

20 LOUIS LAKE TRAIL FROM TWISP RIVER HORSE CAMP

Location: West of Twisp along the Twisp River in the Lake Chelan–Sawtooth Wilderness.

General description: A 10.5-mile round-trip ride to Louis Lake with views of one of the most rugged parts of the Sawtooth Ridge in the Lake Chelan–Sawtooth Wilderness.

Trailhead horse facilities: See Twisp River Horse Camp.

Trailhead elevation: 3,000 feet at the Twisp River Horse Camp.

High point: 5,351 feet.

Maps: Okanogan National Forest; USGS Gilbert.

Season: Mid-July through October.

Water availability: Trail follows South and Louis creeks with ample watering sites.

Feed availability: There is no horse feed at the lake; carry pelletized feed.

Permits/restrictions: Do not camp within 200 feet of the lake. Sites at the lake are marked for revegetation.

Finding the trailhead: From the Twisp River Horse Camp, ride a short distance to the end of Forest Road 4435. At the end, turn to the left and follow the trail until you come to the bridge over South Creek. Continue on to the junction with the South Creek Trail, which begins across the Twisp River at the South Creek campground.

The ride: Riding along the gentle opening stretch of this trail, it's easy to hear South Creek rushing down a slot canyon. After a mile of riding through the Okanogan National Forest, the trail enters the Lake Chelan–Sawtooth Wilderness. Two miles up the trail, at 3,800 feet, is a junction with Louis Lake Trail 428.

The trail to the lake extends 3.2 miles from South Creek Trail 401, crossing a bridge over South Creek. South Creek Butte is identified by its red crest. When the path enters the Louis Creek valley, the trail winds above the creek with frequent inclines and descents. Farther on, the trail parallels the creek, leading to an opening in the seemingly solid mountain walls and to the lake beyond.

Louis Lake is overshadowed by 7,742-foot Rennie Peak on the left and an unnamed 8,142-foot peak on the right. Only a few hours of direct sunshine reach this lake even in midsummer, due to the deep valley. On the far shore of the lake is a small island with trees. The surface of the lake is filled with floating timbers deposited by winter avalanches.

Although very scenic, the area is difficult to camp in because of the sensitive terrain. Several areas by the lake are marked for revegetation projects. The best place to camp is at a site several hundred feet before the trail reaches the lake.

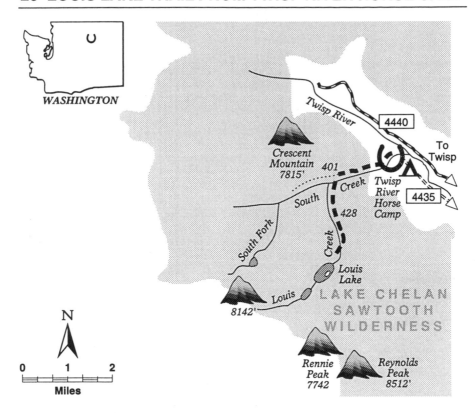

21 TWISP RIVER TRAIL FROM TWISP RIVER HORSE CAMP

Location: Along the Twisp River west of Twisp in the Okanogan National Forest.

General description: 7 miles of pleasant riding along the river valley. The trail is also open to hikers and mountain bikes.

Trailhead horse facilities: See Twisp River Horse Camp.

Trailhead elevation: 3,000 feet at horse camp.

Maps: Okanogan National Forest; USGS Gilbert.

Season: Late June through October.

Water availability: Plentiful along the Twisp River.

Feed availability: Forage is limited along the river. For an extended ride carry pelletized feed.

Permits/restrictions: The trail crosses Twisp River Road (Forest Road 4440) three times; use caution and watch for traffic.

21 TWISP RIVER TRAIL FROM TWISP RIVER HORSE CAMP

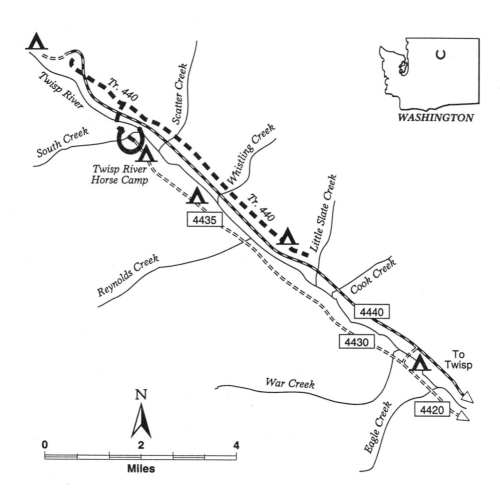

Finding the trailhead: From Twisp River Horse Camp on Forest Road 4435, ride 50 feet down the road to its end, then follow the trail on the left to a bridge over South Creek. Ride to the junction with South Creek Trail 401, rein right onto 401, and cross FR 4440 to the Twisp River Trail.

The ride: This is an easy trail that follows the Twisp River and the Twisp River Road, providing a scenic ride through the river valley. Numerous small creeks flow into the Twisp River along the trail route. Riders can travel up the trail toward the North Creek/Twisp Pass trailhead or downstream toward the town of Twisp, almost to Little Slate Creek.

22 CRATER CREEK TRAIL TO CRATER LAKE

Location: West of Methow and east of Lake Chelan in the Twisp Ranger District.

General description: A 6.4-mile round-trip to Crater Lake, a larch-adorned tarn ringed by rugged, glaciated peaks.

Trailhead horse facilities: Stock ramp, hitch rail, water trough, and campsites.

Trailhead elevation: 4,760 feet.

High point: Upper Crater Lake, 6,969 feet.

Maps: USGS Martin Peak 7.5-minute quad; Okanogan National Forest.

Season: July through mid-October.

Water availability: Abundant at Crater Lake.

Feed availability: Limited forage; carry processed feed.

Permits/restrictions: No permits are required, but riders are allowed to camp only at the horse campsite, not at other campsites. Camping is limited to one night at this site.

Finding the trailhead: From Twisp, drive 3 miles east on Washington Highway 20 and then south on Washington Highway 153 for 18.5 miles. Turn right on Gold Creek Loop Road for 0.8 mile, which follows the west bank of the Methow River. Then turn right again, about 1 mile later, as the route becomes Gold Creek Road (Forest Road 4340), heading west. A sign marks this junction for Crater Creek Camp and other destinations. Travel another 6.5 miles along the north side of Gold Creek, past the Foggy Dew campground, to Forest Road 300. Follow this switchbacked road, marked for the Crater Creek trailhead, about 4.4 miles to the trailhead parking area, signed "Eagle Lakes Trail."

The ride: The Sawtooth Range east of Lake Chelan is an eastern subrange of the Cascade Mountains, with open and dry forests and a variety of rock types, vegetation, and climate. Glaciers have carved the mountain slopes into sharp crests and pinnacled peaks rising above the U-shaped valleys. The rugged granite mountains here rise to 8,000 feet, overshadowing numerous cirque basins on the northeast slope of the range.

Visiting this remote, scenic area at Crater Lakes is an opportunity to explore the upper reaches of a peak-rimmed lake basin with timberline forests of Englemann spruce, Lyall larch, whitebark pine, and subalpine fir. Campsites are numerous and both Crater and Upper Crater lakes yield tasty pan-sized trout.

From the trailhead, riders will find an easy grade through an open, grass-carpeted forest. The trail soon reaches a viewpoint overlooking the Martin Creek drainage to the southwest and the Crater Lake drainage to the west.

About 0.6 mile from the trailhead, the trail bridges Crater Creek at a junction. Motorcycles that use the trail to this point typically fork left to the Eagle Lakes Trail, where the lakes are about 4 miles away. No motor vehicles are allowed on Crater Creek Trail to the right.

At this point the trail is generally straight, climbing moderately through a spruce and fir forest with limited views for the next 2 miles until it reaches a series of three

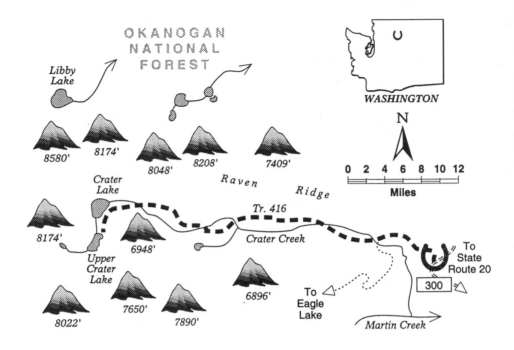

steep switchbacks. The sudden elevation gain provides a scenic view of the grassy hills and scattered trees of the Methow Valley, looking toward the Columbia River basin.

Farther up the trail, the canyon opens up as the trail reaches the level ground of the first of a series of steplike benches so typical of glacial valleys. There are some fine views of rugged granite peaks up the canyon. When the trail leaves that first bench, it climbs steeply for 0.8 mile to another bench at 6,800 feet, reaching a lovely meadow and a campsite frequented by horse packers. A hitching rail is provided here to encourage riders to camp away from the lake.

Now in subalpine forest, the trail climbs gently to Crater Lake at 6,841 feet, a scenic but shallow lake filled with trout. The lake is set in a timberline forest of Lyall larch, Englemann spruce, whitebark pine, and subalpine fir.

Camera-toting riders will be pleased to find a backdrop of rugged, craggy peaks overlooking the lake. Those peaks, including Raven Ridge to the north and 8,174-foot-high Mount Bigelow to the southwest, are on the border of the Lake Chelan–Sawtooth Wilderness area. The sun's morning rays light Mount Bigelow brightly, but by dusk the details of the backlit granite peak are lost in shadows.

A scenic 0.3-mile hike from the campsite reaches to Upper Crater Lake. Follow the sketchy trail rising from the southeast shore of Crater Lake. Those who seek solitude will enjoy this realm, set on a 6,969-foot bench surrounded by stunted timber and inspiring high peaks. Like the lower lake, there are trout here for the catching in this lake decorated with blue gentian, red and white heather, and other alpine cushion plants.

Another tiny lake lies 500 feet higher, on an alpine bench below Peak 8174. This secluded tarn can be reached by a steep trail that offers a few tough spots along with scenic views. The south slopes of Raven Ridge are densely covered with stunted whitebark pines in contrast to the cold-tolerant larches, spruces, and firs that prefer the cooler, glacier-scoured basin.

23 SUIATTLE RIVER TRAIL TO IMAGE LAKE

Location: Mount Baker–Snoqualmie National Forest, Darrington Ranger District, Glacier Peak Wilderness in the North Cascade Mountains.
General description: A popular 17-mile ride from river valley to ridgetop with marvelous views of 10,541-foot Glacier Peak and Fire Mountain. The trail ranges from moderately difficult to strenuous.
Trailhead horse facilities: Stock ramp, water, toilet, and a corral.
Trailhead elevation: 1,600 feet.
High point: 6,210 feet at Miners Ridge Lookout.
Maps: Mount Baker–Snoqualmie National Forest; USGS Glacier Peak.
Season: Mid-May to late October on Suiattle River Trail 784; mid-July to mid-October on Miners Ridge Trail 785.
Water availability: Ample along the Suiattle River but little water is found on the ridges and higher elevations except at Lady Camp near Image Lake.
Feed availability: Pack processed, pelletized feed.
Permits/restrictions: In the wilderness, groups are limited to twelve heartbeats, in any combination of people and horses. Camp at least 200 feet from water sources. No campfires are allowed. Bring small, portable propane camp stoves.

Horse riders may camp at any site except those designated for hikers only, such as at Image Lake, or where any camping is prohibited. When planning your ride, check with rangers for the latest information about road and trail conditions and which campsites are open to horses.
Finding the trailhead: From the Darrington Ranger Station, drive north of Darrington on Washington Highway 530, along the north side of the Sauk River, toward Rockport for 7 miles to Suiattle River Road 26. Turn right (east) and follow the road north, then southeast and east for 23 miles to the parking area at the end of the road.

The ride: From the trailhead follow an abandoned road past the wilderness boundary and ride for 1 mile to the junction with Milk Creek Trail 790. Stay to the left as the Suiattle River trail follows within view of the river, passing over a fairly level grade through groves of old and young trees for 6 miles to the crossing of Canyon Creek. There are several nice campsites here.

Continue another 3.5 miles to the junction with Miners Ridge Trail 785. Check your canteens. Then rein left for the steep switchback route to the ridge. About 3

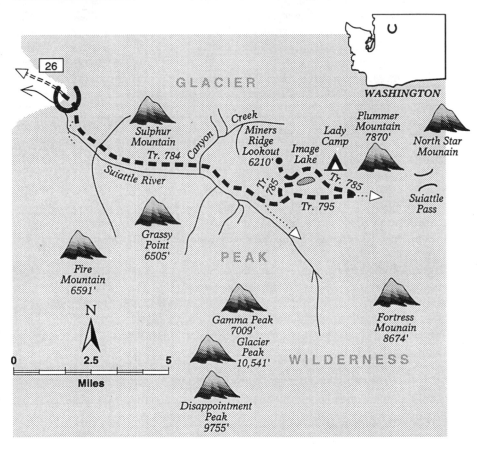

miles up the trail on these dry slopes are two streams at the edge of a meadow. Just 0.5 mile farther is a trail junction with Miners Cabin Trail 795 at 4,800 feet. From the campsites in the area the Miners Cabin route heads east to Suiattle Pass.

Follow Miners Ridge Trail 785 as it heads off to the left at 2,900 feet in elevation. Continue northeast to more switchbacks and an elevation gain of more than 3,000 feet on the way to Miners Ridge. Occasional views of the valley can be seen along the forested trail. The ridge is reached at 15 miles from the trailhead and at 6,150 feet. A side trail to the north from this point leads 0.25 mile to Miners Ridge Lookout at 6,210 feet. Wilderness rangers use this lookout during the summer.

After returning to Miners Ridge Trail 785 from the lookout site, head east about 1 mile to Image Lake, descending slightly to the 6,060-foot contour. The Forest Service is trying to protect this lake from heavy use by prohibiting camping close to the shoreline. Hitching posts are provided at the lake since it's open to day use for horses, so riders can relax or walk around the lake. Don't expect to find much solitude. This is a heavily traveled trail route for both hikers and horse riders and the lake is a major horse trek destination.

About 400 yards below the lake is a hikers' camp. But riders should use Lady Camp, designated for horses. It is 1 mile east of the lake. Above the trail to Lady Camp, around 1916, a sheepherder carved a woman's image in a tree. See if you can find it.

Rising above Lady Camp to the east is 7,870-foot Plummer Mountain, adjacent to Lady Camp Basin, a grassy area near the horse camp. Views of volcanic, snow-covered Glacier Peak and the forests along the Suiattle River are among the many sights to enjoy.

For the return trip the trail from Lady Camp descends 500 feet over a 0.5-mile path to the Suiattle Pass trail (Miners Cabin Trail 795). Rein right and ride 1.75 miles to the junction with the Miners Ridge Trail 785 you rode to the ridge and Image Lake. From there ride west on the Miners Ridge Trail and then right on Suiattle River Trail 784 to get back to the trailhead.

CHIWAWA HORSE CAMP

Location: Northeast of Lake Wenatchee and north of Washington Highway 2 in the Wenatchee National Forest.

Horse camp facilities: Twenty-one campsites, barrier-free toilets, potable water, a group fire pit area and individual campsite fire pits, steel poles for stringing highlines, a stock watering trough, stock ramps, and parking for five large trailers and rigs.

A loop road allows for pull-through handling of trucks and horse trailers, making it easy to unload stock without having to turn trailers around. A second loop road accesses the campground area.

This is one of the newer horse camps in Washington State, completed through a cooperative effort between the Lake Wenatchee Ranger District and the Cascade Horse Club of Lake Stevens, affiliated with Back Country Horsemen of Washington. Faced with the need to create equestrian camping facilities in the Chiwawa River drainage and wanting to reduce the trail activity by hikers and horseback riders into the Glacier Peak Wilderness, the Forest Service accepted the horse club's offer to develop a combination horse camp and riding trail network at Rock Creek.

The horse campground provides a scenic site on the upper Chiwawa River. When the system of trails is completed, riders will have access to a combination of loop trails, day rides, and overnight camping opportunities. Presently, there is access to hiking/horse trails in the area and several short bridle trails, including two that are appropriate for young or physically challenged riders. A 2-mile bridle trail loop around the horse camp was completed in 1993. The main loop trail from the camp, expected to be completed during 1995, is the scenic Basalt Ridge Trail.

Horse club members worked with the Forest Service, volunteering their time, to plan and build the camp and trail systems. Club members have also built trails to connect with Finner Creek Campground and helped to reconstruct other trails in the area.

Work remains to be done, and both the Cascade Horse Club and Lake Wenatchee Ranger District welcome other individuals or groups who want to volunteer. Contact Paul Sanford at the Lake Wenatchee Ranger District, (509) 763-3103.

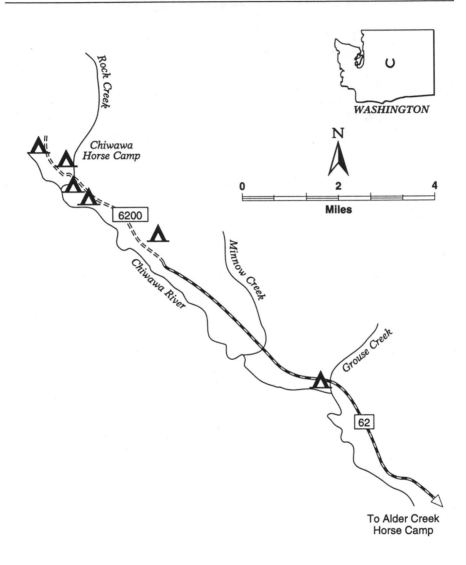

Locating the horse camp: The Chiwawa Horse Camp is 32 miles north of Leavenworth and 20 miles north of Lake Wenatchee. From U.S. Highway 2 at Coles Corner (14.6 miles west of Leavenworth and 19.5 miles east of Stevens Pass) turn northwest on Washington Highway 207 and follow the paved road past the south end of Lake Wenatchee to County Road 22 and Forest Road 6200, the Chiwawa River Road.

The road turns to gravel at Finner Creek, a few miles before reaching Rock Creek Campground on the left. Chiwawa Horse Camp is just past the campground on the right side of the road.

Horse camp elevation: 2,500 feet.

Trails: There are a variety of trails available from Chiwawa Horse Camp. The Basalt Ridge Trail from Chiwawa Horse Camp (see Trail Ride 24) is a scenic valley-and-ridge loop trip that encompasses trails up Rock Creek along Basalt Ridge, past Basalt Peak.

This new route is expected to be open during the summer of 1995. Both Rock Creek Trail from the horse camp and Basalt Ridge Trail from Finner Creek Campground already exist. But the old Rock Tie Trail that forms the top part of the loop ride is in poor condition for horse travel. When this part of the ride is rerouted, the completed ride will be one of the most scenic in Washington State.

Until then, both the Rock Creek and Finner Creek/Basalt Ridge trails are open to horses, offering scenic valley and ridge rides.

24 BASALT RIDGE FROM CHIWAWA HORSE CAMP

Location: Northeast of Lake Wenatchee and U.S. Highway 2, near the western edge of the Glacier Peak Wilderness.

General description: A 12-mile loop through meadows and along a high ridge with beautiful mountain scenery.

Trailhead horse facilities: See Chiwawa Horse Camp.

Trailhead elevation: 2,500 feet.

High point: 5,100 feet at Basalt Pass.

Maps: USGS Wenatchee Lake.

Season: Mid-June through October.

Water availability: Abundant at the horse camp and along the Rock Creek Trail; scarce on the Basalt Ridge Trail.

Feed availability: Carry pelletized feed.

Permits/restrictions: No permits required.

Finding the trailhead: See Chiwawa Horse Camp.

The ride: The Basalt Ridge Trail is a new loop created by connecting portions of the existing Rock Creek Trail 1509 and Basalt Ridge Trail 1515 with a newly relocated segment of Rock Tie Trail 1538 between the two older trails. Work on the loop should be completed by 1995. Until the new Trail 1538 link is finished, stay off the old link—it's extremely steep and in poor condition for horse travel. The new link will rely on switchbacks to handle the steep grade and will be designed to accommodate horse use.

Until then, both the Rock Creek and Basalt Ridge trails are blessed with scenery that makes them worthwhile as separate out-and-back rides. Here's how the loop ride will look when it's completed.

From the Chiwawa Horse Camp ride up Rock Creek Trail 1509 by crossing the Rock Creek Bridge or fording the creek from camp. The trail follows the creek, crossing several side streams in the first 2 miles and easing through meadows of wildflowers. The first mile is a gentle climb, but the grade increases over the next

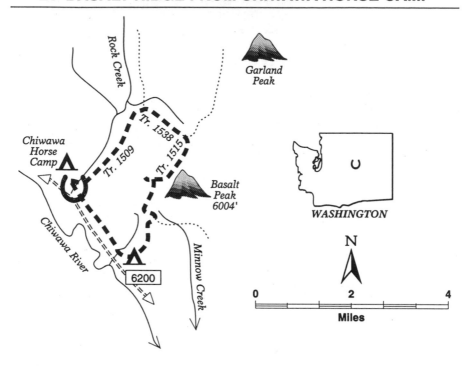

mile. At 2.25 miles and 3,400 feet in elevation the trail meets with the rerouted Rock Creek Tie Trail 1538.

Rein right and ride southeast along the contours and switchbacks, enjoying spectacular scenery as you climb 1.5 miles to 5,100-foot Basalt Pass and Basalt Ridge Trail 1515. Rein right again and climb south, gaining more than 900 feet in 1 mile. The trail then levels off and heads toward 6,004-foot Basalt Peak. The trail skirts the wooded summit with views of Garland Peak, the Rock Creek valley, and the logging roads of Chikamin Creek.

South of the summit is a spur trail to the west. Rein right and ride less than 0.5 mile on a dead-end trail to a stupendous rock cliff viewpoint. Then return to the main trail and head south again along the ridge.

Near the end of the ridge, at about 4,600 feet, the Minnow Creek Trail comes in from the left. Shortly, the main trail begins its steep, 1.25-mile descent to Finner Creek Campground and the Chiwawa River Road at 2,500 feet. Rein right and follow the new horse trail that parallels the road for about 2 miles back to the horse camp.

ALDER CREEK HORSE CAMP

Location: North of Leavenworth and northeast of Lake Wenatchee and Washington Highway 2, in the Wenatchee National Forest.

Horse camp facilities: Eighteen horse stalls in three sets of six each. Stalls include a place to tie horses and a manger for feeding hay. Also a horse watering barrel; stock ramp; one group campsite with a table, fire ring, and vault toilet. Parking is available for six or seven horse trailers and trucks, maximum length 30 feet. Maximum horse capacity at the site is twenty-four.

Finding the horse camp: From U.S. Highway 2 at Coles Corner (14.6 miles west of Leavenworth and 19.5 miles east of Stevens Pass) turn northwest on Washington Highway 207 and follow this paved road past the south end of Lake Wenatchee to County Road 22 and Forest Road 6200, the Chiwawa River Road. Turn right; the camp is just off the Chiwawa River Rd., about 2 miles northeast of Fish Lake.

Horse camp elevation: 2,400 feet.

Trails: The main riding trail served by Alder Creek Horse Camp is the Lower Chiwawa Trail. It passes by the horse camp, leading to a wooded, lower-elevation ride with views of distant mountains (see Trail Ride 25).

Over the years Alder Creek has become popular as a base for spring rides. The rest of the season it is predominantly an off-road-vehicle campsite, since the nearby Lower Chiwawa Trail 1548 is built for motorcycles. Horse riders rarely use the camp during the summer months.

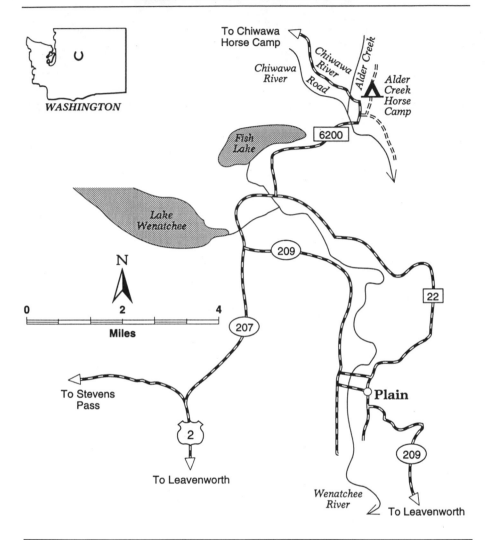

To Chiwawa
Horse Camp

Chiwawa
River

Chiwawa
River
Road

Alder Creek

Alder
Creek
Horse
Camp

WASHINGTON

6200

Fish
Lake

Lake
Wenatchee

N

0   2   4

Miles

209

22

207

To Stevens
Pass

2

To Leavenworth

Plain

209

Wenatchee
River

To Leavenworth

25 LOWER CHIWAWA RIVER FROM ALDER CREEK HORSE CAMP

Location: Northeast of Lake Wenatchee and U.S. Highway 2 on the Lake Wenatchee Ranger District.

General description: An easy ride along the hillside above Chiwawa River Road (Forest Road 6200).

Trailhead horse facilities: See Alder Creek Horse Camp.

Trailhead elevation: 2,400 feet at Alder Creek Horse Camp.

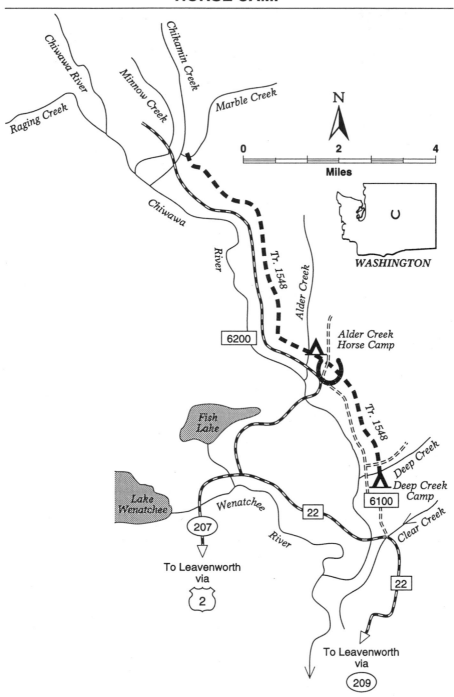

High point: 2,400 feet.
Maps: USGS Wenatchee Lake.
Season: Early spring, May through mid-June.
Water availability: Abundant at the horse camp.
Feed availability: Grazing is not allowed at the horse camp but hay can be used here, along with pelletized, processed feed.
Permits/restrictions: No permits needed.
Finding the trailhead: The trail passes a short distance south of the Alder Creek Horse Camp.

The ride: Over the years, the Alder Creek Horse Camp has become a popular starting point for early season rides. The rest of the season it is predominantly an off-road vehicle (ORV) campsite, since the nearby Lower Chiwawa Trail 1548 is designed for motorcycles. Horse riders rarely use the camp during the summer months. Campsites are available on a first-come, first-served basis.

This is an easy ride that stretches for 8.5 miles along the hillside just above Chiwawa River Road (FR 6200). The trail stretches from Deep Creek campground at the southern end to the junction of Trail 1534 at 2,200 feet elevation on the north end, just 1.5 miles north of Grouse Creek Campground.

There are several places along the wooded trail where distant mountains can be seen to the north and west, along with views of the Chiwawa River and its valley. Most of this low trail is through forests of mixed pine, including some ponderosa.

26 WEST CADY RIDGE

Location: 21 miles northeast of Index, off U.S. Highway 2, in the Henry M. Jackson Wilderness.
General description: An excellent 14-mile round-trip day ride through some of the most spectacular mountain scenery in the Henry M. Jackson Wilderness.
Trailhead horse facilities: Stock ramp and space for primitive roadside camping.
Trailhead elevation: 2,500 feet.
High point: 5,600 feet at Benchmark Mountain.
Maps: Mount Baker–Snoqualmie National Forest; USGS Blanca Lake and Benchmark Mountain quads.
Season: Mid-July through late September.
Water availability: Available from lowland streams but no water on West Cady Ridge.
Feed availability: Carry pelletized feed.
Permits/restrictions: Groups traveling in the wilderness are limited to twelve heartbeats, in any combination of riders and stock.
Finding the trailhead: From U.S. Highway 2 at Index, turn northeast onto the North Fork Skykomish River Road (Forest Road 63) and then drive north 6 miles before crossing the river. Then head east another 8.5 miles. The West Cady Ridge trailhead is on the south side of the road, across from Quartz Creek trailhead. FR 63 continues beyond this point about 1.4 miles, ending at the trailhead for North Fork Skykomish River Trail 1051.

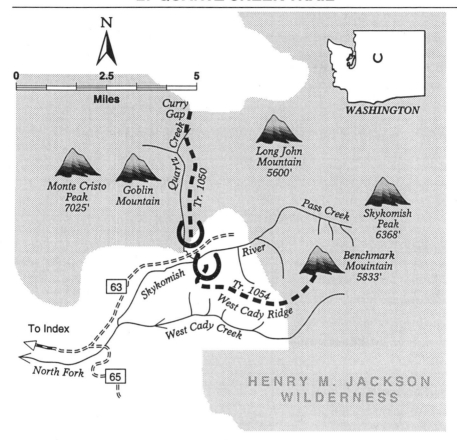

The ride: The lower portion of West Cady Ridge Trail 1054 begins in a forest of big trees, crossing the North Fork Skykomish River and then switchbacking up West Cady Ridge.

After about 3 miles the top of the 4,800-foot ridge is reached. The trail continues along the top. No water sources are available on the ridge, and there are some loose, rocky sections. But open meadows here offer broad vistas in every direction. Views include fields of heather and flowers, as well as Sloan Peak, Skykomish Peak, the Monte Cristo peaks, Glacier Peak, Mount Baker, and Mount Rainier.

The trail gradually climbs another 4 miles to 5,833-foot Benchmark Mountain. Trail elevation on the mountain is 5,600 feet. This ridge trail is heavily traveled during deer and bear hunting seasons. There are no good campsites along West Cady Ridge. It's very exposed and is best traveled during fair weather. Simply reverse the route for the return trip. If you go farther, Saddle Gap is 1 mile east of Benchmark Mountain, at the junction with Pacific Crest Trail 2000, at 4,900 feet in elevation.

27 QUARTZ CREEK TRAIL

Location: 21 miles northeast of Index, off U.S. Highway 2, in the Henry M. Jackson Wilderness.

General description: An 8.8-mile round-trip day ride through meadows with limited views of mountain scenery.

Trailhead horse facilities: A stock ramp is across the road near the West Cady Ridge 1054 trailhead. Riders sometimes camp in this area.

Trailhead elevation: 2,500 feet.

High point: 3,900 feet at Curry Gap.

Maps: Mount Baker–Snoqualmie National Forest; USGS Blanca Lake and Benchmark Mountain. See map on p. 101.

Season: Mid-July through late September.

Water availability: Water is plentiful in lowlands along Quartz Creek; little or no water as the trail climbs to Curry Gap.

Feed availability: Carry pelletized feed.

Permits/restrictions: Groups in the wilderness are limited to twelve heartbeats, in any combination of riders and stock.

Finding the trailhead: From US 2 at Index, turn northeast onto the North Fork Skykomish River Road (Forest Road 63) and then north along the east side of the river for 6 miles before crossing to the other side. Then head east along the north side of the river another 8.5 miles. The Quartz Creek 1050 trailhead is on the north side of the road, across from the West Cady Ridge 1054 trailhead. FR 63 continues beyond this point about 1.4 miles, ending at the trailhead for North Fork Skykomish River Trail 1051.

The ride: The trail climbs gradually, passing through tall timber and following the route of Quartz Creek almost straight north from the trailhead. This lower section can be very muddy at times, so it's best to wait for a dry spell. Though it's nearly always passable, keeping stock off muddy trails saves both the animals and the land from damage.

When the trail reaches higher elevations, it passes through small meadows. There are only limited views of Goblin Mountain to the west, rising above Quartz Creek.

At a little more than 4 miles from the trailhead, the trail ends at Curry Gap and the intersection with Bald Eagle Mountain Trail 650, at an elevation of 3,900 feet. Curry Gap is on the boundary between the Skykomish Ranger District and the Darrington Ranger District to the north. Several excellent campsites are set in a small saddle area of the ridge.

Be aware that Bald Eagle Mountain Trail 650 has some sections rated "most difficult" by the Forest Service. That means narrow tread and steep side slopes. This trail is recommended only for very experienced riders—and, even more importantly, for very experienced horses. It's best to rest a while at Curry Gap and then head back down Quartz Creek Trail 1050 to the trailhead at FR 63.

BLACK PINE HORSE CAMP

Location: 19 miles southwest from Leavenworth in Wenatchee National Forest.
Horse camp facilities: The only developed horse camp in the Leavenworth Ranger District; it has eight campsites, hitch rails, two restrooms, tested drinking water, fire rings, a stock ramp, and limited parking for trailers and stock trucks. The maximum horse capacity is six per campsite.
Finding the horse camp: Drive to Leavenworth on U.S. Highway 2. Just west of town, turn south on Icicle Creek Road and drive 17.5 miles to the Rock Island campground. Turn left on Forest Road 7600 and travel 1.5 miles to the end and the entrance to Black Pine Horse Camp.
Horse camp elevation: 2,900 feet.
Trails: Icicle Creek Trail 1551 leads from the horse camp to several other trails, including loop trails, all in the Alpine Lakes Wilderness.

- One of the most scenic is the Lorraine Ridge Trail 1568, a 14-mile round-trip to Lake Lorraine that includes steep climbs, multiple switchbacks, and rewarding scenery on the high ridges of the wilderness.

- Jack Creek Trail, being built by the Wenatchee Chapter of Back Country Horsemen of Washington, may be ready for use in 1995. The trail will begin 1.5 miles down the road from the horse camp, toward Leavenworth. The trail will be linked to others to make a loop ride. Check with rangers about the completion schedule and the condition of the trail.

BLACK PINE HORSE CAMP

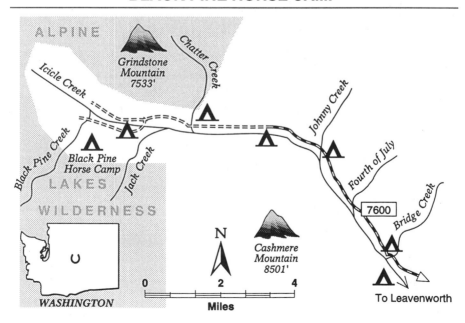

28 LORRAINE RIDGE FROM BLACK PINE HORSE CAMP

Location: Southwest of Leavenworth in the Alpine Lakes Wilderness.

General description: A 14-mile round-trip ride through old-growth forest to Lake Lorraine.

Trailhead horse facilities: See Black Pine Horse Camp.

Trailhead elevation: 2,900 feet at the horse camp.

High point: 4,681 feet on the Icicle Creek trail and 5,451 feet on the Lorraine Ridge trail.

Maps: Wenatchee National Forest; USGS Chiwaukum Mountains and Stevens Pass quads.

Season: July through mid-October on the Icicle Creek trail; July through September on the higher Lorraine Ridge trail.

Water availability: Ample at the horse camp and along Icicle Creek. Lorraine Ridge trail is dry except for Lake Lorraine. Carry water with you.

Feed availability: Very limited forage on Icicle Creek trail but some is available on the ridge top. Pack processed feed.

Permits/restrictions: In the Alpine Lakes Wilderness, free permits are required for all day and overnight visitors from May 15 to October 31. These are available at ranger stations and trailheads. Limited permits are available for overnight camping in the Enchantment Lakes area for $5 each.

Campfires are prohibited above 4,000 feet west of the Cascade crest and above 5,000 feet east of the crest. Campfires within 0.5 mile of some areas below these elevations are also prohibited. Check with the nearest ranger station.

Maximum group size in the wilderness, in any combination of people and stock, is twelve. In the Enchantments, maximum party size is eight. More restrictions are due to go into effect in 1995—including new rules for camping with pack or saddle stock in some areas—check with the Leavenworth Ranger District before planning trips into the Alpine Lakes Wilderness.

No permits are required for camping at the horse camp, but there is a $4 vehicle fee. Fording Icicle Creek is not recommended during high-water periods.

Finding the trailhead: The trail begins 0.4 mile west of the horse camp.

The ride: The Icicle Creek Trail is the main path into the northeast part of the Alpine Lakes Wilderness, leading to a variety of wilderness trails and vistas. Riding through the valley for 1.25 miles brings you in sight of French Creek Camp. Ride on along the Icicle River to the next junction, a meeting with Frosty Creek-Wildhorse Trail 1592, just after crossing a bridge over Icicle Creek.

About 4.5 miles from the trailhead cross a bridge over Icicle Creek, at 3,240 feet elevation, the trail rises and crosses two brushy avalanche paths. A campsite marks the Leland Creek junction, 6 miles from the trailhead. From here trails head left to Lake Leland and Wolverine Lake and right to the Chain Lakes, Doelle Lakes, White Pine Creek, and Josephine Lake, then eventually to the Pacific Crest National Scenic Trail beyond Josephine Lake.

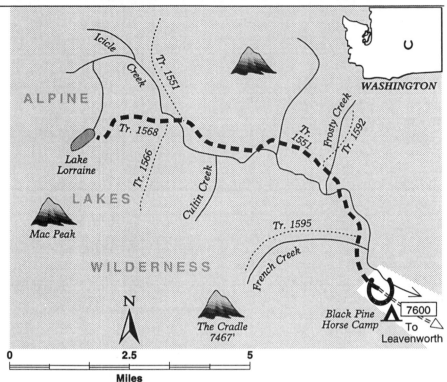

Turn left at this junction and ford Icicle Creek, if the water is low enough to be safe. Then ride along Lake Leland Trail 1566 for a short distance until you come to the junction with Lorraine Ridge Trail 1568 off to the right. The trail is particularly steep for the next 0.5 mile, with multiple switchbacks easing the grade—twenty-one switchbacks in all.

At the end of the last switchback the forest also ends. Riders are greeted by a rocky trail that makes the final ascent to the ridge, a ride filled with views of the Icicle Creek valley and the peaks of the Alpine Lakes Wilderness.

Near the crest of Lorraine Ridge the trail levels out and turns left, west toward Lake Lorraine. A short distance later the trail passes a faint old path to the right, heading uphill 0.1 mile to a lookout point at 5,451 feet, just below the summit of Lake Lorraine Point to the northwest. From here clear weather affords spectacular views of several peaks, including Bulls Tooth to the east and Mac Peak to the southwest.

Back at the main trail, continue 0.5 mile along or near the crest until the trail descends 450 feet to Lake Lorraine, at 5,056 feet elevation. The lake is 2 miles from the Icicle Creek trail and 7 miles from the Black Pine Horse Camp. At last, a place to water the horses and stretch the saddle imprint out of your jeans.

The best place to camp with stock is on the ridge, although these sites may not have water close at hand. Stock can also camp at the Leland/Icicle Junction, at about six miles from the trailhead.

29 DE ROUX TRAIL TO ESMERALDA BASIN

Location: North of Cle Elum, southwest of Mount Stuart and the Alpine Lakes Wilderness.

General description: A relaxing 11.5-mile loop through forest, meadows, streams, and mountain scenery.

Trailhead horse facilities: Stock ramp, large parking lot, picnic tables, and a pit toilet at Esmeralda Basin trailhead. Nearby De Roux Campground has space for horse trailers.

Trailhead elevation: 3,840 feet at De Roux Campground; 4,200 feet at Esmeralda Basin trailhead.

High point: 5,900 feet.

Maps: Wenatchee National Forest; Green Trails 209, Mount Stuart.

Season: Late June through October.

Water availability: Abundant along De Roux Trail 1392. Streams and creeks cross Esmeralda Basin Trail 1394 in the lower elevations. Don't count on stock water at Gallagher Head Lake. The shoreline of this marsh-lake is difficult to approach with horses.

Feed availability: Carry processed feed if you don't want to neglect stock during the riders' lunch stop in mountain meadows. But this and other day rides from De Roux campground are short enough that horses can be fed before and after rides.

Permits/restrictions: No permits are required.

Finding the trailhead: From Cle Elum (a good place to stock up on camping groceries), drive 6 miles east on Kittitas County Road 970, which angles northeast a short distance out of town, heading toward U.S. Highway 97.

Turn left (north) on Teanaway Road and drive 6 miles, past the Teanaway Store, the last supply store for groceries. Bear right and head north on North Fork Road. At 29 Pines Campground, the pavement ends and the road becomes Forest Road 9737. Continue about seven miles to the left turn to De Roux Campground. De Roux Trail 1392 begins nearby.

The ride: Only a short drive from the Puget Sound metropolitan area, De Roux Campground is nestled among tall trees next to the North Fork of the Teanaway River. The campground is popular with trail riders and serves as a good jumping-off point for Esmeralda Basin. The De Roux trailhead is just a few hundred feet north on FR 9737, and the Esmeralda Basin trailhead lies 1.5 miles up the road, offering a convenient loop ride.

Begin by riding from De Roux Campground to the signed trailhead on the left of FR 9737. Cross the shallow, rocky-bottomed North Fork of the Teanaway River and continue up the opposite bank into a cool forest route that follows De Roux Creek west. Along the trail are side meadows of grasses and mountain flowers. Many of the meadows are too marshy to support off-trail exploration, but they're pretty to see from the trail.

About 1 mile up the trail the route crosses De Roux Creek for the first of three times. Then the trail becomes steeper. About 0.25 mile farther is a trail to the left,

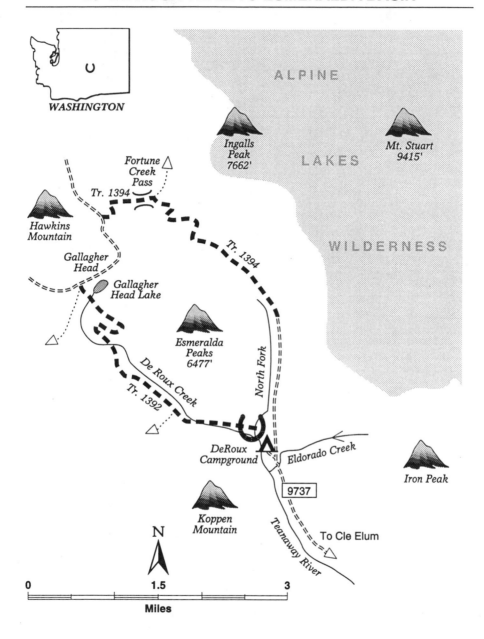

WASHINGTON

ALPINE

Ingalls Peak 7662'

Mt. Stuart 9415'

LAKES

Fortune Creek Pass

Tr. 1394

Hawkins Mountain

Gallagher Head

Gallagher Head Lake

Tr. 1394

WILDERNESS

Esmeralda Peaks 6477'

North Fork

De Roux Creek

Tr. 1392

DeRoux Campground

Eldorado Creek

Iron Peak

9737

Koppen Mountain

N

Teanaway River

To Cle Elum

0			1.5			3

Miles

De Roux Spur Trail 1392A. Pass up the spur trail and continue northwest on the main trail, which climbs even more steeply, sometimes switchbacking through scattered timber and past bluffs until it crosses a small ridge. From that point the trail follows the valley through thicker forest and scattered meadows.

Esmeralda Peaks.

The route is mostly forested along the De Roux Creek Trail. Views of mountains are few until riders reach the higher points of the ride. Forests here are a mix of hemlock; Douglas-fir and grand fir; lodgepole, ponderosa, and white pines; western larch; whitebark pine; and subalpine fir at higher elevations.

Grassy meadows in the mountains host abundant flowers that form fields of color in the spring and early summer. But ridgetops are mostly rocky and dry, with a few scattered trees in the high meadows. Mountain goats can be seen on some of the higher ridges and peaks in the western part of the Teanaway Valley, along with elk and deer. Some black bear live in the hills, as do coyotes and bobcats. Rattlesnakes are encountered only occasionally.

Lunch breaks on the De Roux trail are great times to lay back in a field and watch hawks soaring overhead. Red-tailed hawks and other raptors are frequently seen along roadways and over valley fields and high mountain meadows. Some will investigate horses and riders, swooping low enough to clearly show feather patterns and coloring.

Near the top of the steadily climbing trail the route crosses De Roux Creek two more times, about 1.5 miles apart. The last crossing is just before the trail ends at a junction with an old mining road built in 1910. Now used by jeep enthusiasts, Fortune Creek Road (Forest Road 4330-161) offers a wide, scenic route for riding the 2-mile northeast link to the return route on Esmeralda Basin Trail 1394.

To the right, near the start of the road, is Gallagher Head Lake, set in a small rocky basin. The lake is surrounded by meadows, all filled with flowery colors during the spring and early summer. Gallagher Head rises to the left of the roadway, appearing as a high bluff along the jeep road. At the end of the trek up the old wagon road, rein right onto Esmeralda Basin Trail 1394.

From this point the trail climbs 1,000 feet through a series of steep switchbacks above the South Fork of Fortune Creek, reaching a ridge that overlooks the Esmeralda Basin. About 0.5 mile from the ridge is the junction with County Line Trail 1226.2 (formerly a part of Esmeralda Basin Trail 1394), which heads northeast 1 mile to a cliff overlook at Lake Ann, several hundred feet below. Ridges of mountains can be seen to the north.

Be aware that this is a steep, switchbacking, dangerous trail. There are sections of loose shale that will soak your riding gloves with cold sweat as you try to keep your attention on the scenery instead of the trail. Riders who do take this route often dismount and lead their steeds through the higher, rougher parts of the trail near the Lake Ann overlook. It's best to bypass this trail section and continue the loop ride on the main basin trail.

From that trail junction the path winds down to the valley through a series of hillside switchbacks. To the south, across the valley, are the jagged spires known as Esmeralda Peaks, rising to 6,477 feet. Views of those peaks provide mountain scenery along much of Esmeralda Basin Trail 1394 as it descends along the North Fork Teanaway River Valley.

The trail route along the basin follows a moderate grade through meadows and groves of trees. There are many scenic views of neighboring mountains and many flowered meadows. Even in the fall, with most of the high-country flowers past their bloom, fields gleam with rich golden hues.

Toward the end of the trail a steep slope leads out of the forest to the parking lot at the trailhead. On summer and fall weekends this is a busy trail, but hikers are generally friendly and obliging about finding a wide spot in the narrow trail where they can stand back to let horses pass.

From the Esmeralda Basin trailhead it's only a 1.5-mile ride down FR 9737 to De Roux Campground and a rest for both horses and riders.

For those interested in commercial, outfitter-led rides into the region, watch for Camp Wahoo just before the turn off for De Roux Campground. This is a summer youth horse-riding facility operated by High Country Outfitters of Issaquah (the Green Trails map shows its former name, High Country Packers). The camp is on the left side of the road, and its corral on the right.

SAND FLATS HORSE CAMP

Location: On the eastern boundary of Mount Rainier National Park, near Crystal Mountain Ski Area.

Horse camp facilities: Fifteen parking spaces for trucks and horse trailers, a pit toilet, stock ramp, hitching rails, and several sets of poles for highlines.

"For those who love to ride horses, this is the place!" That's how the White River Rangers describe Sand Flats and the 12.6-mile Crystal Mountain Loop ride in their trail literature. Sand Flats is a popular area with stock riders. Even though the horse facilities here are as good as most horse camps, the White River Ranger District doesn't officially consider it a horse camp but more of a trailhead. There are, however, some bootleg fire grates here and room for camping, which many riders do. So unofficially it has become known as Sand Flats Horse Camp.

Horse camp elevation: 4,100 feet.

Finding the horse camp: From Enumclaw, drive east and south 33.1 miles on Washington Highway 410.

Just before the northeast entrance to Mount Rainier National Park, turn left on Forest Road 7190, heading north and then sharply south for 4.4 miles toward Crystal Mountain Ski Area. Before reaching the ski area, turn right onto FR 7190-510. Follow a double-back turn that's sharp but no problem for horse trailers and drive 0.4 mile to the Sand Flats Horse Camp and the trailhead for Crystal Mountain Trail 1163.

Trails: There are two fine horse rides from Sand Flats.

- Crystal Mountain Trail (Trail Ride 30) leaves the horse camp for a scenic ridge ride through Crystal Mountain Ski Area, offering some of the best close-up views of Mount Rainier to be found anywhere. The trail links with Silver Creek Trail to make a highly enjoyable loop trail.

- A short ride across the road leads to the trailhead for Norse Peak Trail (Trail Ride 31), a scenic route to the summit of Norse Peak, with views of Mount Rainier and surrounding mountains.

30 CRYSTAL MOUNTAIN LOOP TRAIL FROM SAND FLATS HORSE CAMP

Location: At Crystal Mountain Ski Area on the eastern boundary of Mount Rainier National Park.

General description: A 12.6-mile loop along a ridge through a ski area with some of the best close-up views of Mount Rainier found anywhere. Open to hikers and mountain bikers.

Trailhead horse facilities: See Sand Flats Horse Camp.

Trailhead elevation: 4,100 feet.

High point: 6,776 feet on the summit of Crystal Mountain.

Maps: Mount Baker–Snoqualmie National Forest; Green Trails Bumping Lake 271.

SAND FLATS HORSE CAMP
30 CRYSTAL MOUNTAIN LOOP TRAIL FROM SAND FLATS HORSE CAMP
31 NORSE PEAK TRAIL FROM SAND FLATS HORSE CAMP

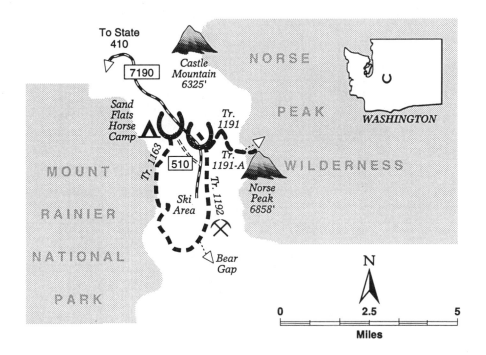

Season: July through September; best in early fall.

Water availability: Available at the horse camp and along a spur stream of Silver Creek. None on the trail.

Feed availability: Pack some pelletized feed for a horse treat at the summit. Little or no grazing.

Permits/restrictions: None.

Finding the trailhead: See Sand Flats Horse Camp.

The ride: Leaving camp early in the morning increases the chances of seeing elk along this trail, before the ski lifts start running. During summer they haul hikers and mountain bikers instead of skiers. When the lifts start running the elk head back into the forest. Much of the summer the trail gets heavy use. It's also a hot trail with little shade and no water, making it a great fall ride.

Rows of scenic peaks near Mount Rainier can be seen from the top of the Crystal Mountain Ski Area.

Crystal Mountain Trail 1163 starts out as a service road beneath power lines, but it soon becomes a simple trail, rising gently through second growth forest, scattered old-growth trees, and subalpine timber.

The route then passes through clearcuts and an old burn before reaching the top of the 5,500-foot ridge on Crystal Mountain about 3 miles from the trailhead. The ridge offers beautiful views of Mount Rainier and the White River Valley to the west and Castle Mountain to the south.

From the first ridge the trail climbs to the summit of Crystal Mountain, passing along the ridge that is also the boundary between the national forest to the east and Mount Rainier National Park to the west. Parts of the ridge trail are narrow, and at one point there is a cliff on the park side. The remainder of this ridge is more broad, rounded terrain.

The summit, at 6,776 feet and 6 miles from the trailhead, is also the top of the main chairlift to the Crystal Mountain Summit House restaurant. From the restaurant area views of Mount Rainier are even better than from the first ridge. Seeing Mount Rainier from Crystal Mountain is the kind of reach-out-and-touch-it closeness that truly inspires awe.

From the summit the Crystal Mountain Trail continues for 3 miles along the ridge and begins descending on a service road for 0.3 mile. Then it drops in a set of switchbacks down the ski hill though Silver Queen Basin. Ride past the junction with Henskin Lake Trail 1193, which leads south to Pacific Crest Trail 2000 at Bear Gap.

Continue on to Lower Henskin Lake, about 8 miles into the trip. Farther on, at mile point 9.1 and 5,500-feet elevation, is the junction with Silver Creek Trail 1192 at Jim Town, site of an old mining camp.

Rein left (north) on the Silver Creek Trail and follow it 1.5 miles to the base of Crystal Mountain Ski Area and a meeting with Forest Road 7190's spur road "410," known locally as the historic "mine-to-market" road. Ride north along the narrow 410 road for 2 miles and then cross FR 7190 to complete the loop and return to Sand Flats Horse Camp.

31 NORSE PEAK TRAIL FROM SAND FLATS HORSE CAMP

Location: On the western boundary of the Norse Peak Wilderness, overlooking Crystal Mountain Ski Area.

General description: A fairly difficult 4.5-mile route to the summit of Norse Peak; outstanding alpine vistas.

Trailhead horse facilities: None. Narrow Forest Road 7190-410 spur dead-ends with no trailer turnaround space. Best to park or camp at Sand Flats Horse Camp (which has trailhead facilities.)

Trailhead elevation: 4,100 feet at Sand Flats Horse Camp.

High point: The summit of 6,858-foot-high Norse Peak.

Maps: Mount Baker–Snoqualmie National Forest; Green Trails Bumping Lake 271; USGS Bumping Lake NW 7.5 quad. See map on p. 111.

Season: Late June through early November.

Water availability: Available at the horse camp; none on the higher elevations of the trail.

Feed availability: Pack pelletized feed. Raw grain and hay are illegal. Grazing is limited.

Permits/restrictions: Permits are required for camping in the wilderness. Groups traveling in the wilderness area are limited to twelve heartbeats, in any combination of riders and stock. Keep stock 200 feet from any lakeshore or stream except when traveling on through trails or watering.

Finding the trailhead: See Sand Flats Horse Camp for directions. From the horse camp, ride down Forest Road spur 510, rein left to cross FR 7190, the road you drove in on, and ride south on the road a couple hundred feet to reach the trailhead for Norse Peak Trail 1191 on the left. Be wary of traffic on FR 7190 during the crossing.

The ride: This trail is rated "more difficult" because of its steep grades, but the scenery is well worth the effort. Apparently the scenery is no secret—the route is highly popular with both trail riders and hikers and tends to be busy during summer. Fall is an ideal time to ride here, when trail traffic is lighter and fall colors enhance the trip.

From the trailhead the route climbs steadily along an almost continuous series of switchbacks from 4,000 feet to 6,500 feet at the junction with Norse Peak View Trail 1191-A. Trail 1191 bears left and crosses the ridge to continue on to Big Crow Basin.

There are some beautiful mountain and valley views as the trail ascends toward the Norse Peak Wilderness. Even in the early sections the snowy, mounded top of

Mount Rainier's volcanic dome appears over the ridge that is Crystal Mountain. Watching Rainier become almost larger than life as the trail ascends is a pleasant distraction from the steepness of the route. Two miles up the trail the whole summit of Rainier is easily seen, but the view gets even better as the trail continues to rise.

The old trail crosses the new from time to time, but stay on the newer one to let the other heal and recover. This is a slow process at these altitudes, where plant growth is inhibited by short seasons and harsh winters.

At the 4-mile mark, as the trail reaches the ridge at 6,480-feet elevation and turns east to cross it, rein right onto Norse Peak View Trail 1191-A, a 0.5-mile path to the summit. This is an old route to Norse Peak, site of an abandoned Forest Service lookout station. At 0.3 mile from the junction, you are within the Norse Peak Wilderness.

The trail summit is 0.5-mile from the junction, at 6,856 feet elevation, only 2 feet below the peak itself. Scenery includes Mount Rainier to the west, Crystal Mountain Ski Area across the Silver Creek Valley, and Castle Mountain to the north. Big Crow Basin is directly northeast below the summit.

Relax, enjoy the views, take pictures, have lunch. Then retrace the trail for the return ride to Sand Flats Horse Camp.

DEEP CREEK HORSE CAMP

Location: West of Yakima, 6 miles south of Bumping Lake on the edge of the William O. Douglas Wilderness Area.

Horse camp facilities: Six small, dispersed campsites, with six hitch rails. No restrooms or drinking water. Parking for up to 15 vehicles. Water stock at Deep Creek. Maximum horse capacity at the camp is 18.

Horse camp elevation: 4,350 feet.

Finding the horse camp: From Yakima, drive 18 miles northwest on U.S. Highway 12 to Washington Highway 410. Drive 26 miles north on WA 410 and turn left (south) on Bumping River Road (also marked as County Road 1050 and Forest Road 1800). Follow the pavement 10.7 miles through the outposts of Goose Prairie and Bumping Crossing until it becomes gravel surfaced near the north end of Bumping Lake.

At that point the route becomes FR 1800-395 and continues south until it makes an S-curve and FR 1800 splits west to Lily Lake. Stay south here, on what is now FR 1808.

Watch for a sign and short spur road for Deep Creek Horse Camp about 19 miles from WA 410 and a mile before reaching Deep Creek Campground. The main road ends at the boundary to the William O. Douglas Wilderness in about another mile.

Trails: Several trail rides are easily accessible from the Deep Creek Horse Camp and provide a fine introduction to the southern part of the William O. Douglas Wilderness.

- Twin Sisters Lakes Trail 980 leads to the lakes and also accesses Tumac Mountain.

- Indian Creek 1105 reaches Blankenship Meadows and Blankenship Lakes, stretching south to Indian Creek Horse Camp, about 2 miles from US 12.

32 TWIN SISTERS LAKES AND TUMAC MOUNTAIN FROM DEEP CREEK HORSE CAMP

Location: West of Yakima in the William O. Douglas Wilderness.

General description: A 10-mile round-trip on a heavily used trail to Twin Sisters Lakes and a 6,339-foot dormant volcano.

Trailhead horse facilities: See Deep Creek Horse Camp.

Trailhead elevation: 4,350 feet.

High point: 6,339 feet on Tumac Mountain.

Maps: Wenatchee National Forest; USGS Bumping Lake and White Pass quads; USFS William O. Douglas Wilderness; Green Trails Bumping Lake 271 or White Pass 303.

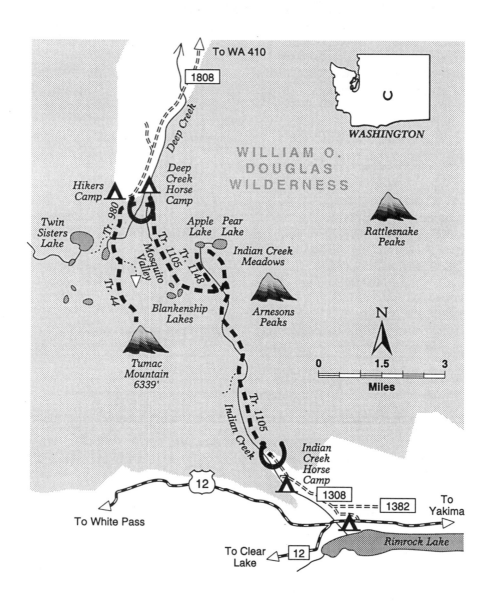

Season: July through October.
Water availability: Abundant.
Feed availability: Carry processed or pelletized feed.
Permits/restrictions: No groups larger than twelve in any combination of people and stock in the wilderness. All visitors must obtain a free wilderness permit at the trailhead. Horses are not allowed on Big Twin Sisters Trail 980A from its junction with Trail 980.
Finding the trailhead: See Deep Creek Horse Camp.

The ride: This trail is a good ride for discovering the scenic attractions of the southern half of the William O. Douglas Wilderness. The area is named for the late U.S. Supreme Court justice who had a home at nearby Goose Prairie.

The route is popular with both hikers and trail riders. You can help this wild but fragile landscape endure such heavy use by leaving no trace—stay on designated trails, keep stock at least 200 feet from streams and lakes except when watering, and avoid soft shorelines and streambanks when watering. Hobble your stock or use a high hitchline and move it frequently to prevent pawing.

Also be sure to take a permit from the box at the trailhead. Horse riders frequently ignore the permitting process, according to USFS studies. Registration is important for helping rangers manage the use of these trail areas. And note that trail signs in this wilderness area indicate trail numbers only, not destinations. A good map is essential to a successful trip.

Twin Sisters Trail 980 leaves the horse camp and parallels the road for about 1 mile to the Deep Creek Campground for hikers, at the end of the road. Then it winds around the campground and heads south into the wilderness through a forest of silver firs, mountain hemlocks, and Alaska yellow-cedars for 1.5 miles to the plateau at Little Twin Sister Lake. Fishing for trout can be productive here, as well as at other deep lakes in the area.

Dozens of lakes and ponds are scattered across the Tumac Plateau, left behind by the glaciers of an earlier era. The surrounding scenery includes the headwaters of the Bumping River to the north, Nelson Ridge to the east, and the jagged ridges and snowy cone of Mount Rainier to the west.

Lovely to look at, the many acres of shallow ponds unfortunately provide superb breeding sites for mosquitos well into August, making this trip especially delightful in the fall when mountain colors are out and most of the pesky bugs are gone.

For the longer ride to Tumac Mountain continue ahead at Little Twin Sister Lake and travel 0.4 mile to the junction with Trail 44 to the summit of Tumac Mountain. On the northwest ridge of the mountain the trail grade rises and meets the Cowlitz Pass Trail just below the summit, leading westward to the Pacific Crest Trail 2 miles away. Stay left on the trail for one last switchback across the heather-blanketed volcanic slopes of the mountain and continue to the 6,339-foot summit.

From this former Forest Service lookout site, decorated with stunted subalpine fir, riders can look down upon dozens of lakes below. Mount Rainier and the Tatoosh Range dominate the western skyline. Look south to the summits of Mount Adams, Goat Rocks, and Mount St. Helens. East stand Arnesons Peaks, and to the north are the peaks of American Ridge rising above the Bumping River Canyon. Also to the north are the unusual volcanic crags known as Fifes Peaks.

33 INDIAN CREEK TRAIL FROM DEEP CREEK HORSE CAMP

Location: West of Yakima in the William O. Douglas Wilderness.

General description: A 10-mile ride visiting Mosquito Valley, Blankenship Lakes, Apple and Pear lakes, and Indian Creek, with views of Mount Rainier.

Trailhead horse facilities: See Deep Creek Horse Camp for information about facilities at the north end of the trail. Indian Creek Horse Camp, at the south end, has a stock ramp, hitch rail, restroom, four dispersed campsites, room for six vehicles, and spring water south of the trailhead.

Trailhead elevation: 4,350 feet at Deep Creek Horse Camp.

High point: 5,200 feet.

Maps: Wenatchee National Forest; USGS Bumping Lake, White Pass quads; William O. Douglas Wilderness; Green Trails Bumping Lake 271 or White Pass 303.

Season: July through October.

Water availability: Abundant.

Feed availability: Pack processed or pelletized feed.

Permits/restrictions: Groups traveling in the wilderness are limited to twelve heartbeats in any combination of people and stock. Obtain a free wilderness permit at the trailhead.

Finding the trailhead: See Deep Creek Horse Camp.

The ride: This wilderness trail links the Deep Creek Horse Camp near Bumping Lake at the north end with the horse facilities at the trailhead of Indian Creek Trail 1105 on the south end.

At the north end the trail leaves the horse camp and heads south through Mosquito Valley. Lovely to look at, the many acres of shallow ponds in this region unfortunately provide superb breeding sites for mosquitos well into August, making this trip delightful in the fall when mountain colors are showing and most of the pesky bugs are gone.

From the valley the trail climbs a steep, rugged grade to the Tumac Plateau and Blankenship Lakes, among the larger of the many high-country lakes found in this realm. The elevation is 5,200 feet. There are views of 6,339-foot Tumac Mountain to the southwest. The volcano's cone is wooded except for open meadows on one side. Mount Rainier is on the western horizon, with Mount Adams and Mount St. Helens to the south.

There are fewer mountain flowers in the meadows than might be expected, but lupines (Texas bluebonnets) and bear grass grow here, even in the woods. This almost level trail section is an enjoyable ride, crossing subalpine meadows that are home to scattered groves of timber.

One mile east of the lakes Trail 1105 arrives at a scenic 3-mile loop ride on Trail 1148—first to shallow Apple Lake and then to the much deeper Pear Lake. Returning to Trail 1105 on Trail 1148, head south through Indian Creek Meadows and follow the creek southeast.

On this stretch of trail Indian Creek Meadows offers 0.5 mile of open scenery. The trail is faint crossing the meadow, then becomes clearer again as it winds south, crossing Indian Creek three times.

From the plateau meadows the trail descends 4 miles south into a narrow, forested valley that is almost a gorge. Water is available along the trail and a roaring waterfall may be heard about 2.5 miles before the end of the trail.

The trail climbs sharply out of the canyon to meet with the end of an old mining road. The road continues through the forest about 2 miles to meet the end of FR 1308. On the south part of the trail is a high bridge that is more than 10 feet above the water. Since the bridge has only a low cable guardrail, some riders prefer to ford the creek on horseback. A short distance down the abandoned road is the Indian Creek trailhead. About 2 miles beyond the trailhead is the junction with U.S. Highway 12.

If someone picks you up with a truck and horse trailer at the southern trailhead for 1105, near US 12, it makes this ride from Deep Creek Horse Camp a nice day outing. Or camp at Indian Creek and ride to Deep Creek Horse Camp, preferably with a ride waiting there. A third option is to camp overnight at either site and retrace hoofprints to your trucks and horse trailers the next day.

To approach Indian Creek Trail 1105 from the south end, near Rimrock Lake, drive 8.3 miles east from White Pass on US 12. Then turn left at Forest Road 1382 and drive 0.8 mile to the left-hand turnoff onto Forest Road 1308 and travel about 1 mile to the end. This 3,400-foot trailhead camp, used by both horse riders and hikers, has four campsites, a hitch rail, stock ramp, and restrooms.

WHITE PASS HORSE CAMP

Location: West of Yakima and east of Chehalis on U.S. Highway 12 at White Pass, southeast of Mount Rainier, on the Wenatchee National Forest.
Horse camp facilities: Six dispersed campsites, two toilets, a stock ramp, eight hitch rails, and parking for eighteen horse trucks and trailers. Spring water is available. Maximum horse capacity is twenty-four.
Finding the horse camp: Travel U.S. Highway 12 from either Chehalis or Yakima to White Pass. Watch for White Pass Horse Camp signs at Leech Lake on the east side of the pass. The camp is adjacent to Pacific Crest National Scenic Trail 2000, also known by its former name on this northern portion, the Cascade Crest Trail.
Elevation: 4,550 feet.
Trails: The primary trail accessible from this horse camp is the Pacific Crest National Scenic Trail 2000.

- Pacific Crest Trail/Cramer Lake Loop leaves from White Pass Horse Camp, accessing the northern portion of the PCT (see Trail Ride 34).

- Access to the southern portion of the Pacific Crest Trail 2000 leaves from the nearby White Pass trailhead. Facilities there include a stock ramp, four hitch rails, and room for four vehicles. There is no water there but that can be found at the White Pass Horse Camp.

34 PACIFIC CREST TRAIL/CRAMER LAKE LOOP FROM WHITE PASS HORSE CAMP

Location: West of Yakima and east of Chehalis on U.S. Highway 12 at White Pass.
General description: A 13-mile round-trip with serene lakes, lush forests, mountain peaks, and bright red huckleberry bush leaves in the fall.
Trailhead horse facilities: See White Pass Horse Camp.
Trailhead elevation: 4,550 feet at White Pass Horse Camp.
High point: 5,600 feet.
Maps: Wenatchee National Forest; USFS William O. Douglas Wilderness; Green Trails White Pass 303.
Season: Mid-July through November.
Water availability: Abundant at the series of lakes.
Feed availability: Carry processed or pelletized feed.
Permits/restrictions: No group larger than twelve in any combination of people and stock in the wilderness. Obtain a free wilderness permit at the trailhead.
Finding the trailhead: See White Pass Horse Camp. The primary trail accessible from this horse camp is Pacific Crest National Scenic Trail 2000, which passes by the camp. The PCT trailhead is near Leech Lake, about 0.25 mile from the campground.

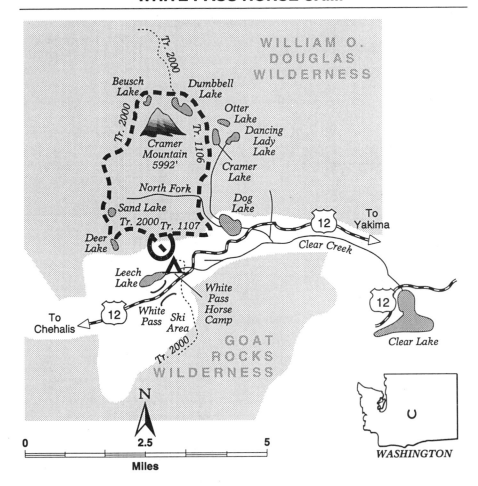

The ride: This is a prime scenic section of Pacific Crest/Cascade Crest Trail 2000, with easy access from US 12, so expect the trail to be busy with hikers and riders even on rainy days. If the weather has been wet for several days, stay off this trail to avoid churning up the mud. Also note that trail signs in this wilderness area list only trail numbers, not destinations. A good map is essential to a successful trip.

The trail begins in forest, ascending about 800 feet over the next 2.75 miles to forested Deer Lake (elevation 5,206). Ride another 0.75 mile to Sand Lake (5,295 feet), a scenic spot, especially with early morning fog rising from the still water. There are also some meadowlands near the lake. The water is generally very clear in this shallow lake. Sand Lake is a convenient turnaround for those on a short trip and a great spot for a break, although it's only 3.5 miles from the trailhead.

121

Leaving Sand Lake, the trail passes several smaller lakes and climbs to 5,600 feet at the 4-mile point. Mount Adams and the Goat Rocks Wilderness to the south are visible from several points on the wooded trail. To the east is Spiral Butte.

The PCT moves from the east side of the crest to the west side at about 5 miles, winding through forest and descending about 500 feet over the next 0.75 mile. In clear weather riders can glimpse Mount Rainier at times through the trees.

At mile 6 the trail arrives at Buesch Lake (5,081 feet). Admire the views and then travel on to a junction with Cramer Lake Trail 1106. Rein right and follow the trail to shallow Dumbbell Lake (5,091 feet) with its intriguing rocky shoreline. Keep stock well away from wet soils and be careful about walking too close to any of the lakes in this wilderness. In many places the shoreline areas are being replanted and cared for by Forest Service staff and volunteers who are trying to renew and preserve plants and soil battered by too many visitors.

From Dumbbell Lake follow the trail past Cramer Lake to within 0.5 mile of Dog Lake, then rein right (west) on Dark Meadow Trail 1107. Ride on to meet the Pacific Crest Trail to complete the loop ride and head south on the PCT for the last mile back to the horse camp.

KEENES HORSE CAMP

Location: East of Swift Creek Reservoir, at the northern tip of the Mount Adams Wilderness.

Horse camp facilities: Stock ramp, corrals, fourteen camping sites, and a watering trough.

Horse camp elevation: 4,300 feet.

Finding the horse camp: The Keenes Horse Camp, about 3.5 hours driving time from the Portland–Vancouver area, can be reached from Interstate 5 via Washington Highway 503. When WA 503 turns south, just before Yale Lake, continue straight on Forest Road 90. Continue past the north end of Swift Creek Reservoir, then follow the road as it winds northeast along the Lewis River.

Drive past Lower Falls Campground and the Lewis River Horse Camp at the junction with Forest Road 9300. Continue for 12.5 miles, mostly along the Lewis River, until a hairpin bend in the road brings you to an intersection with Forest Road 23, a gravel road. Turn north (left) and travel 3 miles to where the road turns to pavement for a short distance. Turn right on Forest Road 2329 and drive 6 miles, past Takhlakh Lake and Horseshoe Lake Campground to Spring Creek. You have arrived at Keenes Horse Camp, named to honor a long-time horse packer for the Forest Service.

Trails: Several non-wilderness trails from this camp offer a variety of river, meadow, and mountain scenery.

- Keenes Trail 120 is an easy trail along Spring Creek. Combined with Spring Creek Trail 115 and High Lakes Trail 116, the three trails create a scenic loop ride (see Trail Ride 35).

- Green Mountain Trail 110 and Spring Creek Trail 115 provide a ride through meadows and semi-open forests to reach panoramic views from the top of Green Mountain (see Trail Ride 36).

- High Lakes Trail 116 is a more difficult trail, taking riders through terrain that includes mountain views, wildflowers, and old volcanic mudflow from Mount Adams on the way to Chain of Lakes (see Trail Ride 37).

35 KEENES TRAIL LOOP FROM KEENES HORSE CAMP

Location: Southeast of Packwood at the northern tip of the Mount Adams Wilderness.

General description: A fine 3.6-mile loop ride to Horseshoe Lake and along Spring Creek, with the 3 trails combined.

Trailhead horse facilities: See Keenes Horse Camp.

Trailhead elevation: 4,300 feet.

High point: 4,630 feet.

Maps: Gifford Pinchot National Forest; USGS Green Mountain quad.

KEENES HORSE CAMP
35 KEENES TRAIL LOOP FROM KEENES HORSE CAMP
36 GREEN MOUNTAIN TRAIL FROM KEENES HORSE CAMP
37 HIGH LAKES FROM KEENES HORSE CAMP

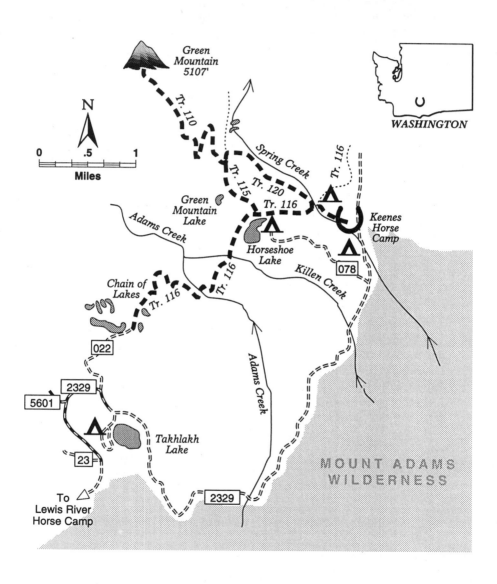

Season: July to October.

Water availability: Ample at Horseshoe Lake.

Feed availability: It's a short trip, but pack processed feed for a horse treat.

Permits/restrictions: No permits are required. Horses are not allowed in any of the regularly designated campsites.

Finding the trailhead: See Keenes Horse Camp.

The ride: The Keenes Trail part of the loop is found on forest maps dating back to 1926. It leaves the horse camp heading northwest along Spring Creek. Semi-open forest borders much of the trail, but open meadows also come into view.

At the end of the 1.9-mile trail is Spring Creek Trail 115, also found on 1926 forest maps. Rein left at this junction and follow the trail south and then southeast to Horseshoe Lake and the junction with High Lakes Trail 116.

Spring Creek Trail is believed to have been one of the main routes for Yakama Indians between berry-picking camps at Horseshoe Lake and fishing sites to the north along the Cispus River. Along the trail are semi-open meadows and stands of peeled cedar trees where Indians gathered bark to make berry baskets. There are also small ponds and an open conifer forest with a view of Mount Adams.

At Horseshoe Lake, where there's usually good fishing, turn left and head east on a 0.5-mile segment of High Lakes Trail 116 that travels back to Keenes Trail 120. Then turn right for the 0.5-mile return trip to camp.

Spring Creek Trail 115 and High Lakes Trail 116 are both rated as "more difficult" by the Forest Service. The Keenes Trail is heavily used, but the Spring Creek and High Lakes trails get only moderate use.

36 GREEN MOUNTAIN TRAIL FROM KEENES HORSE CAMP

Location: Southeast of Packwood at the northern tip of the Mount Adams Wilderness.

General description: A 3-mile ride through semi-open forest and meadows to panoramic views from near the top of Green Mountain.

Trailhead horse facilities: See Keenes Horse Camp.

Trailhead elevation: 4,300 feet.

High point: 4,600 feet on 5,107-foot-high Green Mountain.

Maps: Gifford Pinchot National Forest; USGS Green Mountain quad.

Season: July to October.

Water availability: Ample at the crossing of Spring Creek near the horse camp, at Horseshoe Lake, and near the junction of Spring Creek Trail 115 and High Lakes Trail 116. There is no water available on Trail 110 to Green Mountain.

Feed availability: Pack processed feed for a horse treat after steep grades.

Permits/restrictions: No permits required. Use good trail etiquette.

Finding the trailhead: See Keenes Horse Camp.

The ride: Leave the horse camp on Keenes Trail 120 and ride about 0.5 mile to the junction with High Lakes Trail 116. Then rein left and ride 0.5 mile to the junction with Spring Creek Trail 115.

Spring Creek trail is believed to have been one of the Yakama Indians' routes between berry-picking camps at Horseshoe Lake and fishing sites to the north along the Cispus River. Along the trail are semi-open meadows, stands of peeled cedar trees where Indians gathered bark to make berry baskets, small ponds, and an open conifer forest with a view of Mount Adams.

Rein right and head northwest on Spring Creek Trail 115 for 0.6 mile to the junction with Green Mountain Trail 110, which heads off left to the northwest 1.5 miles to Green Mountain.

From Spring Creek Trail 115 the route to Green Mountain ascends a moderately steep hillside on switchbacks for nearly 1 mile. The route passes through a mixed forest, breaking out periodically into open areas. Riders can see sweeping panoramic views of mountains, meadows, and wildflowers as the trail nears a spot close to the summit. Below the mountain to the west are old clearcuts. Retrace the route to return to Keenes Horse Camp.

37 HIGH LAKES FROM KEENES HORSE CAMP

Location: Southeast of Packwood at the northern tip of the Mount Adams Wilderness.

General description: A 4.2-mile ride with mountain views, wildflowers, huckleberries, and a look at a volcanic mudflow from Mount Adams along the way.

Trailhead horse facilities: See Keenes Horse Camp.

Trailhead elevation: 4,300 feet.

High point: 4,400 feet.

Maps: Gifford Pinchot National Forest; USGS Green Mountain quad. See p. 124.

Season: July to October.

Water availability: Ample at Horseshoe Lake and at several creek crossings en route to Chain of Lakes.

Feed availability: Pack processed oats for a horse treat.

Permits/restrictions: No permits are required. Horses are not allowed in any of the regularly designated campsites.

Finding the trailhead: See Keenes Horse Camp.

The ride: Leave the horse camp on Keenes Trail 120, heading northwest 0.5 mile to the junction with High Lakes Trail 116. Turn left and ride about 0.5 mile to Horseshoe Lake, where there's usually good fishing. The lower section of High Lakes Trail is rated "more difficult" by the Forest Service.

Here the trail descends through an open forest about 0.5 mile to a canyon with a large lava flow near Adams Fork Creek. From that point the trail ascends a switchback trail for about 2.5 miles, then levels off through open forest. There are views of Mount Adams through breaks in the timber as the trail continues to Chain of Lakes.

The trail ends at Forest Road 022, a spur road off Forest Road 2329. An old trail that corresponds with this modern one was noted in the writings of C. E. Rusk, a famous mountaineer who circled Mount Adams on foot in 1890. He described it as a path used by Yakama Indians for gathering berries in the area. The trail also appears on a 1911 Forest Service map.

LEWIS RIVER HORSE CAMP

Location: In Gifford Pinchot National Forest east of Mount St. Helens National Volcanic Monument.

Horse camp facilities: Parking spaces for fifteen truck-and-trailer rigs, plus six single vehicles. Staging area has a stock ramp, water trough, hitch rails, high hitchlines, four small corrals, a mounting assist area, and a horse lounging area. There is a double-tank composting toilet, plus a picnic area with a high hitchline, table, and fire pit.

There are eight separate campsites. Three are double sites that can hold two truck-and-trailer units each and five are single sites for one truck/trailer unit and one single vehicle. All of the sites have tables, fire rings, and a high hitchline. All campsites have easy access to the loop trail that leads to the staging area and main trail connections. This scenic, well-designed, forest-buffered horse camp was created through a joint effort of the Mount St. Helens and Thunder Mountain chapters of Back Country Horsemen, Mount St. Helens National Volcanic Monument, Gifford Pinchot National Forest, and the Interagency Committee for Outdoor Recreation. Donations are welcome to defray maintenance costs.

Finding the horse camp: From Interstate 5 follow Washington Highway 503 past Lake Merwin to Forest Road 90 and the small community of Cougar. Then continue east along the north shore of Swift Creek Reservoir. Past the reservoir, FR 90 turns north and follows the Lewis River. Drive past Lower Falls campground, Middle Falls, and Upper Falls and turn left onto Forest Road 93. Travel 0.1 mile to the horse camp entrance on the right.

Elevation: 1,800 feet.

Trails: All of the trails are in non-wilderness areas east of Mount St. Helens with opportunities for day trips, overnight trips, and week-long campout rides. There are many route combinations and loop options suitable to both novice and experienced riders.

All of the trails are open to horses and hikers, but many are also open to mountain bikes and a few are open to motorbikes. While most motorcycle riders on these trails have a reputation for courteous attitudes toward horse riders (quickly shutting down engines when they see horses, taking helmets off, and talking to the horses so they don't spook them, etc.), mountain bikers have a less enviable reputation. Be alert for traffic on the trails.

WARNING! Riders should be aware that there are dangerous sections on Lewis River Trail 31, south of the horse camp in the area of the four falls on the Lewis River. There are sheer dropoffs at several points above the falls in sections that are heavily used by mountain bikers. Working with the USDA Forest Service, horse riding groups are preparing to construct new area trails that will provide options to riding this hazardous section of the Lewis Creek Trail. Until then, horse riders should avoid the upper sections of this trail overlooking the falls.

The Lewis River Horse Camp trail map shows the preferred, safer trailhead for Trail Ride 38, Lewis River, on the left side of FR 90, opposite the trailhead for Trail Ride 39, Wright Meadow. Both trailheads are accessible by riding south on FR 90 from the horse camp. There are several paths for horses along the shoulder of FR 90 so riders are not on the roadway for the entire length.

LEWIS RIVER HORSE CAMP
38 LEWIS RIVER
39 WRIGHT MEADOW

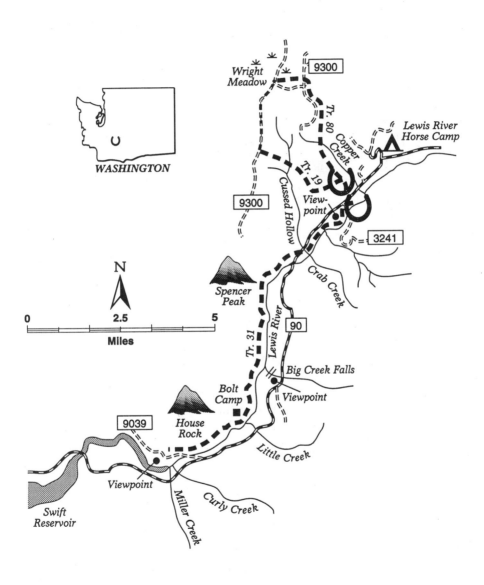

Trails accessible from the Lewis River Horse Camp include:

- Lewis River Trail, which follows the Lewis River 14.4 miles south to Curly Creek (see Trail Ride 38).

- Wright Meadow Trail, a 12.5-mile loop ride into the hills west of the horse camp (see Trail Ride 39).

- Quartz Creek Trail, a 14-mile adventure into Dark Meadow (see Trail Ride 40).

- Sunrise Loop Trail from Dark Meadow, a 10-mile loop trip into scenic high country at Sunrise Mountain (see Trail Ride 41).

38 LEWIS RIVER FROM LEWIS RIVER HORSE CAMP

Location: East of Mount St. Helens National Volcanic Monument on the Gifford Pinchot National Forest.
General description: A 14.4-mile ride along the Lewis River with views of splendid waterfalls, scenic timber-and-stream corridors, and the beauty of Curly Creek Falls.
Trailhead horse facilities: See Lewis River Horse Camp.
Trailhead elevation: 1,800 feet at Lewis River Horse Camp.
High point: 1,800 feet at Lewis River Horse Camp.
Low point: 1,260 feet at Curly Creek Falls Viewpoint.
Maps: Gifford Pinchot National Forest; USGS Burnt Peak, Spencer Butte; Green Trails Lone Butte 365. See map on p. 129.
Season: June through November.
Water availability: Plentiful along entire route.
Feed availability: Some grazing available but pack processed feed for rest stops.
Permits/restrictions: No permits are needed. Use caution to protect plants and soil when traveling along the river shoreline.
Finding the trailhead: See Lewis River Horse Camp.

The ride: Leave Lewis River Horse Camp riding south and then southwest on Forest Road 90 for 1.5 miles. This way riders avoid the upper stretches of Lewis River Trail 31, a narrow route along cliffs (and also popular with mountain bikers). A bridle path follows the shoulder of the road in several spots so riders do not have to be on the road all the way to the trailhead.

When the road reaches the trailhead for Wright Meadow Trail 80, on the right, rein left instead. Cross the road to link with Lewis River Trail 31. There are fascinating waterfalls on this stretch where the trail weaves beside the Lewis River. The river begins on the glacial ice fields of Mount Adams to the east, carving a deep route through the southern Cascades as it flows to the Columbia River. The Lower Falls

Recreation Area, with hitching rails and restrooms, makes a convenient stop for riders who want to enjoy the flow of the falls from the viewpoint.

At 5.5 miles the trail crosses FR 90 about 1 mile south of the Lower Falls campground. It then climbs a canyon wall to the top of a ridge and continues to follow the Lewis River. The trail rises and dips through the timbered hills and ravines along the river. Alternately, the trail is beside and above the river. About 10 miles from the horse camp the trail leaves the canyon and follows the riverbank for the next 4 miles on a predominantly level grade the rest of the way to Curly Creek Falls.

Twelve miles from the horse camp the trail passes Bolt Camp, a shelter built in the early 1930s that has been preserved by Forest Service rangers and others over the years. For the next mile the trail rises and falls steeply, leveling out about where Rush Creek joins the Lewis River.

Less than 2 miles remain, including a 0.5-mile stretch of clearcut and a winding track along bottomland and riverbed. These lowlands are home to huge Douglas-fir, western red cedar, big leaf maple, and western hemlock. Look for Oregon grape among the ground plants. The best forested areas are at the southern end of the trail. Moss is also abundant, since this area is much like a temperate rain forest.

Fishing along the river may yield rainbow trout and large Dolly Vardens (bull trout), but be sure to check current fishing regulations. The season is usually from June through October.

Arriving at the south end of the trail, the route exits a shady forest where the ground is covered with ferns and raspberries, in season. At trail's end there is a parking lot, horse staging area, and barrier-free restroom. Across the road a scenic interpretive trail leads to the Curly Creek Falls viewpoint. It's well worth the walk. The viewpoint and parking lot are off Forest Road 9039, only 1 mile from FR 90.

A popular option for riding this long trail is to have horses and riders dropped off at the Curly Creek trailhead for a ride north to the horse camp. Eager riders get into the saddle sooner and by the time they reach camp several hours later, all of the gear should be set up and a meal prepared—by some kind souls who postponed their own riding opportunities.

39 WRIGHT MEADOW FROM LEWIS RIVER HORSE CAMP

Location: East of Mount St. Helens National Volcanic Monument and Swift Creek Reservoir on the Gifford Pinchot National Forest.
General description: A 12.5-mile loop ride along the Lewis River to the meadow home of elk.
Trailhead horse facilities: See Lewis River Horse Camp.
Trailhead elevation: 1,800 feet at Lewis River Horse Camp.
High point: 3,600 feet.
Maps: Gifford Pinchot National Forest; USGS Burnt Peak, Spencer Butte; Green Trails Lone Butte 365. See map on p. 129.
Season: June to November.
Water availability: Not abundant, but available at two stream crossings.

Feed availability: Some grazing, but pack processed feed for rest stops.

Permits/restrictions: No permits are required. Watch for logging trucks on Forest Road 9300. Use caution to protect plants and soil along river shorelines.

Finding the trailhead: From the horse camp, head south on Forest Road 90. There are shoulder paths in several spots along the road. The trailhead for Wright Meadow Trail 80 is on the right about 1.5 miles down the road from the horse camp.

The ride: Ride northwest on Wright Meadow Trail 80, passing the junction with Cussed Hollow Trail 19 at 0.75 mile. Ride across Copper Creek about 1 mile from the junction, then continue 2 miles north and 1 mile west to Wright Meadow, paralleling Forest Road 9328 along that route and crossing FR 9300 where the trail turns west. At Wright Meadow the trail also meets the Craggy Peak trailhead and FR 9300. Elk herds browse and bed down in Wright Meadow. Scattered campsites are available along the trail.

Follow FR 9300 south for 2.25 miles, then rein left at the junction with Cussed Hollow Trail 19 and ride southeast 1 mile to a crossing of Cussed Hollow Creek. From that point the trail descends steeply through an old burned forest area to the junction with Wright Meadow Trail 80. Rein right for the 0.75-mile ride to FR 90, then rein left and follow the road northeast 1.5 miles to Lewis River Horse Camp.

Use is normally light on these trails. The Cussed Hollow trail is rated "most difficult" because of very steep grades. The easier Wright Meadow trail is rated "more difficult."

40 QUARTZ CREEK TO DARK MEADOW FROM LEWIS RIVER HORSE CAMP

Location: East of Mount St. Helens National Volcanic Monument on the Gifford Pinchot National Forest.

General description: A strenuous and sometimes hair-raising ride (14 miles one way) to a campsite at Dark Meadow, with giant trees, mountain views, and great huckleberries (in season) along the way.

Trailhead horse facilities: See Lewis River Horse Camp.

Trailhead elevation: 1,800 feet at Lewis River Horse Camp.

High point: 5,238 feet.

Maps: Gifford Pinchot National Forest; USGS Quartz Creek and McCoy Peak quads; Green Trails Lone Butte 365.

Season: July to November.

Water availability: Scarce, with only limited access along Quartz Creek. Water stock at stream crossings. No water along the top of Quartz Creek Ridge. Water can be found on the upper Summit Prairie Trail and near Dark Meadow Camp.

Feed availability: Some grazing, but pack processed feed to ride the full 28 miles.

Permits/restrictions: No permits are required. Use caution to protect plants and soil along the shoreline of Quartz Creek.

Finding the trailhead: See Lewis River Horse Camp. Quartz Creek Trail 5 can be accessed from the north side of the horse camp.

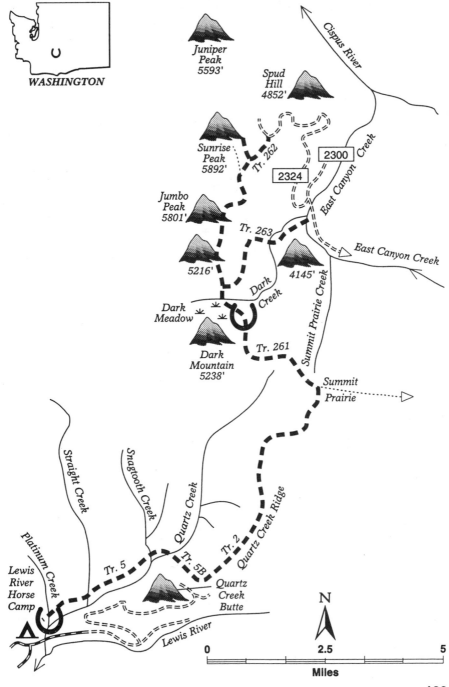

WASHINGTON

Juniper
Peak
5593'

Spud
Hill
4852'

Cispus River

Sunrise
Peak
5892'

Tr. 262

2300

2324

East Canyon Creek

Jumbo
Peak
5801'

Tr. 263

East Canyon Creek

5216'

4145'

Dark Creek

Dark
Meadow

Summit Prairie Creek

Tr. 261

Dark
Mountain
5238'

Summit
Prairie

Straight Creek

Snagtooth Creek

Quartz Creek

Quartz Creek Ridge

Tr. 2

Tr. 5

Tr. 5B

Platinum Creek

Lewis
River
Horse
Camp

Quartz
Creek
Butte

Lewis River

N

0   2.5   5

Miles

133

The ride: The Quartz Creek Trail follows the stream of the same name but has limited access to water. It's a steep trail with 20 percent grades, or steeper. Since the upper part of the trail is hazardous to horses, an alternate horse route to Dark Meadow combines sections of five trails, adding a lot more scenery. The Forest Service rates this route "most difficult" at the bottom and "more difficult" at the top. Expect a lot of ridge riding and straight-down dropoffs. DO NOT ATTEMPT THIS ROUTE UNLESS YOU'RE COMFORTABLE WITH HEIGHTS AND YOUR HORSE IS SURE-FOOTED AND EXPERIENCED. Build extra rest time into your schedule since this trip is hard on horses and riders alike.

The Quartz Creek trails are usually only lightly used, while the higher trails—Summit Prairie, Boundary, and Dark Meadow—generally receive medium use.

A magnificent forest shades the lower portions of Quartz Creek Trail 5 with trees measuring 4 to 8 feet in diameter. The stream can be heard, but mostly it's out of sight in a deep canyon. This lower section of the trail crosses three tributary streams: Platinum, Straight, and Snagtooth creeks.

The first part of the trail follows an old miner's route. Above the trail near Platinum Creek is some rusting mining equipment. From that point the trail rises sharply, crosses a clearcut, and comes to Straight Creek at 2 miles. Across the creek is a campsite, with Quartz Creek Falls a short distance below. From here the trail ascends through the clearcut for 0.5 mile before entering forest again. Three miles in the trail arrives at the Snagtooth Creek crossing and more campsites.

In another 0.5 mile the Quartz Creek trail meets Quartz Creek Butte Trail 5B, a horse bypass route bearing right to Summit Prairie Trail 2, along Quartz Creek Ridge. About 0.25 mile up Trail 5B is Quartz Creek Camp, a fine place to rest surrounded by huge fir trees. Towering over the area to the south is Quartz Creek Butte.

About 0.5 mile farther down Trail 5B is the junction with Summit Prairie Trail 2 to the north, leading to a campsite in Dark Meadow by a route that avoids the hazardous upper stretches of Quartz Creek Trail 5.

Some water is available on this ridge route but only on the lower part below where Trail 5B meets Forest Road 9075. The higher portion of this trail, which begins at 2,400 feet and rises to 5,238 feet, is often covered with snow until mid- to late July.

As the trail follows the Quartz Creek Ridge there are fine views of surrounding forests and mountains for the 4.5 miles to Summit Prairie and a junction with Boundary Trail 1. Rein left onto the Boundary Trail, which follows the southern border of the Randle Ranger District. Follow the trail west 1.25 miles, past Summit Prairie Creek, and turn northwest on Juniper Peak Trail 261.

The route passes Dark Mountain and goes to Dark Meadow, about 1 mile north of Boundary Trail 1. There's nothing sinister about Dark Meadow, Dark Mountain to the west, and Dark Creek to the north. They are named for John Dark, who reportedly built a cabin in the meadow about 1895 while he was prospecting in the area.

Dark Meadow is a wetland with a deep creek running through it. Primitive camping areas are available, but one next to the creek isn't available for horse camping because stock should not be tethered that close to the stream.

Riding to Dark Meadow from Lewis River Horse Camp is a strenuous day ride that wears on horses unless they're in excellent shape. Plan on an overnight stay. There are several fine day rides from Dark Meadow, including a loop trip to

Sunrise Peak (see Trail Ride 41) that passes Jumbo Peak for outstanding views from the middle of Dark Divide.

From Dark Meadow riders can enjoy spectacular views of the peaks in the Goat Rocks Wilderness to the northeast, Mount Adams to the southeast, and the peaks of the Indian Heaven Wilderness to the south, with Mount Hood beyond on the southern horizon. Return to Lewis River Horse Camp by the same route.

41 SUNRISE LOOP FROM DARK MEADOW

Location: East of Mount St. Helens National Volcanic Monument on the Gifford Pinchot National Forest.

General description: A 10-mile loop ride to Sunrise and Jumbo peaks with spectacular views of the Goat Rocks Wilderness, Mount Adams, and the Indian Heaven Wilderness.

Trailhead horse facilities: See Lewis River Horse Camp.

Elevation at Dark Meadow: 4,200 feet.

High point: 5,880 feet at Sunrise Peak.

Maps: Gifford Pinchot National Forest. See map on p. 133.

Season: July to October.

Water availability: Ample at several creek crossings.

Feed availability: Some grazing is available. Carry processed feed for camping in Dark Meadows and on the loop ride to Sunrise and Jumbo peaks.

Permits/restrictions: No permits are required. Use caution to protect soil and vegetation when traveling along any shoreline. Keep stock at least 200 feet from streams except for watering.

Finding the trailhead: The Sunrise Loop Trail begins in Dark Meadow (see Trail Ride 40).

The ride: From Dark Meadow ride across Dark Creek on Juniper Ridge Trail 261 past the right-hand junction with Dark Meadow Trail 263. Continue north on this "more difficult" trail, passing abundant huckleberries in the late summer.

The Juniper Ridge Trail extends several miles farther north, into an area once used by sheepherders as a stock driveway. For this loop ride turn right at the junction with Sunrise Trail 262, breaking out of a forest of dense conifers into an open, scenic ridgetop south of Sunrise Peak.

A short distance along Sunrise Trail 262, passing by Jumbo Peak at 4,300 feet, is a 0.25-mile trail to the left—Trail 262A to Sunrise Peak, the site of a former Forest Service post. The views from there are spectacular, including Mount Rainier, Mount Adams, Mount St. Helens, and peaks of the Cascade Range. Open slopes in this area often bloom with tiger lily, lupine, paintbrush, and bear grass, plus huckleberries in season.

This isn't a designated wilderness area but it might as well be. It's certainly remote; trail signs have been missing for a long time, and the routes are steep and sometimes challenging but always rewarding for their views.

Returning to Sunrise Trail 262, travel about 0.75 mile farther through dense timber to the junction with Forest Road 2324. Rein right and follow the road as it winds north and east for about 1 mile. It then hairpins south, crosses East Canyon Creek, and meets Dark Meadow Trail 263.

The 3.2-mile Dark Meadow Trail 263 leaves the road and crosses various forks of Dark Creek three times on its way south. Scenery is limited along this heavily forested part of the trail. But in season, blackberries are abundant. The route continues, often steep in parts, until it meets Juniper Ridge Trail 261. Turn left to follow the trail for the 0.5-mile ride back to campsites in Dark Meadow.

As an alternative to taking the entire loop trip, follow Juniper Ridge Trail 261 north from the campsites to the Sunrise Peak Trail and back, since the beauty of the scenery is entirely different going each way.

KALAMA HORSE CAMP

Location: Near the town of Cougar in the southwest sector of Mount St. Helens National Volcanic Monument.

Horse camp facilities: Parking for thirteen truck and trailer rigs, plus six single vehicles. Ten campsites each have tables, fire rings, and small corrals. There are also two group sites that can hold three or more truck/trailer rigs. These sites have fire rings, long tables, corrals, and one 20-foot high hitchline.

The site also features a stock ramp, water trough, hitch rails, a composting toilet, a staging area with manure bins, a picnic area with a horseshoe pit, and a mounting assist area that can be used even from a wheelchair. There's even a "horse lounging area" where stock can roll or relax before or after trail trips.

There are no feed restrictions within the camp. Weed-free hay is acceptable here, but processed feed is required on trail rides.

Horse camp elevation: 2,320 feet.

Finding the horse camp: Kalama Horse Camp is east of Interstate 5 off Washington Highway 503 on Forest Road 8100, which leaves eastbound WA 503 from a point where the highway turns south, just west of Cougar.

Turn north on paved FR 8100 and drive about 8 miles, past Merrill Lake and Merrill Lake Campground. About 3 miles past the Merrill Lake Campground, at an intersection, make a sharp right, staying on FR 8100. The horse camp entrance is the next road to the right, about 200 yards from the turn.

Trails: The Kalama Horse Camp provides access to several trails on the south side of Mount St. Helens.

- Toutle River Trail 238 and Blue Lake Horse Trail 237 provide excellent opportunities for riders to create a loop trip that provides a variety of scenic experiences. These trails are open to horses, hikers, and mountain bikers.

- The Cinnamon Peak Trail from the Kalama Horse Camp is expected to be completed during 1995, providing another loop trip in the area. Future plans by the Forest Service and horse groups include a loop trail to reach Goat Marsh and Goat Mountain.

KALAMA HORSE CAMP

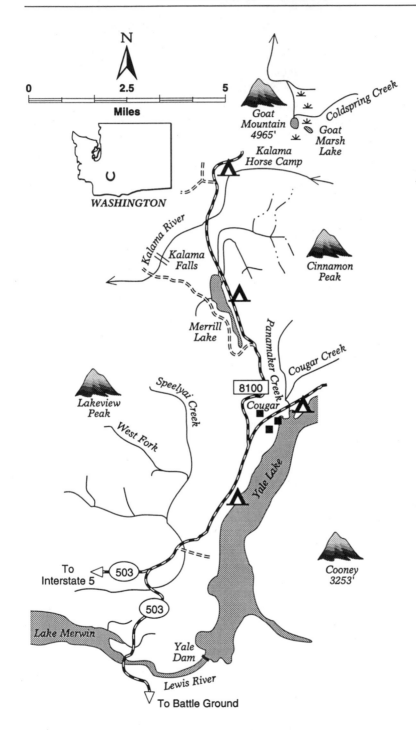

Kalama Horse Camp.

42 TOUTLE RIVER TRAIL FROM KALAMA HORSE CAMP

Location: Near the town of Cougar in the southwest sector of Mount St. Helens National Volcanic Monument.

General description: Rated as "more difficult," this 13-mile ride through old-growth noble fir and new mudflow areas offers excellent views of Mount St. Helens, the Toutle River, and the blast zone from the 1980 eruption.

Trailhead horse facilities: See Kalama Horse Camp.

Trailhead elevation: 2,320 feet.

High point: 3,840 feet.

Maps: Gifford Pinchot National Forest; USGS Mount St. Helens.

Season: Late April to November.

Water availability: Water is available along the Kalama River and at several river crossings.

Feed availability: Pack processed or pelletized feed.

Permits/restrictions: None, except that stock are not allowed beyond the hikers' bridge that crosses Sheep Creek at the bottom of Sheep Canyon.

Finding the trailhead: The Toutle River 238 trailhead can be reached from the staging area at the east side of the horse camp. A perimeter loop trail connects campsites with the staging area.

Mount St. Helens seen from the Toutle River Trail.

42 TOUTLE RIVER TRAIL FROM KALAMA HORSE CAMP
43 BLUE LAKE HORSE TRAIL FROM KALAMA HORSE CAMP

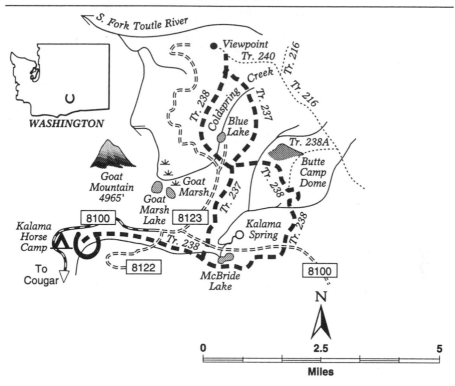

The ride: This scenic trail on the southwestern flank of Mount St. Helens begins with a 3.5-mile ride along the north side of the Kalama River. As the river turns north, ride on 2.1 miles, past McBride Lake, to where the trail crosses Forest Road 8100.

After the trail turns north ride 1.25 miles to the junction with Butte Trail 238A. Continue riding on Toutle River Trail 238. (Horses are not allowed on Butte Trail 238A.) The trail's unusual terrain includes a cooled lava bed with huge boulders. Crushed rock was used to fill some of the area to level the ground when the trail was built. Beyond the lava bed is an open meadow of bear grass and white-plumed squaw grass. The trail enters a forest below Butte Camp.

Continue to the left on the main trail for 0.75 mile, skirting Butte Camp Dome, which overshadows the camp. This part of the trail travels across a shifting ash flow that changes its location and grooves with each spring runoff. By the time the trail is in use, however, the ash has dried. There are still some ruts and grooves but nothing dangerous for horses. Just let them pick their way through it.

The trail across the 150 yards of ash flow is well marked. On the other side it enters a stand of lodgepole pine that towers over low growth chaparral and huckleberries. Another 0.75 mile and the trail reaches the Blue Lake trailhead, near the Forest Roadjunction of Coldspring Creek and Forest Road 8123.

Toutle River Trail cuts through a lava flow from the 1980 eruption.

About 0.5 mile up this trail, through a forest of noble fir, is Blue Lake, usually a good fishing stop. The trail continues through old-growth noble fir forest, believed to be the largest such stand in the nation and one of only two stands of this size in the world.

About 1.5 miles farther north, Toutle River Trail 238 enters Sheep Canyon, where mudflow from the 1980 eruption destroyed all vegetation in its path. Here the trail meets a junction with Sheep Canyon Trail 240. Horses are not allowed on Trail 240 to the east, which connects with Loowit Trail 216, a route that is also closed to stock.

Stock is allowed, however, on a short portion of Sheep Canyon Trail 240 to the left off Toutle River Trail 238. It leads to the Sheep Canyon Viewpoint, overlooking the Toutle River and flows of mud from the volcano. There's also a trailhead parking lot at the viewpoint, which is the end of FR 8123. For those who don't want to camp at Kalama, there is stock water and room for four truck-and-horse-trailer rigs to park at the end of FR 8123, so riders can take day rides into the area.

From the junction of Trails 238 and 240, Toutle River Trail 238 continues north, switchbacking down through regrown clearcuts. The trail ends at the South Fork of the Toutle River, which now runs through the remains of the giant mudflow created during the 1980 eruption of the volcano.

But you'll have to walk the 2 miles to the South Fork from the junction of Trails 238 and 240 because stock are not allowed past the hiker bridge across Sheep Creek. Unfortunately there is no place at the bridge to tie horses for that hike. Riders usually stop at the overlook for a while and then ride the trail back to Kalama Horse Camp.

Also, several loop or figure-eight rides can be planned from Kalama Horse Camp by using a combination of three sections of Toutle River Trail 238 and Blue Lake Horse Trail 237 (Trail Ride 43).

43 BLUE LAKE HORSE TRAIL FROM KALAMA HORSE CAMP

Location: Near the town of Cougar in the southwest sector of Mount St. Helens National Volcanic Monument.

General description: A 16-mile ride through old-growth noble fir and lodgepole pine, with occasional spectacular views of Mount St. Helens.

Trailhead horse facilities: See Kalama Horse Camp.

Trailhead elevation: 2,320 feet at Kalama Horse Camp.

High point: 3,840 feet.

Maps: Gifford Pinchot National Forest; USGS Mount St. Helens. See p. 141.

Season: Late April to November.

Water availability: Water is available where Toutle River Trail 238 follows the Kalama River, but there is no water on Trail 237 until the upper section.

Feed availability: Pack processed or pelletized feed.

Permits/restrictions: None.

Finding the trailhead: The Toutle River 238 trailhead can be reached from the staging area at the east side of the horse camp. A perimeter loop trail connects campsites with the staging area. Toutle River Trail 238 meets the southern end of Blue Lake Horse Trail 237 after a 2.5-mile ride east from the horse camp.

Blue Lake Horse Trail 237 can also be accessed at that point by driving east of Kalama Horse Camp on Forest Road 8100. Also, access to Blue Lake Horse Trail is available by driving north of Kalama Horse Camp on FR 8100 to the Blue Lake trailhead, or to the end of Forest Road 8123 where there is stock water and room for four truck-and-horse trailer rigs.

The ride: Travel east 2.5 miles on Toutle River Trail 238, along the north side of the Kalama River, to the junction with Blue Lake Horse Trail 237. Turn left and head north 5.5 miles, crossing Trail 238 and then meeting it again near a short trail to the viewpoint over Sheep Canyon.

The lower section of Blue Lake Horse Trail 237 passes through two stands of old-growth noble fir and more open stands of lodgepole pine. Many of the noble firs are 300 feet tall and so stout that it takes three to four people to reach around a single tree touching hands. After 2 miles the trail crosses an east-west trail that is part of Toutle River Trail 238.

On the 1.75-mile upper section of Blue Lake Horse Trail 237, the trail moves into lodgepole pine forest. This area has a variety of unusual lava formations. Many of the rocks have trees growing out of them or around them. Two-thirds of the way up this section of trail is a fresh mudflow that is usually passable. After crossing the mud flow, the trail skirts the edge between the mudflow and a stand of noble fir, then drops into the fir forest and ends at a clearcut in Sheep Canyon, meeting Toutle River Trail 238 for the third time.

From this point the ride continues north on Toutle River Trail 238, switchbacking down through regrown clearcuts to a junction with Sheep Canyon Trail 240, coming in from the east. Horses are not allowed on Trail 240 to the right, which connects

Mount St. Helens mudflow on the Blue Lake Horse Trail.

with Loowit Trail 216. To the left of that junction, Sheep Canyon Trail 240 is open to horses. A short ride leads to a viewpoint overlooking the Toutle River and mudflow from the volcano. There is also a suitable trailhead and parking lot here on FR 8123.

Toutle River Trail 238 continues north 2 miles, ending at the South Fork of the Toutle River, which now runs through the remains of the giant mudflow created during the 1980 eruption of the volcano. Riders must walk if they want to see the river because stock are not allowed past the hiker bridge that crosses Sheep Creek.

To see new scenery on the way back riders can follow Toutle River Trail 238 south past the northern Blue Lake Horse Trail 237 junction to the Blue Lake trailhead and then head east to the southern junction with Blue Lake Horse Trail 237. From that junction ride south to the junction with Toutle River Trail 238, rein right, and head west for 2.5 miles to Kalama Horse Camp.

Both the Blue Lake Horse Trail and the Kalama Horse Camp were built by the Washington Trail Riders Association and other volunteer horsemen in partnership with the Gifford Pinchot National Forest, Mount St. Helens National Volcanic Monument, and the Interagency Committee for Outdoor Recreation.

FALLS CREEK HORSE CAMP

Location: At the western edge of the Indian Heaven Wilderness, east of Swift Creek Reservoir, on the Gifford Pinchot National Forest.

Horse camp facilities: Undeveloped site with pit toilets, tables, and fire rings. Stock ramp and four campsites with room for truck and trailer rigs up to 20 feet long.

Finding the horse camp: From Interstate 5 drive east on Washington Highway 14 along the Columbia River Gorge. Travel east to Carson and turn north through town on County Road 30, the Wind River Road. Continue north 2 miles, then northwest about 3 miles on CR 30 to Forest Road 65.

Stay on FR 65 past Panther Creek Campground and the Wind River Experimental Forest, through a hairpin switchback and on northward through forested areas. When you cross the bridge over Falls Creek, the Falls Creek Horse Camp will be on the left. This is about a 2-hour drive from the Vancouver area.

Elevation: 3,500 feet.

Trails: A variety of trails leave from this camp, in both non-wilderness and the Indian Heaven Wilderness areas.

- McClellan Meadow Trail 157 and Terminator Trail 159 provide a non-wilderness loop leaving from the west side of the horse camp (see Trail Ride 44).

- Indian Race Track Trail 171 leads to the summit of Red Mountain in the Indian Heaven Wilderness of the Mount Adams Ranger District, east of the camp (see Trail Ride 45).

- Indian Race Track Trail 171, the Pacific Crest Trail 2000, and Thomas Lake Trail 111 provide a scenic loop ride through the Indian Heaven Wilderness (see Trail Ride 46).

44 MCCLELLAN MEADOW LOOP FROM FALLS CREEK HORSE CAMP

Location: At the western edge of Indian Heaven Wilderness, east of Swift Creek Reservoir.

General description: An easy 3.1-mile ride to McClellan Meadows, past several small waterfalls along the way. Can also be done as a 9.9-mile loop.

Trailhead horse facilities: See Falls Creek Horse Camp.

Trailhead elevation: 3,500 feet.

High point: 4,000 feet on the Terminator trail. Lowest point is 3,000 feet at McClellan Meadows.

Maps: Gifford Pinchot National Forest; Indian Heaven Wilderness; USGS Gifford Peak, Terminator Point, and Lone Butte quads.

Season: July or August to October.

Water availability: McClellan Meadow Trail crosses two forks of the Wind River;

FALLS CREEK HORSE CAMP
44 MCCLELLAN MEADOW LOOP
45 INDIAN RACE TRACK TO RED MOUNTAIN
46 INDIAN HEAVEN LOOP

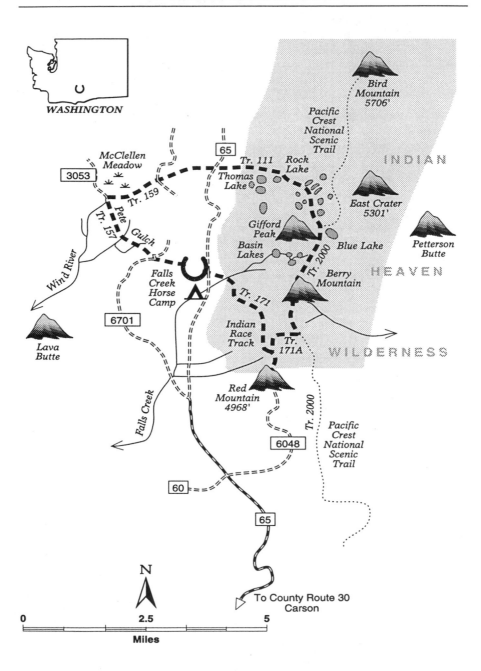

WASHINGTON

Bird
Mountain
5706'

Pacific
Crest
National
Scenic
Trail

INDIAN

65

Tr. 111

Rock
Lake

McClellen
Meadow

Thomas
Lake

East Crater
5301'

3053

Tr. 159

Petterson
Butte

Pete
Tr. 157

Gulch

Gifford
Peak

Basin
Lakes

Blue Lake

HEAVEN

Tr. 2000

Wind River

Falls
Creek
Horse
Camp

Berry
Mountain

6701

Tr. 171

Lava
Butte

Indian
Race
Track

Tr. 171A

WILDERNESS

Falls Creek

Red
Mountain
4968'

Tr. 2000

6048

Pacific
Crest
National
Scenic
Trail

60

65

N

To County Route 30
Carson

0   2.5   5

Miles

also a stream crossing on Forest Road 65 on the return loop trip.

Feed availability: Pack processed feed in any wilderness ride from Falls Creek Horse Camp; weed-free hay can be used in the campground.

Permits/restrictions: No permits are required. Use leave-no-trace methods to protect and preserve the environment.

Finding the trailhead: See Falls Creek Horse Camp. The trailhead is just north of the camp.

The ride: This easy 3.1-mile trail travels gently downhill, from 3,500 feet to 3,000 feet elevation, to McClellan Meadow. The route passes several small waterfalls and travels through Pete Gulch. The trail eventually arrives at the end of Forest Road 3053, a spur road.

By returning to camp along a 3.8-mile trip on Terminator Trail 159 and 3 miles of riding on FR 65, this becomes a 9.9-mile loop trip.

Rein right at the spur road, FR 3053, and head northeast on Terminator Trail 159. The route climbs from the meadows through second-growth timber to FR 65. Ride the road south for 3 miles to return to Falls Creek Horse Camp.

45 INDIAN RACE TRACK TO RED MOUNTAIN FROM FALLS CREEK HORSE CAMP

Location: In the Indian Heaven Wilderness east of Mount St. Helens on the Gifford Pinchot National Forest.

General description: A "more difficult" 3.1-mile ride to the historic site of an Indian race track and the Red Mountain lookout, with views of Mount St. Helens, Mount Adams, and other peaks.

Trailhead horse facilities: See Falls Creek Horse Camp.

Trailhead elevation: 3,500 feet.

High point: 4,700 feet on Red Mountain.

Maps: Gifford Pinchot National Forest; Indian Heaven Wilderness; USGS Gifford Peak, Terminator Point, and Lone Butte quads; Green Trails Wind River 397.

Season: July and August to October. Late summer and fall are best.

Water availability: Falls Creek is the only year-round flowing water on this trail, overly abundant in the spring and early summer.

Feed availability: Pack processed feed.

Permits/restrictions: Groups traveling in the Indian Heaven Wilderness are limited to twelve heartbeats, in any combination of people and horses.

Finding the trailhead: The trail begins on the north side of the horse camp.

The ride: Ride Race Track Trail 171, proceeding east a short distance across Forest Road 65 to the wilderness boundary where the trail turns right and heads southeast.

This is a heavily used trail for hikers and horses that runs through second-growth timber, crossing Falls Creek about 0.25 mile from the trailhead. Then it climbs moderately through rocky terrain for 1 mile to a flat meadow area known as the Indian Racetrack, at 4,300 feet elevation.

More than 100 years ago, Klickitat and Yakama Indians visited this area late in the summer to pick huckleberries and race their horses along a 2,000-foot run that became known as the "racetrack." Today about 200 feet of it can still be found where horses hooves have worn a track several inches deep into the terrain.

From the racetrack, pass by side Trail 171A, which leaves the racetrack area and ascends 0.5 mile to the east to connect with the Pacific Crest National Scenic Trail 2000. Race Track Trail 171 continues on to meet with Forest Road 6048, near the lookout at the summit of 4,968-foot Red Mountain. Clear days offer views of Mount St. Helens, the Racetrack area, and Mount Adams.

Late summer and fall are the best times to travel here, when mosquitos are fewer and trails drier.

46 INDIAN HEAVEN LOOP FROM FALLS CREEK HORSE CAMP

Location: In the Indian Heaven Wilderness, east of Swift Creek Reservoir.
General description: A scenic 13-mile loop ranging from easy riding to most difficult, including 2.5 miles along the Pacific Crest National Scenic Trail.
Trail horse facilities: See Falls Creek Horse Camp.
Trailhead elevation: 3,500 feet.
High point: 5,000 feet along most of the Pacific Crest National Scenic Trail.
Maps: Gifford Pinchot National Forest; Indian Heaven Wilderness; USGS Gifford Peak, Terminator Point, and Lone Butte quads; Green Trails Wind River 397.
Season: July to November; late summer and fall are best.
Water availability: Falls Creek is the only year-round flowing water on this trail, overly abundant in the spring and early summer. Water is in short supply along the Pacific Crest Trail and Thomas Lake Trail 111.
Feed availability: Pack processed feed.
Permits/restrictions: Riding parties in the Indian Heaven Wilderness are limited to 12 people and horses, including pack stock.
Finding the trailhead: See Falls Creek Horse Camp. The trail begins on the north side of the horse camp.

The ride: This 13.2-mile loop ride explores the southwest portion of the Indian Heaven Wilderness. Late summer and early fall are the best times to ride here, when trails are drier and mosquitos not so numerous. The ride begins near the Falls Creek Horse Camp, at the trailhead for Indian Race Track Trail 171. The trail proceeds east a short distance across Forest Road 65 to the wilderness boundary where it turns right and heads southeast.

This heavily used trail for hikers and horses stretches through second-growth timber, crossing Falls Creek about 0.25 mile from the trailhead. It then climbs moderately through rocky terrain for 1 mile to a flat meadow area known as the

Indian Racetrack, at 4,300 feet.

More than 100 years ago, Klickitat and Yakama Indians visited this area late in the summer to pick huckleberries and race their horses along a 2,000-foot run that became known as the "race track." Today about 200 feet of it can still be found where horses have worn ruts several inches deep into the terrain.

At the junction with Trail 171A, near Red Mountain, rein left for a 0.5-mile ascent to Pacific Crest National Scenic Trail 2000. Turn left again and head north on this ridge trail for 3.5 miles. The route offers views of neighboring mountains and numerous lakes. The Pacific Crest Trail traverses deep forest, fingers of alpine trees, and grassy meadows, and affords glimpses of Mount Adams and other local peaks.

Ride along the ridge, past Gifford Peak west of the trail, to the junction of Thomas Lake Trail 111 at Blue Lake. Rein left and head northwest, riding a curving trail that turns due west as it descends 3.2 miles to FR 65.

Thomas Lake Trail 111 is rated as "most difficult" and requires a well-conditioned trail horse and good riding skills by the passenger. If you're unsure about being able to go on, turn around at Blue Lake and retrace hoof prints to Indian Race Track Trail 171 for an easier ride to Falls Creek Horse Camp. Although Thomas Lake Trail 111 is steep, it is heavily used by both hikers and horse riders.

Continuing northwest on the Thomas Lake Trail from the Pacific Crest Trail, the forested route passes by Lake Sahalee Tyee, then ascends a slope out of the woods into a meadow. The trail then passes Lake Umtux and scattered other lakes in the area before reaching Rock Lake, where the trail heads west.

A short distance beyond Rock Lake the trail enters thick woods and descends to FR 65. Rein left and head south 3 miles to Falls Creek Horse Camp.

47 ANTOINE TRAIL

Location: Northeast of Tonasket on the Okanogan National Forest, near the Canadian border.

General description: A "more difficult" 4.2-mile ride to the top of Mount Bonaparte with marvelous clear-day views of Bonaparte Lake and Mount Phoebe.

Trailhead horse facilities: None. Parking for three to four trailers.

Trailhead elevation: 4,400 feet.

High point: 7,258 feet.

Maps: USGS Mount Bonaparte; Okanogan National Forest.

Season: Mid-June through October.

Water availability: Ample along lower trail, but none on the climb up Mount Bonaparte.

Feed availability: Pack processed feed.

Permits/restrictions: None.

Finding the trailhead: From the north end of Tonasket, travel east and northeast on Okanogan County Road 9467. Signs point the way to "Sitzmark Ski Area-Havillah." About 15 miles from Tonasket and 0.5 mile before Havillah, turn right (east) on gravel Forest Road 3230. Then turn left on Forest Road 150, traveling about 3.5 miles from CR 9467 to the trailhead.

47 ANTOINE TRAIL
48 FOURTH OF JULY RIDGE TRAIL
49 MOUNT BONAPARTE–SOUTH SIDE TRAIL

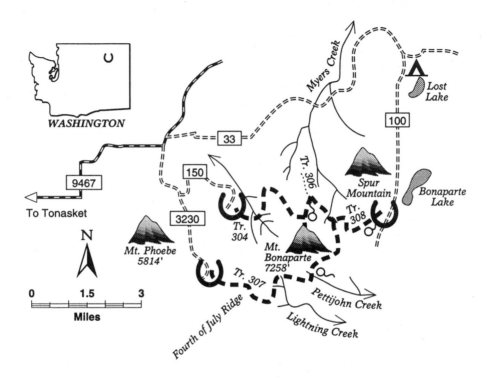

The ride: This region of highlands is a sub-realm of the Selkirk Mountains, farther to the east in Washington and northern Idaho. The destination—7,258-foot Mount Bonaparte—is one of the westernmost peaks of the Rocky Mountains within the United States.

The newly reconstructed Antoine Trail, rebuilt in 1992 when two bridges were replaced, is rated "more difficult" by rangers but its prime recommended use is for pack and saddle explorers.

Although the Antoine Trail is not marked on the Okanogan National Forest map, roads to the trailhead are shown, along with other guiding locations. The trail is shown on the map in the foldout "Okanogan National Forest Travel Plan 1993-1995." Ask rangers for a copy of the plan.

From the roadside trailhead the path winds eastward along the hillside, crosses two streams, then turns sharply and heads north for nearly 1.5 miles. Then it makes a hairpin turn to the southeast and begins climbing. The trail passes an old pole cutter's cabin and enters a thick stand of old-growth trees. There are good scenic viewpoints as the trail turns to head north.

At higher levels the trail passes through lodgepole pine with many scenic views of the hills and valleys to the north, including Canadian mountains in the distance. At the upper end the trail meets with the Myers Creek/Bonaparte Mountain Trail 306 about 1 mile below the mountain lookout site. Be aware that the Bonaparte Trail is open to motorbikes.

Rein right and ride the last mile of the trail through lodgepole pines and subalpine fir to open meadows and clear views near the top. On the summit are the sites of two lookouts, offering a historical contrast. The older building, built in 1914 and now missing its former tower on top, is on the National Register of Historic Buildings. Until recently the building was leaning precariously but rangers recently restored the lookout with new timbers for the walls and new flooring. The building is open to the public when rangers are on duty at the new lookout, built nearby in 1961.

The newer tower rises high above the summit for a marvelous view of the surrounding countryside. This is the highest fire lookout in eastern Washington forests. Inside is a mural of wilderness scenes painted around the top of the four walls by the ranger on duty during 1986 and 1987.

Sights include 5,814-foot Mount Phoebe to the west and Bonaparte Lake to the east. On clear days, the summits of the eastern North Cascades are also visible, from the Sawtooth Ridge to the southwest to the Canadian Cascades to the northwest. Osoyoos Lake to the northwest crosses the U.S.-Canada border. Looking east, the Kettle Range in northeastern Washington State can easily be seen. Beyond is the Selkirk Crest in Idaho.

A few campsites have been cleared below the lookout. One has a picnic table and fire pit. There are sparse trees at the top, along with granite boulders around the area. Be sure to bring your own water up here.

48 FOURTH OF JULY RIDGE TRAIL

Location: Northeast of Tonasket in Okanogan County, near the Canadian border.
General description: A "more difficult" 7.3-mile ride to historic lookouts on the summit of Mount Bonaparte.
Trailhead horse facilities: None.
Trailhead elevation: 5,200 feet.
High point: 7,258 feet.
Maps: USGS Mount Bonaparte, Okanogan National Forest.
Season: Mid-June through October.
Water availability: The trail crosses three or four streams.
Feed availability: Pack processed feed.
Permits/restrictions: None.
Finding the trailhead: From the north end of Tonasket, drive east and northeast on Okanogan County Road 9467. Signs will read "Sitzmark Ski Area–Havillah." About 15 miles from Tonasket (at Havillah), turn right (south) on gravel Forest Road 3230, past Forest Road 150, and drive about 4 miles to the trailhead. There is room to park trucks and horse trailers at a wide area in the road.

The ride: This region of highlands is a sub-realm of the Selkirk Mountains farther to the east in Washington and northern Idaho. The destination—7,258-foot Mount Bonaparte—is one of the westernmost peaks of the Rocky Mountains within the United States.

From the roadside trailhead the path winds eastward across Fourth of July Ridge, past several old cabins. There are many scenic views from the high spots along this trail. About 3 miles from the trailhead the route crosses Lightning Creek, then proceeds 1 mile to cross Pettijohn Creek. At that point, Mount Bonaparte is close by and due north of the trail.

Continue about 1.25 miles to the junction with South Side Trail 308. Rein left to follow it about 1 mile to meet Bonaparte Lookout Trail 306, a northbound motorcycle trail that horses should avoid at the northern end. Rein left again and ride 1 mile of switchbacks on Trail 306 through lodgepole pines and subalpine fir to open meadows and clear views near the top of the mountain.

Stunted by short growing seasons and cold weather, the trees at this altitude include Englemann spruce, subalpine fir, and whitebark pine. After passing by the junction with Antoine Trail 304 from the west, it's only 0.5 mile to the summit.

At the top are two lookouts, offering a historical contrast. The slightly leaning building, minus its former tower on top, was built in 1914 with hand-cut logs and is now on the National Register of Historic Buildings. Until recently the building was leaning precariously but rangers recently restored the lookout with new timbers for the walls and new flooring. The building is open to the public when rangers are on duty at the new lookout, built nearby in 1961.

That tower rises high above the land for a marvelous view of the surrounding countryside. This is the highest fire lookout in eastern Washington forests. Inside is a mural of wilderness scenes painted around the top of the four walls by the ranger on duty during 1986 and 1987.

Sights include 5,814-foot Mount Phoebe to the west and Bonaparte Lake to the east. On clear days, the summits of the eastern North Cascades are also visible on the western horizon, from the Sawtooth Ridge in the south to the Canadian Cascades in the north. Osoyoos Lake to the northwest crosses the U.S.-Canadian border. Looking east, the Kettle Range in northeastern Washington can easily be seen. Beyond is the Selkirk Crest in Idaho.

A few campsites have been cleared below the lookout. One has a picnic table and firepit. Be sure to bring your own water up here. There are sparse trees at the top, along with granite boulders around the area.

There are no developed campsites along this route, but there are many places to set up camp, such as the flat areas near some of the stream crossings. Also, there is a campsite trail about 1 mile from the trailhead, off to the left 0.25 mile. The log cabin at the site has caved in, but it's a nice area to camp. There's a fire pit and a creek for water, about 50 feet from the cabin.

49 MOUNT BONAPARTE–SOUTH SIDE TRAIL

Location: Northeast of Tonasket on the Okanogan National Forest, near the Canadian border.

General description: A 5.6-mile ride from Bonaparte Lake up a wooded trail to the summit of Mount Bonaparte.

Trailhead horse facilities: None. Parking for trucks and horse trailers on the road.

Trailhead elevation: 4,400 feet.

High point: 7,258 feet.

Maps: USGS Mount Bonaparte; Okanogan National Forest. See map on p. 150.

Season: Mid-June through October.

Water availability: There is always water in Duffy Springs, about 0.25 mile in. Next water is at the new bridge near the junction with Fourth of July Ridge Trail 307.

Feed availability: Pack processed feed.

Permits/restrictions: None.

Finding the trailhead: From the north end of Tonasket, travel east and then northeast on Okanogan County Road 9467. Signs point to Sitzmark Ski Area–Havillah. About 16 miles from Tonasket at Havillah, turn right (east) on gravel Forest Road 33 and follow it 10 miles northeast and then south to Forest Road 100, off to the right. Continue on FR 100, past Lost Lake, about 4 miles to an overlook above Bonaparte Lake. Less than 0.25 mile beyond the overlook, on the right, is the trailhead for the Mount Bonaparte/South Side Trail 308. A sign indicates where to park.

Riders enjoy the wooded hills near Mount Bonaparte and Bonaparte Lake.

The ride: Leaving the trailhead on this wooded path, head southwest for 0.5 mile, then north 0.5 mile before heading west and northwest. The trail crosses a small branch of Myers Creek near the junction with Fourth of July Ridge Trail 307, coming in from the left (west).

Continue about 1 mile, crossing another feeder to Myers Creek, and then go 0.25 mile to the junction with Bonaparte Lookout Trail 306, a northbound motorcycle trail that horses should avoid at the northern end.

Rein left on Trail 306 to head south toward Mount Bonaparte. Ride 1.5 miles of switchbacks through lodgepole pine and subalpine fir to open meadows and clear views near the top of the mountain. Stunted by short growing seasons and cold weather, the trees at this altitude include Englemann spruce, subalpine fir, and whitebark pine. After passing by the junction with the Antoine Trail from the west, it's only 0.5 mile to the summit.

For information about views and facilities at the summit, see Trail Ride 47.

WAPALOOSIE HORSE CAMP

Location: 20 miles east of Republic, north of Washington Highway 20, in Colville National Forest.

Horse camp facilities: Small but well designed and scenic, this horse camp was completed during 1993. Facilities include a parking area, small corral, unloading ramp, hitch rails, wooden feeders, a toilet, and three campsites with fire pits.

Finding the horse camp: Travel about 20 miles east of Republic on WA 20, which is designated the Sherman Pass National Scenic Byway from 2.5 miles east of Republic until it reaches the Columbia River. Sherman Pass elevation is 5,575 feet. This is the state's highest all-weather highway and has enjoyable scenery.

About 3.5 miles east of Sherman Pass, near a hairpin curve, is the gravel Albian Hill Road (Forest Road 2030). Turn north on this road and travel for about 2.75 miles, along the North Fork of Sherman Creek, to the horse camp. The trailhead for Wapaloosie Trail 15 is at the horse camp.

Horse camp elevation: 5,000 feet.

Water availability: The North Fork of Sherman Creek flows near the horse camp.

Trails: This horse camp offers a short loop ride.

- Wapaloosie Trail 15 leaves the camp for a relatively easy westward trek to the north leg of the popular Kettle Crest Trail. Farther south on Kettle Crest the trail picks up Jungle Hill Trail 16, which returns to FR 2030 for the return ride to the horse camp.

50 WAPALOOSIE TRAIL LOOP FROM WAPALOOSIE HORSE CAMP

Location: 20 miles east of Republic on Washington Highway 20.

General description: A 6.5-mile loop ranging from "easy" to "most difficult," with panoramic views of surrounding mountains

Trailhead horse facilities: See Wapaloosie Horse Camp.

Trailhead elevation: 5,000 feet.

High point: 6,850 feet on Kettle Crest Trail 15.

Maps: Colville National Forest; USGS Sherman Peak quad.

Season: Late June through early October; fall is best.

Water availability: The trail crosses streams at several points.

Feed availability: Pack processed food for a stock snack.

Permits/restrictions: None.

Finding the trailhead: See Wapaloosie Horse Camp.

The ride: Wapaloosie Trail 15 leaves the camp for a short, relatively easy westward trek past Albian Hill to the junction with Kettle Crest Trail 13. This loop trip from the Wapaloosie Horse Camp includes only a 1-mile segment of the Kettle Crest trail. After heading south on Kettle Crest to the junction with Jungle Hill Trail 16, the trail returns to Forest Road 2030 for the ride north to the horse camp.

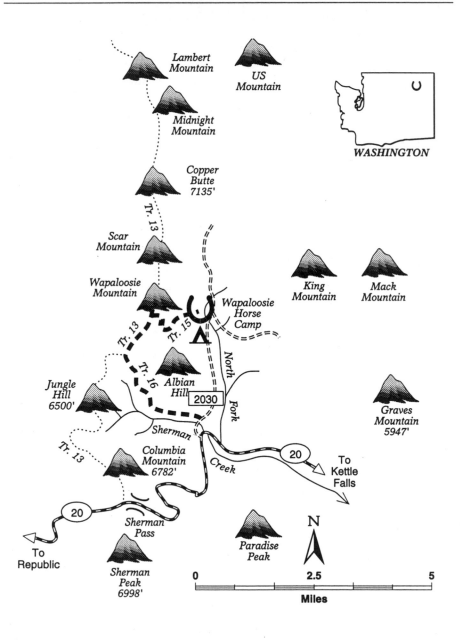

Lambert Mountain

US Mountain

Midnight Mountain

Copper Butte 7135'

Tr. 13

Scar Mountain

Wapaloosie Mountain

King Mountain

Mack Mountain

Tr. 13

Tr. 15

Wapaloosie Horse Camp

Tr. 16

North Fork

Albian Hill

2030

Jungle Hill 6500'

Graves Mountain 5947'

Sherman

Tr. 13

Columbia Mountain 6782'

Creek

20

To Kettle Falls

20

Sherman Pass

Paradise Peak

N

To Republic

Sherman Peak 6998'

0   2.5   5
Miles

WASHINGTON

Riding the Wapaloosie Trail makes a pleasant, scenic day outing. At the beginning, the trail crosses the North Fork of Sherman Creek. Although there are some steep-pitched areas and numerous switchbacks, for the most part the grade is moderate, passing through semi-open stands of lodgepole pine. Near the top of the ridge the trail crosses a meadow near the summit of 7,018-foot Wapaloosie Mountain and winds along the south side of the mountain to join the Kettle Crest Trail.

To the north of the mountain riders may get glimpses of the burned area around Copper Butte, 2.5 miles from the trail junction. A 1994 forest fire destroyed more than 10,000 acres of timber between the butte and Lambert Mountain, some 5 miles north. There are horse camps and trails in that area but the fires have temporarily eliminated access.

From Wapaloosie Mountain the trail descends gently through meadows, heading south along the eastern edge of the crest. Initially there is an area of weather-polished snags, giving way to open, grassy slopes and stunted stands of subalpine fir and lodgepole pine.

The high point of the trip, in elevation at least, is 6,850 feet on the Kettle Crest Trail. That's perhaps the high point for the scenery, too, since the forested crown of Wapaloosie Mountain generally obstructs panoramic views.

Along Kettle Crest Ridge there are spectacular views of neighboring mountains and valleys, with more forests of lodgepole and ponderosa pine to the north. Riders should be able to see Graves Mountain, 5 miles to the southeast, and Mack Mountain, 4.5 miles to the northeast.

The Kettle Crest Trail is one of the most popular in the Colville National Forest, although its isolated location in this part of the state keeps crowds to a minimum. Winding through flowery meadows and along rolling, rounded mountaintops, this trail stretches for 42 miles, reaching 29 miles north of Sherman Pass and another 13 miles on the south (see Trail Ride 51, Sherman Pass to Sherman Peak).

A mile south of Wapaloosie Mountain, near the junction with Jungle Hill Trail 16, is an old outfitters' camp in a tree grove about 300 feet from a spring. From the campsite there's a view of the valley to the southeast.

At the junction with Jungle Hill trail the route is faint, heading to the east for the 2.5-mile trip back to FR 2030. This is the most difficult section of the loop because the trail is hard to follow. Orange markers help to guide riders for the first 0.25 mile as the trail leaves Kettle Crest Ridge.

Then the route descends through a forest with few open areas, ending near Sherman Creek, on the west end of a large gravel pit on Albian Hill Road (FR 2030). From this point ride Albian Hill Road north 2.75 miles to the Wapaloosie Horse Camp.

51 SHERMAN PASS TO SHERMAN PEAK

Location: About halfway between Republic and Kettle Falls on Washington Highway 20 in Colville National Forest.

General description: A 6.6-mile round-trip ride along the southern Kettle Crest mountain range from Sherman Pass to the summit of Sherman Peak.

Trailhead horse facilities: None.

Trailhead elevation: 5,500 feet.

High point: 6,500 feet near the summit of 7,011-foot Sherman Peak.

Maps: Colville National Forest; USGS Sherman Peak.

Season: Mid-June through September.

Water availability: Some creeks along the trail provide water, but riders should take plenty of water with them.

Feed availability: Pack processed feed.

Permits/restrictions: No permits are required. Avoid riding through this old forest fire burn during stormy, windy weather due to the danger from falling snags.

Finding the trailhead: Drive about 17 miles east of Republic, or 26 miles west of Kettle Falls, on Washington Highway 20 to Sherman Pass. Then turn north on Forest Road 495, which has a sign for the Kettle Crest Trail. Trailhead parking is about 0.1 mile up the road. This area serves as the trailhead for both the north and south Kettle Crest trails.

The ride: Kettle Crest South Trail 13 leaves the parking lot and travels south toward the highway, then heads east about 300 feet through lodgepole pine along the roadway until it reaches a signed junction. Rein right and continue downhill into a draw, then up a switchback trail to the highway. Use extreme caution crossing WA 20 to pick up Kettle Crest Trail South 13.

On the south side of WA 20 the trail follows a switchback route up a gentle slope from Sherman Pass. Granite boulders are seen along the early part of the trail, which is sheltered by a shady forest of lodgepole pine, western larch, and Douglas-fir. Enjoy the shade while you can—much of this ride covers open, parched terrain very different from western Washington's damp landscape. Trail difficulty is rated from easiest to more difficult along the route, which gets only light to medium use from hikers, horse riders, and the deer that often use the same trail.

About 0.7 mile from the highway the trail bridges a small, spring-fed creek. About 0.2 mile farther the trail curves around a low ridge and enters a forest of charred and bleached snags, heading into a small cirque basin. After curving through the basin the trail switchbacks up hill four times to a 6,300-foot saddle that is about 0.5 mile east of Sherman Peak. Now 2.8 miles from the trailhead, peaks within view to the south are Snow Peak, Barnaby Buttes, and White Mountain.

Wildlife is abundant in this area, including deer, coyotes, black bears, and lynx, plus an assortment of songbirds. The Washington Wildlife Department manages this area as mule deer habitat. Lucky riders may see four-point bucks along the way.

It's only a short distance from the saddle to the summit of Sherman Peak, about 0.5 mile. Leave the trail and ride toward the peak through a mixture of charred snags

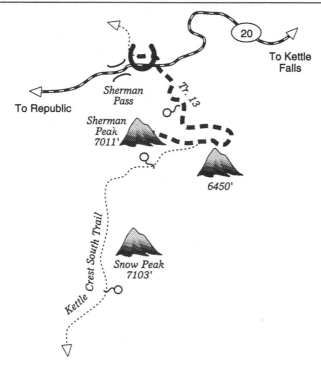

and live trees, traveling up an increasingly steep slope covered with boulders and a few stunted pine trees and junipers.

Be cautious near the top, where the ridge turns to loose rubble. Horses will have a difficult time keeping their footing. It may be best to dismount and walk the remaining distance to the peak for a 360-degree view of the area.

To the west, beyond the rolling Okanogan Highlands, is the eastern range of the Okanogan Cascade mountains with the jagged peaks of the Sawtooth Range to the southwest. To the east, beyond the Columbia River, are the Selkirk Mountains near the horizon, 75 miles away in the northern Idaho panhandle. North are the rolling highlands of the Kettle Crest Ridge and other high ranges that stretch into Canada. To the south rise Snow Peak and White Mountain.

52 SALMO BASIN LOOP

Location: In the extreme northeast corner of the state, east of Sullivan Lake, on the Colville National Forest.

General description: An 18-mile loop ride through the old-growth forests of the Salmo-Priest Wilderness Area, one of the state's wildest mountain regions. Nearly half of the loop is in Idaho.

Trailhead horse facilities: Two hitch rails, two campfire rings, a toilet, an intermittent stream, and parking for four two-horse trailers.

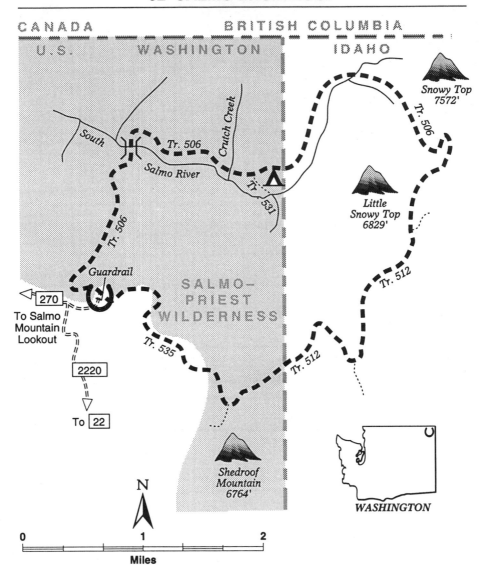

Trailhead elevation: 5,910 feet.

High point: 6,400 feet near Snowy Top Mountain in Idaho.

Maps: Colville National Forest; USGS Salmo Mountain and Continental Mountain quads; Salmo–Priest Wilderness.

Season: July through mid-October.

Water availability: Ample at several perennial streams along the route, particularly on Salmo Basin Trail 506. Little or no water on ridgetops, especially in Idaho near Snowy Top Mountain.

Feed availability: Scant forage; carry processed feed.

Permits/restrictions: No permits are required. Groups in the wilderness are limited to twelve heartbeats, in any combination of people and stock.

Finding the trailhead: From Tiger and the junction of Washington Highways 20 and 31, drive north 15 miles on WA 31 to Metaline Falls (2 miles north of the town of Metaline).

Continue north across the Pend Oreille River 2 miles and turn right on paved County Road 9345, toward Sullivan Lake. After about 3 miles, follow the road south 1.5 miles to a landing strip near the top of Sullivan Lake and the junction with Forest Road 22.

Turn left and head east on graveled FR 22, along the north bank of Sullivan Creek. About 4.75 miles from the paved road, FR 22 continues as 2220 to the trailhead, about 13 miles away. The road ends, after a series of switchback curves, at the trailhead and the boundary of the Salmo–Priest Wilderness. A guardrail across the road blocks an old road grade (you'll recognize it on the return trip). Nearby is a sign and arrow pointing to the trailhead.

The ride: The Salmo–Priest Wilderness Area was named for the Salmo River and the Catholic missionary priests who visited the area more than 100 years ago. Jointly managed by the Colville and Idaho Panhandle national forests, this region is home to two endangered species, the grizzly bear and woodland caribou. There are also black bears, mountain lions, gray wolves, moose, elk, deer, and Rocky Mountain bighorn sheep in this wilderness.

This is an important recovery area for grizzlies, so be sure to observe normal bear precautions. Tie bells to your horses and keep together in a group to warn bears of your approach. Ride only during daylight hours. If you see a bear, ride downwind from it. Leave dogs at home to avoid problems on the trail.

If you camp, check the area for bear droppings or tracks first. Keep your camp clean and hang food at least 15 feet up a tree and 5 feet away from the trunk. Cook away from the camp and don't sleep in clothes filled with cooking aromas. Be alert while picking berries, a favorite bear food.

From the deep South Salmo River valley to high ridges along the Washington–Idaho border, this trail offers a wide variety of scenic vistas and trail experiences. Riders may be surprised to find a lush, inland rain forest on this valley trip, one of the few rain forests of this type in the northern Rocky Mountains. The area should feel familiar to those accustomed to rides in the green forests of the western Cascades.

Most riders here make day trips rather than overnight campouts. Trail use in this neglected corner of the state is usually rated as light to moderate on most trails. Some 85 miles of trails here are open to stock use.

From the trailhead the route descends 3.1 miles to the South Salmo River, on an average 12-percent grade, reaching the river at 4,150 feet elevation and less than 1 mile from the U.S.-Canada border. This is a pleasant ride, switchbacking through a forest of old-growth cedars and hemlocks, mossy logs, and green undergrowth of ferns and bunchberry dogwood.

Glimpses through the trees reveal a Canadian mountain ridge rising 3,000 feet above the canyon. Stands of western red-cedar and hemlock line both sides of the river, which harbors some small cutthroat trout.

After crossing the river on a bridge follow the trail to the right (east) and along the north side of the river, heading upstream. It passes a junction with Crutch Creek at 1.3 miles from the river crossing as the trail nears the Idaho border, 0.7 mile ahead. Where the trail swings gradually north marks the boundary between the two states.

About 0.25 mile before the border there's a camping site with water at Salmo Cabin, built in the 1930s and used as a backcountry ranger station until 1951. To reach it, ride south an easy 0.25-mile on Trail 531 to the South Fork of the Salmo River. The building is deteriorating but the campsite is relatively roomy. Remember to keep stock at least 200 feet from the river, except when watering. Other campsites are found along this loop through the Salmo Basin, but most of them are close to small streams, suitable for hikers but not for horses. Rangers want to discourage camping with horses so close to the water.

The trail begins to climb, leaving behind the tall stands of cedar, spruce, and hemlock in the river valley. It climbs more steeply after reaching the top of the northward route, at 1.3 miles from the border crossing. The trail then crosses two forks of the river before climbing 2.5 miles to the southeast. Along this stretch riders enjoy panoramic views of neighboring mountains and valleys, particularly 7,572-foot Snowy Top to the northeast, less than 0.5 mile from the Canadian border.

At a switchback south of Snowy Top and 8.8 miles from the trailhead is the end of Trail 506 and the beginning of Shedroof Divide Trail 512 on a ridge that is the highest point on the loop at 6,400 feet elevation.

From the ridge continue southeast on Shedroof Divide Trail 512. Less than 1 mile from the ridge is the Little Snowy Top way trail, a 1-mile scramble to the lookout building at the summit.

But even the main trail boasts plenty of scenic eastern views, with the Upper Priest River Valley below and the Idaho Selkirk Mountains beyond. Pass by an eastbound trail that descends sharply through repetitive switchbacks to the river valley below. It's a very steep 4.5-mile journey that would mean a rugged return climb.

Continue on the dry, waterless ridge trail for 6 miles toward 6,764-foot Shedroof Mountain. A campsite with water is located on Shedroof Divide Trail 512 about 0.25 mile west of its junction with Upper Hughes Ridge Trail 315, which originates to the south in Idaho.

About 1.5 miles from the trail junction, part company with Shedroof Divide Trail 512, which heads south at a junction with the Salmo Divide Trail 535. Along this trail there's no water and only limited seasonal forage.

There are intermittent panoramic views through the woods as the route winds 1.7 miles along the 6,200- to 6,400-foot ridge from Shedroof Mountain northwest to the trailhead. The loop trail ends in the old road bed, which was part of FR 2220 before it was closed to vehicles when the new trailhead was built. Ride around the guardrail to return to the Salmo Pass trailhead.

53 NOISY CREEK TRAIL TO HALL MOUNTAIN

Location: In the extreme northeast corner of the state, at the southern end of Sullivan Lake, the Colville National Forest.

General description: A 7.1-mile round-trip ride in the Selkirk Mountains with spectacular views of Sullivan Lake from near the top of Hall Mountain.

Trailhead horse facilities: Parking space for two small horse trailers.

Trailhead elevation: 2,600 feet at Noisy Creek campground.

High point: 6,223 feet at summit of Hall Mountain.

Maps: Colville National Forest; USGS Metaline Falls, Pass Creek quads.

Season: Late June through October.

Water availability: Ample water along Noisy and Harvey creeks. But water is scarce on the Hall Mountain Ridge Trail 540.

Feed availability: Forage is scarce; carry processed feed.

Permits/restrictions: No permits required.

Finding the trailhead: From Colville, drive east 36 miles on Washington Highway 20 to Tiger. Turn left (north) on Washington Highway 31 for 4 miles to Ione. Just before town, turn right (east) on paved County Road 9345 and drive about 9 miles to the Noisy Creek campground at the southern end of Sullivan Lake. The campground is to the right, about 0.25 mile down the gravel road off CR 9345. The trailhead is in the camp's overflow area. Signs for the trailhead point the way from the end of the county road.

The ride: Trail riders can camp at the campground in the field to the right and south of the restrooms near the trailhead. Signs indicate where national forest land ends and private land begins. Stay on national forest land. Remember to clean up all hay and manure before leaving the camping area.

The trail, which begins behind a new restroom near the parking area, rises up a moderately sloped trail, climbing gradually for the first 3 miles before turning sharply northward. Some areas of Noisy Creek Trail 588 are rocky and faint in the northbound section, especially where the trail has been washed out in places. In general, the trail remains in timber.

On the northern portion of the trail the route rises steeply as it climbs to the ridge junction with Hall Mountain Trail 540 from the north and Grassy Top Mountain Trail 533 from the east. From the junction, at 5,540 feet, follow Hall Mountain Trail 540 westward to the summit at 6,223 feet.

The route to Hall Mountain gains only 800 feet in the 2.5 miles between the ridge trail junction and the mountain top. While there is a lot of rocky trail, the path is easy to follow and riders can enjoy outstanding panoramic vistas along the way.

Much of the trail travels along the side of an open grassy ridge on its way to the top of Hall Mountain, where there is a 360-degree view of the Sullivan Lake area. Hall Mountain is also home to the state's most famous, and prolific, local band of Rocky Mountain bighorn sheep. Sheep sightings are most common during the early morning and late afternoon hours. Salt blocks are set out for them each year on the mountaintop.

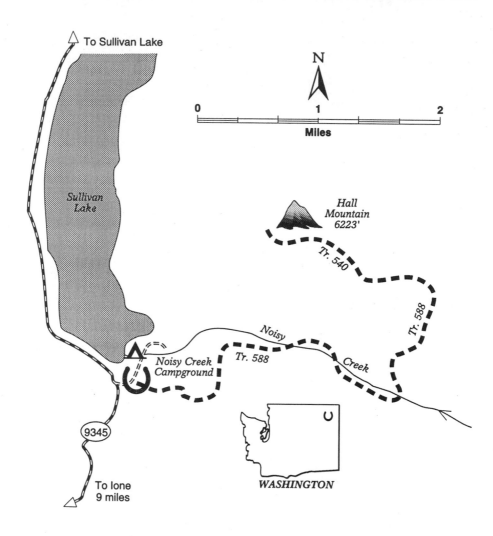

The area is also within grizzly bear habitat, but there have been no incidents involving horses, riders, or hikers and the bears. Rangers advise stock users that horses aren't likely to attract bears. But a messy camp and food smells will catch a bear's attention. So keep a clean camp, don't bury garbage, hang food (including horse feed) at least 15 feet off the ground and 5 feet from the nearest tree, and keep food away from tents and sleeping areas.

Most of the horse riders on Sullivan Lake Ranger District trails are day riders and there are few developed campsites, which reduces the chances of a clash between bears and visitors to this scenic realm.

54 TUCANNON RIVER TRAIL

Location: Near Dayton and Pomeroy on Washington Highway 12, in southeast Washington's Blue Mountains.

General description: An easy 10.2-mile round-trip ride along the edge of the Wenaha–Tucannon Wilderness, with a good chance of seeing Rocky Mountain elk.

Trailhead horse facilities: None.

Trailhead elevation: 3,400 feet.

High point: 4,200 feet.

Maps: Umatilla National Forest; USGS Stentz Spring and Panjab Creek 7.5-minute quads; Wenaha-Tucannon Wilderness.

Season: June through mid-October.

Water availability: Ample from the river along entire route.

Feed availability: No forage; pack processed feed.

Permits/restrictions: No permits are required on this trail. But the endangered spring chinook salmon spawn in the Tucannon River so all camping and livestock must be kept at least 75 feet from the river in this narrow canyon.

Finding the trailhead: From Dayton, drive 10 miles north on WA 12. Just after crossing the Tucannon River, turn sharply right onto Tucannon River Road and drive south about 35 miles. At 28 miles, ignore the left-forking road to the Camp William T. Wooten State Park and Tucannon Campground. The pavement ends here but a good gravel road continues. Drive on about 4 miles to a fork in the road. Bear left and continue on Forest Road 4712—a sometimes rough and narrow road—for 4 miles. Park where signs indicate no parking beyond that point. From the parking area, ride 1 mile to the trailhead at the end of the road.

The ride: Tucannon River Trail 3135 runs nearly straight and climbs gently for 4.1 miles along the river. There are many camping areas available along the river and good fishing spots for rainbow trout. This trail is rated as "easy-to-moderate" by rangers, and it's well maintained.

Until recently there were two trails leaving the trailhead, the upper one for motorbikes. That trail has been closed. The lower trail begins as an old logging road under a shady canopy of western larch, ponderosa pine, Douglas-fir, and lodgepole pine. Farther on the roadway narrows to a trail. Wildflowers along the way include lupine, spirea, larkspur, wild strawberry, and yarrow, plus scatterings of wild rose and huckleberry.

Area ranchers hold grazing permits for about 10,000 cattle and 8,000 sheep on the Umatilla National Forest. Local wildlife includes white-tailed and mule deer, bighorn sheep, black bear, and mountain lion. Bald eagles and peregrine falcons are sometimes seen in the forest. Other attractions are the hummingbirds that often approach colorfully dressed riders. But much of the buzzing may be coming from the horseflies that are just as numerous. A dry climate makes mosquitos rare, however. At lower elevations, be wary of rattlesnakes.

Elk hunting camps are passed at several trail points. Elk hunters are the main users of this trail network. The Umatilla National Forest is home to an estimated 22,000

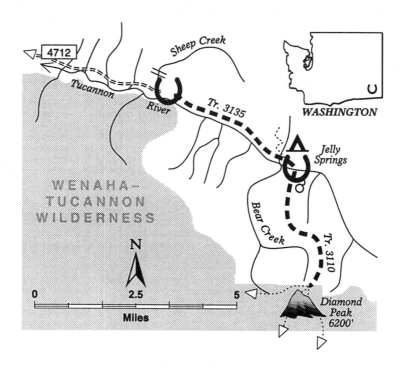

elk, one of the largest concentrations of elk in any national forest. Each hunting season the elk are outnumbered by about 30,000 hunters. During the rest of the year elk wander near the trail with less concern for their safety. As many as a dozen sightings a day are not uncommon along this trail.

The Tucannon River, a small mountain stream at this point, is always close to the trail. At times there are views of wooded slopes across the creek. Just past the point where Bear Creek flows from the south into the Tucannon River, at 4,200 feet elevation, the river route ends at the junction with Bear Creek Trail 6144, coming in from the north. Several campsites dot the area.

Bear Creek Trail climbs sharply north to Hunter Spring and Forest Road 40. For a view of the surrounding terrain, ride 0.5 mile up the Bear Creek trail to an open area.

From this point riders can retrace their hoofprints back to the trailhead or travel on 0.3 mile past the Bear Creek Trail 6144 junction to the junction with the right-hand, southbound Jelly Springs Trail 3110, which climbs 4.5 miles to Diamond Peak (see Trail Ride 55).

55 JELLY SPRINGS TRAIL TO DIAMOND PEAK

Location: Near Pomeroy in the Blue Mountains, Umatilla National Forest.
General description: A 4.5-mile ride up the Tucannon River to Diamond Peak and the northeastern edge of the Wenaha–Tucannon Wilderness.
Trailhead horse facilities: Campsites at the end of the Tucannon River Trail (Trail Ride 54) provide facilities for the start of Jelly Springs Trail 3110.
Trailhead elevation: 4,200 feet.
High point: 6,200 feet on Diamond Peak.
Maps: Umatilla National Forest; USGS Stentz Spring, Panjab Creek, and Diamond Peak 7.5-minute quads; Wenaha–Tucannon Wilderness.
Season: Mid-June through mid-October.
Water availability: Along the Tucannon River route and at Jelly Spring on Trail 3110; also at campsites on Diamond Peak.
Feed availability: Limited forage; pack processed feed.
Permits/restrictions: No overnight camping permits are required for the Wenaha–Tucannon Wilderness. Groups are limited to a total of eighteen riders and stock, in any combination, in the wilderness. No stock allowed within 200 feet of any lake or stream shoreline in the wilderness except during watering.
Finding the trailhead: See Tucannon River Trail, Trail Ride 54. At the end of the trail, 0.3 mile past Bear Creek, is the start of Jelly Springs Trail 3110 to the south, heading up the side of Diamond Peak.

The ride: From campsites at the end of the Tucannon River Trail, the 4.5-mile trail to Diamond Peak is steep, rising 1,000 feet in the 1-mile trek to the ridge above Jelly Springs, a reliable source of water and a good camping location. Although the trail is well maintained, it's characterized by an 8-percent grade.

At the ridge riders will have their first views of the surrounding mountains and timber. Similar scenic vistas and panoramic views are part of the ridge ride, with the best views gained from higher elevations on Diamond Peak.

Arrival at the campsite near Diamond Peak coincides with entry into the Wenaha–Tucannon Wilderness. The boundary is posted on the trail. A short distance farther the trail meets the crossing of Mount Misery Trail 3113. Then the Jelly Springs Trail continues on about 0.5 mile to the 6,200-foot level below Diamond Peak's summit, which rises to 6,379 feet.

The route offers a panoramic view of the Blue Mountain Wilderness where large numbers of Rocky Mountain elk are often seen. Jelly Springs Trail 3110 is easily accessible from the end of Tucannon River Trail 3135 (see Trail Ride 54).

APPENDIX A: THE TRAIL RIDER'S CHECKLIST

Refer to the following list as a reminder of all the items you might want to carry with you on your next trail ride. Some—such as rain gear—are essential, but many are merely aids to comfort and convenience on the trail. Pack light—take only what you need—but don't forget the essentials.

For Camp

- ❑ Tent
- ❑ Ground cloth
- ❑ Tarp
- ❑ Rope
- ❑ Shovel
- ❑ Water bucket
- ❑ Folding rake
- ❑ Lantern
- ❑ Propane fuel
- ❑ Stove
- ❑ Lantern mantles
- ❑ Fry pan
- ❑ Griddle
- ❑ Kettles and lids
- ❑ Butcher knife
- ❑ Coffee pot
- ❑ Can opener
- ❑ Spoon (large)
- ❑ Potato peeler
- ❑ Plates
- ❑ Hotcake turner
- ❑ Silverware
- ❑ Cups
- ❑ Dish soap
- ❑ Scouring pad
- ❑ Dish pan
- ❑ Dish towel
- ❑ Paper towels
- ❑ Dish rag
- ❑ Axe, hatchet, or saw (use only for clearing downfall on the trail)

Food

- ❑ Salt and pepper
- ❑ Sugar
- ❑ Hotcake flour
- ❑ Biscuit mix
- ❑ Shortening
- ❑ Coffee
- ❑ Tea
- ❑ Cocoa
- ❑ Milk (canned and fresh)
- ❑ Syrup
- ❑ Butter
- ❑ Catsup
- ❑ Mayonnaise
- ❑ Jam
- ❑ Honey
- ❑ Bacon
- ❑ Eggs
- ❑ Meats (fresh/canned)
- ❑ Lunch meat
- ❑ Cheese
- ❑ Soup
- ❑ Fruit (canned/fresh)
- ❑ Vegetables (canned/fresh)
- ❑ Onions
- ❑ Potatoes
- ❑ Oatmeal
- ❑ Juice
- ❑ Kool-Aid/Tang drink mixes
- ❑ Candy
- ❑ Snacks
- ❑ Beverages

Personal

- ❏ Money
- ❏ Sleeping bag
- ❏ Soap
- ❏ Toothbrush
- ❏ Camera and film
- ❏ Alarm clock
- ❏ Clothes
- ❏ Shoes/boots
- ❏ Bootjack
- ❏ Chaps
- ❏ Rain gear
- ❏ Gloves
- ❏ Towel
- ❏ Washcloth
- ❏ Toothpaste
- ❏ Toilet paper (non-perfumed, biodegradable)
- ❏ Prescription drugs
- ❏ First-aid kit
- ❏ Matches
- ❏ Knife
- ❏ Binoculars
- ❏ Sunglasses
- ❏ Flashlight
- ❏ Extra batteries and bulbs
- ❏ Thermos
- ❏ Handwarmer
- ❏ Tools
- ❏ Insect repellent
- ❏ Fishing gear
- ❏ Hunting gear
- ❏ Maps
- ❏ Snake bite kit

For horses

- ❏ Halter and lead rope
- ❏ Warming blanket
- ❏ Hoof pick
- ❏ ❏ Comb and brush
- ❏ Bridle
- ❏ Saddle and pad
- ❏ Saddlebags
- ❏ Breast strap
- ❏ Britchin/crupper
- ❏ Hobbles
- ❏ Lariat
- ❏ Pack saddle and pad
- ❏ Lash cinch and tarp
- ❏ High hitchline/tree savers
- ❏ Feed bags
- ❏ Manties
- ❏ Grain/pellets
- ❏ First-aid kit (horses)
- ❏ Fly repellent
- ❏ Horseshoes and nails
- ❏ Horseshoe hammer and rasp

APPENDIX B: AGENCY ADDRESSES

For statewide information on trails, public lands, and trail riding, write to the following addresses:

USDA Forest Service
Pacific Northwest Regional Office
333 S.W. 1st Ave.
P.O. Box 3623
Portland, OR 97204

National Park Service
Pacific Northwest Regional Office
83 South King St., Suite 212
Seattle, WA 98104

For more information about specific trail rides, write to the offices listed below.

Trail Ride 1: Olympic NF, Sol Duc Ranger District, Route 1, Box 5750, Highway 101, Forks, WA 98331.

Trail Rides 2, 3, 4, 5: Olympic NF, Quilcene Ranger District, 202482 Highway 101, P.O. Box 280, Quilcene, WA 98376.

Trail Rides 6, 7, 8, and Brown Creek Horse Camp: Olympic NF, Hood Canal Ranger District, N. 150 Lake Cushman Road, P.O. Box 68, Hoodsport, WA 98548.

Trail Rides 9, 10, 11: Olympic NF, Quinault Ranger District, 353 South Shore Road, P.O. Box 9, Quinault, WA 98575.

Trail Ride 12: Mount Baker/Snoqualmie NF, Mount Baker Ranger District, 2105 Highway 20, Sedro Woolley, WA 98284.

Trail Rides 13, 14: North Cascades National Park (Ross Lake National Recreation Area and Lake Chelan National Recreation Area), 2105 Highway 20, Sedro Woolley, WA 98284.

Trail Rides 15, 16, 17: Okanogan NF, Winthrop Ranger District, 24 W. Chewuch, P.O. Box 579, Winthrop, WA 98862.

Trail Rides 18, 19, 20, 21, 22, and Twisp River Horse Camp: Okanogan NF, Twisp Ranger District, 502 Glover, P.O. Box 188, Twisp, WA 98856.

Trail Ride 23: Mount Baker/Snoqualmie NF, Darrington Ranger District, 1404 Emmens St., Darrington, WA 98241.

Trail Rides 24, 25, and Chiwawa and Alder Creek Horse Camps: Wenatchee NF, Lake Wenatchee Ranger District, 22976 Highway 207, Leavenworth, WA 98826.

Trail Rides 26, 27: Mount Baker/Snoqualmie NF, Skykomish Ranger District, 74920 NE Stevens Pass Highway, P.O. Box 305, Skykomish, WA 98288.

Trail Ride 28 and Black Pine Horse Camp: Wenatchee NF, Leavenworth Ranger District, 600 Sherbourne St., Leavenworth, WA 98826.

Trail Ride 29: Wenatchee NF, Cle Elum Ranger District, 803 W. 2nd St., Cle Elum, WA 98922.

Trail Rides 30, 31, and Sand Flats Horse Camp: Mount Baker/Snoqualmie NF, White River Ranger District, 857 Roosevelt Ave. E., Enumclaw, WA 98022.

Trail Rides 32, 33, 34, and Deep Creek and White Pass Horse Camps: Wenatchee NF, Naches Ranger District, 10061 Highway 12, Naches, WA 98937.

Trail Rides 35, 36, 37, and Keenes Horse Camp: Gifford Pinchot NF, Randle Ranger District, 10024 U.S. Highway 12, Randle, WA 98377.

Trail Rides 38, 39, 40, 41, 42, 43, and Lewis River and Kalama Horse Camps:
Mount St. Helens Volcanic National Monument, 42218 NE Yale Bridge Rd.,
Amboy, WA 98601.

Trail Rides 44, 45, 46, and Falls Creek Horse Camp: Gifford Pinchot NF, Wind
River Ranger District, MP 1.26R Hemlock Road, Carson, WA 98610.

Trail Rides 47, 48, 49: Okanogan NF, Tonasket Ranger District, 1 West Winesap,
P.O. Box 466, Tonasket, WA 98855.

Trail Rides 50, 51, and Wapaloosie Horse Camp: Colville NF, Kettle Falls Ranger
District, 255 W. 11th, Kettle Falls, WA 99141.

Trail Rides 52, 53: Colville NF, Sullivan Lake Ranger District, 12641 Sullivan Lake
Road, Metaline Falls, WA 99153.

Trail Rides 54, 55: Umatilla NF, Pomeroy Ranger District, Route 1, Box 54-A,
Pomeroy, WA 99347.

Other National Forest Offices (including Ranger Districts not listed above)

Colville National Forest, 695 S. Main St., Colville, WA 99114.
Colville Ranger District, 755 S. Main St., Colville, WA 99114.
Newport Ranger District, 315 N. Warren, P.O. Box 770, Newport, WA 99156.
Republic Ranger District, 180 N. Jefferson, P.O. Box 468, Republic, WA 99166.

Gifford Pinchot National Forest, 6926 E. Fourth Plain Blvd., P.O. Box 8944,
Vancouver, WA 98668.
Mount Adams Ranger District, 2455 Highway 141, Trout Lake, WA 98650.
Packwood Ranger District, 13068 U.S. Highway 12, Packwood, WA 98361.

Mount Baker/Snoqualmie National Forest, 21905 64th Ave. W., Mountlake
Terrace, WA 98043.
North Bend Ranger District, 42404 SE North Bend Way, North Bend, WA 98045.

Okanogan National Forest, 1240 2nd Ave. S., P.O. Box 950, Okanogan, WA 98840.

Olympic National Forest, 1835 Black Lake Blvd. SW, Olympia, WA 98502.

Wenatchee National Forest, 301 Yakima St., P.O. Box 811, Wenatchee, WA 98801.
Chelan Ranger District, 428 W. Woodin Ave., P.O. Box 189, Chelan, WA 98816.
Entiat Ranger District, 2108 Entiat Way, Entiat, WA 98822.

Umatilla National Forest, 2517 S.W. Hailey Avenue, Pendleton, OR 97801.
Walla Walla Ranger District, 1415 West Rose Street, Walla Walla, WA 99362.

National Park Service Addresses
Mount Rainier National Park, Tahoma Woods, Star Route, Ashford, WA 98304.
Olympic National Park, 600 E. Park Ave., Port Angeles, WA 98362.

APPENDIX C: FOR MORE INFORMATION

Leave No Trace Horsepacking and Camping

Back Country Horseman Guidebook, published by Back Country Horsemen of American, P.O. Box 597, Columbia Falls, MT 59912, in partnership with the USDA Forest Service's Pacific Northwest, Northern, Intermountain, and Pacific Southwest Regions.

Horse Packing in Pictures, Francis W. Davis, Charles Scribner's Sons, New York, New York, 1975.

Horse Sense, Packing Lightly on Your National Forests (pamphlet), USDA Forest Service, Pacific Northwest Region, 319 SW Pine St., P.O. Box 3623, Portland, Oregon 97208; (503) 326-2971.

Lightweight Camping and Stock Equipment, September 1993, USDA Forest Service Technology and Development Program, Missoula, Montana 59801.

Low-Impact Horse Camping (video), Idaho Back Country Horsemen, HC 66, Box 248, Kooskia, Idaho 83536.

Mountain Manners (video), Idaho Back Country Horsemen, HC 66, Box 248, Kooskia, Idaho 83536.

Techniques and Equipment for Wilderness Travel With Stock, October 1993, USDA Forest Service Technology and Development Program, Missoula, Montana 59801.

Treading Lightly With Pack Animals, A Guide to Low-Impact Travel in the Backcountry, Dan Aadland, 1994, Mountain Press Publishing Co., P.O. Box 2399, Missoula, Montana 59806.

Wild Country Companion: The Ultimate Guide to No-Trace Outdoor Recreation and Wilderness Safety, Will Harmon, 1994, Falcon Press, P.O. Box 1718, Helena, MT 59624; (800) 582-2665.

Trail Information and Maps

Outdoor Recreation Information Center, 1018 First Ave., Seattle, WA 98104. Operated by USDA Forest Service, National Park Service, and Washington State Parks—maps, brochures, pamphlets, guidebooks, and the computerized Trails Information System (TRIS) showing trail conditions, including stock trails in Washington State.

Other Washington State Outdoor Recreation Information Centers That Have the TRIS Computerized Trail Information System.

Sol Duc Ranger Station
Route 1, Box 5750
Forks, WA 98331

Hood Canal Ranger Station
P.O. Box 68
Hoodsport, WA 98548

North Cascades National Park
Mount Baker Ranger District Office (USFS)
2105 Highway 20
Sedro Woolley, WA 98284

Horse Groups and Publications

Horseman's Directory, The All-Breed Horse Industry Directory, State of Washington, P.O. Box 2571, Kirkland, WA 98083; (800) 735-7235. White pages, yellow pages, and cross-directory for tack shops, veterinarians, and horse groups in Washington State.

Stock and Camping Equipment

Dale Pack Station
321 Wiseacre Road
Yakima, WA 98901

Gene "Grizzly" Morgan
2901 S. Skagit Highway
Sedro Woolley, WA 98284

Spokane Tent & Awning
E. 410 Trent
Spokane, WA 99202

Indiana Harness & Saddlery Co.
3030 East Sprague Ave.
Spokane, WA 99202

Whip & Spur Saddlery
E. 3527 Sprague #7
Spokane, WA 99036

Tornow's Custom Saddle & Pack Equipment
P. O. Box 984
Monroe, WA 98272

Rocking M Ranch Feed & Supply
1025 Commercial Street
Darrington, WA 98241

The Bony Pony
1676 Old Hwy 99 South
Mount Vernon, WA 98273

Trail Rides With the Pros

James Murphy
Backcountry Horsemen of Washington
11839 Glenwood Road SW
Port Orchard, WA 98366

Washington Outfitters and Guides Association (WOGA)
22845 NE 8, Suite 331
Redmond, WA 98053

Lorri Bisconer
Washington Trail Riders Association
111 S. 17th Ave.
Battle Ground, WA 98604

U.S. Geological Survey

Earth Sciences Center
678 US Courthouse
W. 920 Riverside Ave.
Spokane, WA 99201

Direct orders for USGS topographic maps.

APPENDIX D: RIDING WITH THE PROS

Many horse owners may be experienced riders, but that doesn't mean that they have experienced all of the varied situations encountered on mountain trails. For those who would like to travel with the "pros" to experience backcountry trails and camping, there are a variety of options. For those who are physically disabled but want to ride, there are resources for you, too.

Back Country Horsemen of America (and Washington Chapters)

Based in Columbia Falls, Montana, Back County Horsemen of America was formed in 1973 to perpetuate the common-sense use and enjoyment of horses in America's backcountry and wilderness, as well as to work to ensure that public lands remain open to recreational stock use. Local chapters of the group also clear and build trails, create horse camps, and promote Leave No Trace environmental ethics.

The group has statewide organizations in ten Western states, including Washington, Montana, California, Idaho, Nevada, Wyoming, Utah, Colorado, Oregon, and New Mexico, plus affiliated groups in British Columbia and Alberta, Canada.

Recognizing the noble place of the horse in Western heritage, BCH of America and its state organizations have dedicated themselves to promoting wise horse use with minimum damage to the backcountry. Members also work to educate, and to encourage and solicit active participation in the "wise and sustaining use of the backcountry resource by horsemen and the general public commensurate with our heritage."

Adverse impact has already forced the closure of a few areas to horse use, a closing that the BCH of America says is because of "horse misuse rather than overuse." The education of horse riders should create a proper regard for the environment that will help eliminate the need for further closures, the group believes.

With more than thirty chapters throughout Washington State, this is the most active horse group promoting trail riding and working with federal and local government agencies to build horse camps and improve trail conditions.

The BCHW publishes *The Trailhead News,* a monthly newsletter, and provides a variety of publications and literature on its "Tread Lightly" program for protecting wilderness and other backcountry environments. Local chapters around the state are also aware of trailhead facilities that provide horse mounting from wheelchairs.

James Murphy
Backcountry Horsemen of Washington
11839 Glenwood Road SW
Port Orchard, WA 98366
(360) 876-7739

Washington Outfitters and Guides Association (WOGA)

Trail rides and camping trips with professional pack-and-saddle outfitters in Washington State are an excellent way to see spectacular country while you experience the reality of trail travel before planning your own treks.

A free WOGA information brochure, listing all of the horse trail outfitters of this statewide association, is available at 22845 NE 8th, Suite 331, Redmond, WA 98053. Since the members are scattered in many areas, there may be one or more who could show you trails in places you want to ride.

Back Country Wilderness Outfitters in Longview, WA, (800) 553-8185, travels in the Mount St. Helens National Volcanic Monument area.

Blue Mountain Outfitting, Enterprise, OR, (503) 828-7878, rides into the Blue Mountains of Umatilla National Forest in southeast Washington.

Cascade Corrals, Stehekin, WA, (509) 682-4677, hits the trails of the Glacier Peak and Lake Chelan–Sawtooth wildernesses [Lake Chelan National Recreation Area] and North Cascades National Park.

Cascade Wilderness Outfitters, Carlton, WA, (509) 997-0155, provides trips into the Pasayten Wilderness and Lake Chelan–Sawtooth Wilderness.

Early Winters Outfitting, Mazama, WA, (800) 737-8750, packs riders into the Pasayten Wilderness, Okanogan National Forest, Glacier Peak Wilderness, and Lake Chelan–Sawtooth Wilderness.

Happy Trails Horseback Riding Ranch, Easton, WA, (509) 656-2634, offers trail rides in the Snoqualmie Pass area east of Seattle.

High Country Outfitters, Issaquah, WA, (206) 392-0111, rides into the Teanaway Valley trails in Esmeralda Basin and the Mount Stuart range east of Seattle. High Country Outfitters also offers spring and fall high-country cattle roundups, a spring horse drive, and the state's only American Campground Association-accredited youth horse camp, **Camp Wahoo!,** in the Teanaway Valley for ages 9-16.

Icicle Outfitters & Guides, Leavenworth, WA, (800) 497-3912, rides the trails of the Leavenworth, Lake Wenatchee, and Entiat Ranger Districts.

Indian Creek Corral, Naches, WA, (509) 672-2400, provides trail and pack trips into the Goat Rocks Wilderness and the William O. Douglas Wilderness near Mount Rainier.

Jorgenson Enterprises, Duvall, WA, (360) 788-5103, offers high-country pack trips in several areas.

North Cascade Outfitters, Twisp, WA, (509) 997-1015, packs high-country trips into the Pasayten Wilderness and the Okanogan National Forest.

North Cascade Safari, Winthrop, WA, (509) 996-2350, offers overnight to ten-day trips into the Pasayten and Lake Chelan–Sawtooth wildernesses and the Okanogan and Wenatchee national forests.

Sawtooth Outfitters, Pateros, WA, (509) 923-2548 or (509) 923-2448, operates in the Okanogan and Wenatchee national forests in the Methow Valley.

Susee's Skyline Packers, Tacoma, WA, (206) 472-5558, provides guided trail rides and pack trips into the Wenatchee National Forest.

Three Queens Outfitter/Guide Service, Cle Elum, WA, (509) 674-5647, operates in Wenatchee National Forest and the Alpine Lakes Wilderness, providing day rides and extended overnight camp trips.

Gray Wolf Outfitters, Poulsbo, WA (360) 692-6455, provides Olympic Mountain pack trips and day rides.

Rock 'N' Tomahawk Ranch, Ellensburg, WA (509) 962-2403, offers hourly, day or overnight scenic rides in Ellensburg's Green Canyon, including children's rides.

Highland Stage Company, Tonasket, WA, (509) 486-4699, offers horse-drawn wagon train camping adventures along historic routes in the Okanogan and Colville National Forests, also scenic pack trips and Pioneer Heritage tours.

Seahorse Ranch, Hoquiam, WA, (360) 532-6791, offers horse and pony rides on the beach at Ocean Shores or at the ranch, plus an indoor riding arena.

Tiger Mountain Outfitting, Issaquah, WA, (206) 392-5090, offers three-hour guided rides in state forests; instruction and boarding available.

Washington Outfitters and Guides Association (WOGA)
22845 NE 8th, Suite 331
Redmond, WA 98053
(206) 392-6107

Washington Trail Riders Association (WTRA)
Based in the Vancouver, Washington, area, the Washington Trail Riders Association was founded in 1979 by Lorri Bisconer and others who wanted to organize and share trail rides for recreational and social experiences.

Today WTRA membership numbers nearly 120 families. Besides trail riding together, much of the group's time has been devoted to designing and building horse camps in the Gifford Pinchot National Forest in cooperation with state and federal agencies.

Lorri Bisconer
Washington Trail Riders Association
111 S. 17th Ave.
Battle Ground, WA 98604
Phone: (360) 687-5697

Little Bit Riders and EquiFriends

Two therapeutic riding programs in Washington open new vistas for disabled persons, even without going into the high country. In fact, they usually never ride on backcountry trails, preferring level terrain for their riders. But horse owners who know of physically impaired people who want to ride horses may want to contact these groups for assistance.

Little Bit Therapeutic Riding Center
19802 NE 148th
Woodinville, WA 98072
Phone: (206) 882-1554

EquiFriends
22610-A State Rd 2
Monroe, WA 98272
Phone: (360) 794-5688

APPENDIX E: PACKSTOCK REGULATIONS ON WASHINGTON PUBLIC LANDS

The trail rides in this book range over seven national forests, including a dozen designated wilderness areas, two national recreation areas, and a national monument. Each of these areas regulates recreational visitors to protect the land and its inhabitants from overuse and abuse. Some regulations apply specifically to trail riders and the use of packstock.

The following list highlights some of the most important of these regulations. It is in no way all-inclusive, and riders should bear in mind that regulations tend to change from season to season and over the years. Land managers may also tighten or loosen some standards as needed to reflect the changing nature of many environmental, recreational, and land-use concerns. Always call or write the district ranger or regional office for updated information before you begin your trip.

- Most designated wilderness areas in Washington limit party size to twelve heartbeats, in any combination of riders and pack-and-saddle animals. In the Lake Chelan–Sawtooth and Pasayten wilderness areas party size is limited to no more than twelve persons and eighteen pack-and-saddle animals.
- In the Olympic National Forest wilderness areas the limit is twelve persons and eight pack-or-saddle stock. In the Wenaha-Tucannon Wilderness in southeastern Washington the limit is a total of eighteen riders and stock, in any combination.
- All visitors are prohibited from leaving equipment, personal property, or supplies unattended for more than 48 hours in a designated wilderness. This means that you cannot cache supplies at a campsite a week ahead of time, nor are you allowed to leave any equipment (tents, fencing, etc.) for a return trip later in the season.
- No types of wagons, carts, or other wheeled vehicles are allowed in designated wilderness areas.
- No livestock feed except certified processed feed is allowed in designated wilderness areas within Washington. Certified weed-free hay may contain viable plant seeds and is not considered to be processed feed.
- In most areas, no pack or saddle animals are allowed to graze, or to be hobbled, tethered, or hitched, within 200 feet of the shoreline of any lake, stream, or river. Some areas enforce a less-stringent 100-foot buffer zone.
- Permits are required for overnight camping in many, but not all, wilderness areas. Permits are issued on a first-come, first-served basis. Check with Forest Service ranger districts or National Park Service offices about permit requirements for the trails you expect to ride.

APPENDIX F: CAMP COOKING WITH DUTCH OVENS

Just as a trail ride is an adventure, camp cooking with Dutch ovens can be an adventure into a creative style of cooking that is rewarded with satisfied appetites.

Dutch oven cooking has deep roots in the Old West, through wagon trains, cattle drives, homesteaders, and pioneers. Mealtime usually centered around several heavy, black cast-iron pots that held rich stews, or vegetable-covered pot roasts, or buttery chicken and dumplings, or flaky sourdough biscuits. The sweet tooth was satisfied with bubbling fruit crisps, fragrant bread puddings, or moist trail cakes—all prepared in Dutch ovens.

Years ago these versatile multi-use black pots were a mainstay around campfires and cabins. And today they should be a mainstay of your trail camp.

Packing ironware into the backcountry adds weight, but since the Dutch oven can be used for one-pot meals it usually replaces another pot or two. Once you're set up at camp, you'll be glad you brought it.

Pick the Right Size

Various Dutch oven sizes serve a predictable number of people and are good for specific types of dishes. A 10-inch Dutch oven is fine for two people and cooks vegetable recipes well. A 12-inch Dutch oven usually serves up to four people and is fine for baking cakes, breads, and desserts. A 14-inch Dutch oven provides enough food for a large family or a hungry trail crew. A 16-inch Dutch oven, for large crowds, requires more heat and cooks a little differently than the smaller versions. Be prepared to experiment to get used to it.

Charcoal for Best Heat

Using charcoal briquettes for camp cooking provides a proven method of heating that can be controlled by the number of briquettes and the distance between them. Briquettes provide uniform, accurate heat that allows you to achieve predictable temperatures.

Using charcoal, you don't need to have an open fire or burn wood at all, an advantage in many camping situations. One of the easiest ways is to used a ventilated metal can-with-a-handle charcoal starter. Place paper and charcoal in the can, ignite, and in a few minutes you have gray, hot coals for cooking.

To start briquettes without a charcoal starter, build a fire with wood. If it's a grassy area, cut out a piece of sod, roll it up, water it, and set it aside so it can be replaced when you're finished. Then place the charcoal on the fire. After the briquettes are started, remove them with a shovel. If you have the luxury of a wood-burning camp stove, place the briquettes in the fire and remove them with tongs when they start burning.

To use briquettes to create a 350-degree oven (a temperature you'll use for many Dutch oven recipes), place gray, heated coals spaced 1.5 to 2 inches apart under the bottom of the oven. That's a good rule-of-thumb that works for figuring the right amount of charcoal briquettes for any size oven. Use the same spacing rule when you place coals on the lid.

When you can hold your hand under the bail of the oven and over the lid coals for no more than seven to eight seconds, your oven is heated to about 350 degrees.

Dutch ovens provide great camp cooking in a single pot that is easy to clean.

Dutch oven cooking.

A certain amount of experimenting will be necessary until you become accustomed to cooking with briquettes. But this rule-of-thumb should help you get started successfully.

If you don't have briquettes for your Dutch oven, or run out of them, use hot coals from your wood fire. Hard woods make the best coals, particularly oak—if you can find it—and alder. Some woods such as white fir and soft pine make hot coals but don't hold the heat long. They fall apart or go out while you're cooking, so they must constantly be replaced.

Whenever you're baking in a Dutch oven, line it with heavy-duty aluminum foil so you can remove your cake or bread easily.

You can buy either cast-iron or cast-aluminum Dutch ovens, but if weight isn't a packing or traveling problem, cast-iron pots usually perform better because they hold heat longer and distribute it more evenly.

If you're doing a lot of cooking with Dutch ovens, particularly stacking them, you may want to use a long hook to lift oven lids, or for moving the Dutch ovens themselves when they're hot. It can be difficult finding the right types of heavy-duty hooks in hardware or retail stores so most trail cooks just find a blacksmith to make one for them.

To clean your Dutch oven, fill it with enough water to cover stuck-on food and place it over the campfire until the sticking food comes loose. After you wipe it clean and dry with a paper towel, cure it with a rubbed-on coating of shortening. Properly cared for Dutch ovens will give generations of good cooking and enjoyment.

Dutch Oven Recipes

Whether you are just thinking about getting into Dutch oven cooking or are a trail-tested pro, here are some recipes to try. All are from professional trail cooks who often serve a dozen hungry riders at a time.

Dutch Oven Breakfast

"My Dutch Oven Breakfast is a good recipe for beginners because the oven temperatures aren't as critical as with 'real' baking," says Marianne LeSage, a former trail cook and outfitter from Brewster, Washington.

1 pound bacon
1 2-pound bag frozen hash brown potatoes
18 eggs
8 ounces grated Cheddar cheese

Cut bacon into 1-inch pieces. Brown in 12-inch Dutch oven over medium cooking fire.
Remove bacon from oven. Pour off excess bacon fat and use remaining fat to brown the hash browns. Add bacon pieces to hash browns.
Beat eggs and pour over bacon-potato mixture. Put lid on Dutch oven and add coals to lid, keeping bottom heat fairly low.
When eggs are cooked, sprinkle cheese on top. Remove oven from bottom heat, return lid with coals to oven and bake until cheese is melted.
Serves 8 - 10.

This recipe can be successful with as few as 10 eggs. Sausage or cubed ham can be substituted for the bacon. Also, onions and/or green pepper may be added for a 'new' taste!

"Sit-on" Turkey Sandwich

"This sandwich carries well in saddlebags or on a pack horse. Our guests love these sandwiches! If you can't find round sourdough bread, a long loaf will work well, too," says Debby Miller of High Country Outfitters of Redmond, Washington. "Save the bread you scoop out to make the 'Sausage and Egg Casserole' for breakfast."

1 large round sourdough French bread
1/2 lb thin sliced turkey
3 oz sliced pastrami
3 large tomatoes
1 small jar marinated artichokes
1/4 lb cheese, thinly sliced
1/2 cup mayonnaise
1 purple onion, thin sliced
1 can (2 1/2 oz) sliced olives, drained

Cut bread in half horizontally (remove top). Hollow out, leave 3/4" thick.
Combine artichoke liquid and mayonnaise. Spread 1/3 mixture on inside of bottom bread shell, 1/3 on inside of top bread shell and 1/3 on filling when sandwich is half-filled.
In bottom half, layer with tomatoes, meat, onion, cheese, artichokes and olives, until mounded high.
Put top back on. Wrap in plastic wrap. Refrigerate 2 to 8 hours.
Just before serving — SIT ON IT!! This is necessary! Cut into wedges and serve.
Serves 6.

Sausage and Egg Casserole

"This dish satisfies even the largest appetite and keeps everyone satisfied when they have a long day ahead in the saddle," says Debby Miller.

1 pound ground or link sausage
8 slices bread, cubed
6 eggs
3/4 tsp dry mustard
1/2 tsp salt
2 1/2 cups milk
2 cups grated cheese
1 can cream of mushroom soup
1/2 soup can milk
1 can, mushrooms, drained

Brown 1 pound ground (or link) sausage.
Put slices of bread (without crust and cut into small cubes) into a 12-inch Dutch oven. (Or use bread scooped from loaf used in making the "Sit-on" Turkey Sandwich.)
Drain sausage and crumble meat over bread.
Whip eggs. Add dry mustard, salt, and 2 1/2 cups of milk and beat together. Pour over bread and sausage.
Sprinkle cheese over mixture. Mix together cream of mushroom soup, 1/2 can of milk, and mushrooms. Pour over mixture (or heat and add as sauce over mixture after it is baked). Bake at 350 degrees for 45 minutes. Let stand 10-15 minutes before serving.

Methow Chicken and Bedsprings

"I cook this one quite a bit on mountain trips and everywhere else," says Andy Mills, who cooks for Cascade Wilderness Outfitters of Carlton, Washington. "One of the great things about it is that it all cooks in one pot!"

1/2 cube margarine
2 or 3 medium onions, chopped
1 pound fresh mushrooms, sliced
2 tsp thyme
2 T of granulated chicken bouillon, not cubed
2 cut-up fryers
1 small package spiral noodles (Bedsprings!)
2 cans condensed cream of mushroom soup
5 strips bacon
2 or 3 bay leaves
Red wine
Water
Salt and pepper to taste

Melt margarine in 12-inch, deep Dutch oven. Saute onions and mushrooms with thyme and chicken bouillon. Remove from oven, set aside.
In frying pan, brown chicken pieces. Place browned chicken in Dutch oven intermingled with uncooked noodles. On top of chicken and noodles, add sauteed onions and mushrooms. Cover with two cans mushroom soup, undiluted.
Lay strips of bacon on top of soup, place bay leaves on bacon. Pour in two soup cans of red wine and two soup cans of water. Cover Dutch oven and cook for 60 to 80 minutes, or until chicken is done. Time will depend on heat.
Serves 8 - 10.

Sourdough Chocolate Cake

"The sourdough gives this cake a distinctive flavor and it's not too sweet," says trail cook Bill Buchanan of Icicle Creek Outfitters in Leavenworth, Washington.

6 T butter
1 cup sugar
2 eggs
1 cup sourdough starter
3/4 cup milk
3 ounces semi-sweet chocolate, melted
1 tsp vanilla
1 3/4 cups sifted flour
1 tsp baking soda
1/2 tsp salt

Mix ingredients together as given.
Line large Dutch oven with aluminum foil.
Pour cake batter into Dutch oven, cover and bake at 350 degrees until done, about 30 - 40 minutes.
(If you bake this cake at home, use a 350-degree oven—40 minutes for a 9 x 13-inch pan, 25 minutes for two 8-inch pans.)
An excellent topping can be made by mixing together a package of 'Lite' cream cheese and 1 small can of chocolate syrup.

[Recipes reprinted from *Pacific Northwest Trail Cook Book* by John and Roberta Wolcott, Features Northwest, Copyright 1991.]

Photo by Debby Miller.

ABOUT THE AUTHORS

John and Roberta Wolcott, owners of Features Northwest in Marysville, Washington, are full-time freelance writers and photographers specializing in outdoor travel adventures and business publications.

They have written extensively about trail rides and high-country cattle and horse drives with members of the Washington Outfitters and Guides Association (WOGA), and published the Pacific Northwest Trail Cook Book with recipes from WOGA trail cooks in 1991.

Their articles and pictures have been published in *Western Horseman, American Forests, Adventure Northwest, Travelin', Northwest Parks & Wildlife, Northwest Travel, Snow Country,* and other outdoor publications.

FALCON GUIDES® are available for where-to-go hiking, mountain biking, rock climbing, walking, scenic driving, fishing, rockhounding, paddling, birding, wildlife viewing, and camping. We also have FalconGuides on essential outdoor skills and subjects and field identification. The following titles are currently available, but this list grows every year. For a free catalog with a complete list of titles, call FALCON toll-free at 1-800-582-2665.

BIRDING GUIDES
Birding Arizona
Birding Minnesota
Birder's Guide to Montana
Birding Texas
Birding Utah

FIELD GUIDES
Bitterroot: Montana State Flower
Canyon Country Wildflowers
Great Lakes Berry Book
New England Berry Book
Plants of Arizona
Rare Plants of Colorado
Rocky Mountain Berry Book
Southern Rocky Mtn. Wildflowers
Tallgrass Prairie Wildflowers
Western Tree
Wildflowers of Southwestern Utah
Willow Bark and Rosehips

FISHING GUIDES
Fishing Alaska
Fishing the Beartooths
Fishing Florida
Fishing Maine
Fishing Michigan
Fishing Montana

PADDLING GUIDES
Floater's Guide to Colorado
Paddling Montana
Paddling Oregon

HOW-TO GUIDES
Bear Aware
Leave No Trace
Mountain Lion Alert
Wilderness First Aid
Wilderness Survival

ROCK CLIMBING GUIDES
Rock Climbing Colorado
Rock Climbing Montana
Rock Climbing New Mexico
    & Texas
Rock Climbing Utah

ROCKHOUNDING GUIDES
Rockhounding Arizona
Rockhound's Guide to California
Rockhound's Guide to Colorado
Rockhounding Montana
Rockhounding Nevada
Rockhound's Guide to New Mexico
Rockhounding Texas
Rockhounding Utah
Rockhounding Wyoming

WALKING
Walking Colorado Springs
Walking Portland
Walking St. Louis

MORE GUIDEBOOKS
Backcountry Horseman's
    Guide to Washington
Camping California's
    National Forests
Exploring Canyonlands &
    Arches National Parks
Exploring Mount Helena
Recreation Guide to WA
    National Forests
Touring California & Nevada
    Hot Springs
Trail Riding Western
    Montana
Wild Country Companion
Wild Montana
Wild Utah

■ *To order any of these books, check with your local bookseller
    or call FALCON® at **1-800-582-2665**.*

Visit us on the world wide web at:
www.falconguide.com

get
FALCONGUIDED

Hiking Guides

Hiking Alaska
Hiking Alberta
Hiking Arizona
Hiking Arizona's Cactus Country
Hiking the Beartooths
Hiking Big Bend National Park
Hiking Bob Marshall Country
Hiking California
Hiking California's Desert Parks
Hiking Carlsbad Caverns
    and Guadalupe Mtns. National Parks
Hiking Colorado
Hiking the Columbia River Gorge
Hiking Florida
Hiking Georgia
Hiking Glacier & Waterton Lakes National Parks
Hiking Grand Canyon National Park
Hiking Glen Canyon
Hiking Great Basin National Park
Hiking Hot Springs
    in the Pacific Northwest
Hiking Idaho
Hiking Maine
Hiking Michigan
Hiking Minnesota
Hiking Montana
Hiker's Guide to Nevada
Hiking New Hampshire
Hiking New Mexico
Hiking New York
Hiking North Cascades
Hiking North Carolina

Hiking Northern Arizona
Hiking Olympic National Park
Hiking Oregon
Hiking Oregon's Eagle Cap Wilderness
Hiking Oregon's Three Sisters Country
Hiking Shenandoah
Hiking Pennsylvania
Hiking South Carolina
Hiking South Dakota's Black Hills Country
Hiking Southern New England
Hiking Tennessee
Hiking Texas
Hiking Utah
Hiking Utah's Summits
Hiking Vermont
Hiking Virginia
Hiking Washington
Hiking Wisconsin
Hiking Wyoming
Hiking Wyoming's Wind River Range
Hiking Yellowstone National Park
Hiking Zion & Bryce Canyon National Parks
The Trail Guide to Bob Marshall Country

Best Easy Day Hikes

Beartooths
Canyonlands & Arches
Best Hikes on the Continental Divide
Glacier & Wateron Lakes
Glen Canyon
North Cascades
Olympics
Shenandoah
Yellowstone

■ *To order any of these books, check with your local bookseller*
or call FALCON® at **1-800-582-2665** .

Visit us on the world wide web at:
www.falconguide.com

FALCON®

get
FALCON GUIDED

SCENIC DRIVING GUIDES

Scenic Driving Alaska and the Yukon
Scenic Driving Arizona
Scenic Driving the Beartooth Highway
Scenic Driving California
Scenic Driving Colorado
Scenic Driving Florida
Scenic Driving Georgia
Scenic Driving Hawaii
Scenic Driving Idaho
Scenic Driving Michigan
Scenic Driving Minnesota
Scenic Driving Montana
Scenic Driving New England
Scenic Driving New Mexico
Scenic Driving North Carolina
Scenic Driving Oregon
Scenic Driving the Ozarks including the
    Ouchita Mountains
Scenic Driving Texas
Scenic Driving Utah
Scenic Driving Washington
Scenic Driving Wisconsin
Scenic Driving Wyoming
Back Country Byways
National Forest Scenic Byways
National Forest Scenic Byways II

HISTORIC TRAIL GUIDES

Traveling California's Gold Rush Country
Traveler's Guide to the Lewis & Clark Trail
Traveling the Oregon Trail
Traveler's Guide to the Pony Express Trail

WILDLIFE VIEWING GUIDES

Alaska Wildlife Viewing Guide
Arizona Wildlife Viewing Guide
California Wildlife Viewing Guide
Colorado Wildlife Viewing Guide
Florida Wildlife Viewing Guide
Idaho Wildlife Viewing Guide
Indiana Wildlife Vewing Guide
Iowa Wildlife Viewing Guide
Kentucky Wildlife Viewing Guide
Massachusetts Wildlife Viewing Guide
Montana Wildlife Viewing Guide
Nebraska Wildlife Viewing Guide
Nevada Wildlife Viewing Guide
New Hampshire Wildlife Viewing Guide
New Jersey Wildlife Viewing Guide
New Mexico Wildlife Viewing Guide
New York Wildlife Viewing Guide
North Carolina Wildlife Viewing Guide
North Dakota Wildlife Viewing Guide
Ohio Wildlife Viewing Guide
Oregon Wildlife Viewing Guide
Tennessee Wildlife Viewing Guide
Texas Wildlife Viewing Guide
Utah Wildlife Viewing Guide
Vermont Wildlife Viewing Guide
Virginia Wildlife Viewing Guide
Washington Wildlife Viewing Guide
West Virginia Wildlife Viewing Guide
Wisconsin Wildlife Viewing Guide

■ *To order any of these books, check with your local bookseller*
*or call FALCON® at **1-800-582-2665**.*

Visit us on the world wide web at:
www.falconguide.com

FALCON®